THE  TIMES
GUIDE TO
1992

First published by Times Books Limited,
16 Golden Square
London W1R 4BN

© Times Books Limited, London 1989

Reprinted with revisions 1989
2nd Edition 1990
Reprinted 1990

British Library Cataloguing in Publication Data
Owen, Richard
  The Times guide to 1992: a complete handbook
  to Europe without frontiers
  1. European Economic Community
  I. Title   II. Dynes, Michael
  311.24'22

ISBN 0 7230 0341 6

Typeset by Rowland Phototypesetting Limited,
Bury St Edmunds, Suffolk

Printed in Great Britain by
Richard Clay Limited, Bungay, Suffolk

THE  TIMES
GUIDE TO
1992

BRITAIN IN A EUROPE WITHOUT FRONTIERS
A Comprehensive Handbook
by RICHARD OWEN and MICHAEL DYNES

SECOND EDITION

TIMES BOOKS

About the Authors

Richard Owen was *The Times* Brussels Correspondent from 1985 to 1988, reporting extensively on EC affairs from around Europe. He was educated at Nottingham University, Stanford University, California, and the London School of Economics, where he received a PhD in Government and Politics. He joined the BBC in 1973 and transferred to *The Times* as a leader writer in 1980. Owen was Moscow Correspondent of *The Times* from 1982 to 1985. His previous books are *Letters From Moscow* (1985), and *Crisis in the Kremlin: Soviet Succession and the Rise of Gorbachov* (1986), both published by Gollancz. Since January 1989 Richard Owen has been *The Times* Correspondent in Jerusalem.

Michael Dynes joined *The Times* in 1986 as a reporter, and has written extensively about the internal market from both London and Brussels. He was educated at the University of Kent in Canterbury, the University of Indiana and Linacre College, Oxford, where he received an MPhil in International Relations. Before joining *The Times* he worked on the Middle and Far East desks at an Oxford-based commercial consultancy. He is currently *The Times* Transport Correspondent.

CONTENTS

15 COLDITZ EUROPE?
Protectionism and global trade   198
16 ARMS AND 1992:
Defence and security in a united Europe   213
17 YALTA TO MALTA AND BEYOND: REDRAWING THE MAP?
Eastern Europe, German reunification and the EC   226
CONCLUSION:
Britain, 1992 and European union   235
APPENDICES

PREFACE

The past five years in the EC have been dominated by the conflict of ideas over 1992 and the Single European Act, or in more humdrum terms, the completion of the internal market. Since the first edition of this book was published in early 1989, the national debate on Europe has, if anything, intensified. Scarcely a single area of political life is untouched by the European dimension, from taxation to defence, from transport to broadcasting, and hardly a single area of business and professional life unaffected by 1992, from accountancy to pharmaceuticals, from engineering to the law.

The explosion of demands for democracy in Eastern Europe, and the disintegration of Communist regimes, has opened up the question of whether 1992 should be 'broadened' to include 'the other Europeans'. A new Chapter 17 for this edition, 'Yalta to Malta and Beyond', discusses these dramatic changes, while the new defence implications are dealt with in Chapter 16. Moreover, Soviet bloc upheaval, above all in East Germany, raises the issue of whether—as Mrs Thatcher argued at the EC Summit in Strasbourg at the end of 1989—moves towards accelerated integration should be slowed down rather than speeded up while Europe takes stock. At Strasbourg, Britain voiced strong objections to the convening of an inter-governmental conference in December 1990 to pave the way for full economic and monetary union, including proposals to create a new European Development Bank to promote economic development in Eastern Europe, and approval of the European Social Charter outlining basic workers rights. Britain was outvoted on all three.

The controversy over Mrs Thatcher's attitude to European integration has put the issue of national sovereignty and 1992 in the forefront of British and European affairs. It would hardly be an exaggeration to say that Britain's role in the EC is the most contentious issue in British politics today, and will remain so as 1992 approaches. Equally, Britain's attitudes to 1992 have helped to shape the debate on Europe which is being conducted on the Continent and followed closely by the United States, the Soviet Union and Japan.

The Times can claim to have recognized earlier than most what the 1992 target date could mean for industry, commerce and finance, as well as for ordinary travellers and consumers and, ultimately, for our national sovereignty. This book draws on the work of *The Times'* home and foreign reporters on various aspects of 1992, as well as on our own experience and observation.

We owe thanks to Charles Wilson, Editor of *The Times*, who consistently gave the theme of 1992, Britain and Europe prominence, and who sanctioned this project; to George Brock, Foreign Editor, who encouraged 1992 coverage in depth; and to Piers Akerman, who as Deputy Foreign Editor oversaw *The Times'* week-long series on 1992 in November 1987, and provided the germ of this book. As an Australian, and thus an 'outsider', he perceived perhaps better than many Europeans the significance of the integration process then taking shape.

Our thanks go also to numerous anonymous British and EC officials who provided information—much of it sensitive—on behind-the-scenes negotiations on 1992 in the Commission, the Council of Ministers and the European Parliament, as well as between London, Bonn, Paris and other EC capitals. The views of many business executives encountered on trains and planes criss-crossing Europe have also contributed to what we hope is as comprehensive a picture as possible of the shifts taking place under the 1992 impulse—and the limitations of integration.

The 1992 process and the question of Britain's future in Europe have aroused passionate debate, with hopes and fears more strongly expressed than at any time since Britain joined the EC sixteen years ago. *The Times Guide to 1992* is intended to provide a concise but detailed explanation of the facts.

All journalists owe a debt to their colleagues, and the British press corps in Brussels and around the EC has provided stimulating company while carrying out the difficult, often unsung task of mastering EC processes, and explaining them for British readers.

Our thanks also go to Julia Owen, for sustaining us since the beginning with advice, encouragement and back-up despite the commitment of running the growing Owen household in postings abroad and in the Cotswolds. This edition is dedicated to Eleanor, Isabel and Laurence, for whom 1992 will be an event in history which shaped the world they live and work in.

Richard Owen and Michael Dynes
London/Brussels, December 1989

INTRODUCTION

The plan for a Europe without frontiers has been implemented because of a unique combination of circumstances at a turning point in European history. Senior EC officials were determined to fulfil the promise of the Treaty of Rome by taking the EC further towards union. Leading British and Continental industrialists perceived that only a pooling of resources can match the economic strength of America and Japan on a global scale. Finally, national leaders wanted an economic strategy—supranational if necessary—which would guarantee growth and jobs within an expanded EC market. On their own, none of these factors would guarantee a major step forward or a change in our lives and ways of doing business. Combined by chance and history, they add up to a potential revolution.

For some, this is exhilarating but for others, it is a disastrous slide towards the surrender of sovereignty and the ending of Britain's proud island tradition. Attacks by IRA terrorists on British servicemen on the Continent, from West Germany to Ostend, have highlighted the problems of policing open frontiers. A third school of thought argues that the more 1992 is talked about as a magic number, the less likely it is to mean anything. But the fact remains that we can still be caught off-guard.

The rest of the world is also on the alert. Despite vows by Mrs Thatcher and other European leaders to keep an integrated EC open to the outside world, the United States and Japan fear exclusion from a protectionist 'Fortress Europe', as does Moscow. The impact on Eastern Europe is potentially profound, with newly democratized countries such as Poland and Hungary looking to the EC for support, perhaps even membership, but Moscow anxious about the implications for German unity and Soviet control. On an historic visit to Strasbourg in July 1989, shortly before the popular uprisings gathered pace, and the Berlin Wall was breached, Gorbachov allowed for changes in Eastern Europe, with Communist parties going into opposition without Soviet intervention, but warned the West that 'to overcome the division of Europe by overcoming socialism is a course for confrontation, if not something worse'. The EC states, meanwhile, have to decide collectively whether extending trade credits to Moscow reinforces hopes for *perestroika* and Soviet reform or merely subsidizes inefficiency and military spending. The long-term political implications of 1992 for the twelve EC states raise basic issues of sovereignty and integration. The consequences for the European continent as a whole could be incalculable.

A CBI survey of 200 companies issued in the autumn of 1988 shows that only 7% had appointed an executive or team to prepare for 1992; the same percentage had introduced language training; 20% had carried out a 'strategy review'; 10% had done 1992 market research; and 31% had done nothing at all.

Abolishing frontier controls and other barriers

After a slow start, both the Government and British industry have accepted that 1992 does add up to something. They are backing the integration of the twelve national markets of the EC, not least because of the business opportunities that 1992 opens up. But 1992 goes further than that: it represents an additional stage on the road to European Union. For the Government, this second concept of 1992 is less attractive, even unacceptable. Plans for a European Central Bank (for example) are seen by Mrs Thatcher as 'airy-fairy' (the same phrase the Prime Minister once used about the Single European Act, which laid the legal basis for 1992). 1992 not only gives rise to fears of European federalism, it also arouses more immediate anxieties over how to control drugs or crime in a frontier-free Europe. The single European market is a 'welcome development,' Mrs Thatcher declared in August 1988 during a tour of Asian countries, but 'you must still have barriers and boundaries to stop crime and illegal immigration'. British officials believe that police checks must be retained even if customs barriers are removed, so that criminals are deterred.

In her controversial speech to the College of Europe in Bruges on 20 Sept. 1988 the Prime Minister laid out her approach in even clearer terms:

> Of course we must make it easier for goods to pass through frontiers. Of course we must make it easier for our people to travel throughout the Community. But it is a matter of plain common sense that we cannot totally abolish frontier controls if we are also to protect our citizens and stop the movement of drugs, of terrorists, of illegal immigrants.

Mrs Thatcher also attacked the centralization of power in Brussels, the folly of trying to create 'an identikit European personality' and the vision of a 'European superstate'. This brought charges in the Continental press that she was being 'neo-Gaullist', and that although the British approach was pragmatic it was also 'myopic and egotistical' (*Corriere della Sera* in Italy) and 'shockingly limited' (*Frankfurter Rundschau* in West Germany). In fact, no 'European superstate' has been proposed, and holding up the abolition of internal frontiers is against the spirit and letter of the Single European Act. Nonetheless, the Prime Minister's intervention—which was not meant to be 'anti-European' since it specifically pointed to Britain's European destiny—had the salutary effect of concentrating minds on key 1992 dilemmas.

In the European election campaign in 1989 Mrs Thatcher called for a

'Europe of enterprise' rather than the Europe of 'red tape and regulation, state intervention and control' she claimed her opponents wanted. Equally, Mrs Thatcher's objections at the Madrid summit of June 1989 to far-reaching plans for monetary union sharpened the debate on national sovereignty (see Chapter 8). Her Cabinet reshuffle a month later, catapulting John Major into the Foreign and Commonwealth Office in place of Sir Geoffrey Howe, may have been designed to narrow the obvious divisions between Downing Street and the FCO over Europe, with the relatively untried Major—unlike Howe—backing Thatcher-style resistance to far-reaching integration. Howe's differences with the Prime Minister, not least over full membership of the European Monetary System (EMS), reached breaking point at Madrid. On the other hand, as Chief Secretary to the Treasury, Major was sympathetic to the pound joining the EMS, and on taking over as Foreign Secretary he declared that 1992 opened up 'exciting prospects' for Europe in which Britain was to play 'a leading role'. Similarly, Douglas Hurd, who took over from Major as Foreign Secretary in the hasty re-shuffle which followed Lawson's resignation as Chancellor of the Exchequer in October 1989, is also thought of as pro-European. With France warning that it could press ahead with the other Ten on a new treaty on economic and monetary union without Britain if necessary, the pace of European integration is becoming one of the most contentious issues of our time, threatening not only to dominate EC affairs but also to cause deep and damaging divisions within the Conservative Party in Britain ten years after Mrs Thatcher came to power.

Similarly, Britain found itself fighting a rearguard action over the so-called 'Workers Charter' in the run-up to the European summit in Strasbourg in December 1989. Although little more than a declaration of rights, devoid of concrete legislative proposals, Britain feels its emphasis on strengthening trade unions, together with its 'collectivist tone,' could help 'undermine' the new atmosphere of industrial relations in Britain. The European Commission now intends to submit a separate 'action programme' codifying the rights outlined by the charter into Community legislation at a later date. The document is therefore simply a declaratory position rather than a legislative programme, and thus not subject to a vote. However, France remained determined to secure its adoption at Strasbourg in the face of British opposition.

In this book we look at these and other controversial issues raised by the 1992 programme. We examine both the practical impact of 1992, area by area, and its wider implications for Britain and Europe. In terms of theory, the internal market programme means the removal of physical, technical and fiscal barriers. In everyday life and business it means that we—the 320 million citizens of the EC—should be able to move around Europe without hindrance in an integrated transport network based on free competition; to work in any of the twelve member states on the basis of harmonized qualifications; to sell our goods in any other EC country as if it were our home market on the basis of harmonized standards; to deposit and borrow money anywhere in the EC, perhaps with a European Central Bank to control the money supply; in short, to think, work and act as if Europe were one country.

The natural reaction tends to be 'I'll believe it when I see it'. Longer-term plans such as a single European currency, a European athletics team or a common European defence (none of which are, strictly speaking, part of the 1992 programme) add to the impression that this is just another Euro-scheme. But in fact, much of 1992 is already in effect. We are already being governed to a large extent by EC laws without realizing it.

Integration: the never-ending story

For Britain, the story of the Common Market began in 1973, with British accession. One of the great themes of British politics and history since then has been the nature of the relationship between Britain and the Continent, and the question of whether Britain's destiny lies in an integrated Europe or not. The plan to complete the single market by the end of 1992 has focused this debate more sharply than ever.

The story of 1992 really began not in 1973 but in 1957, with the signing of the Treaty of Rome. 'Europe will not be created at a stroke or according to a single plan. It will be built through concrete achievements', observed Robert Schuman, one of the EC's founding fathers, and the man still revered in Brussels—together with Jean Monnet—as the originator of the post-war dream of a united Europe. If he has a modern successor, it is probably Jacques Delors, the mercurial, often underestimated ex-Finance Minister of France who is now into his second term as President of the European Commission. From his office on the thirteenth floor of the Berlaymont in Brussels, the plate-glass headquarters of the Commission, Delors is directing the next phase of progressing towards European union, a plan which—like the original Treaty of Rome itself—is based on the assumption that dreams are only realized through specific, painfully negotiated steps. 1992 is nothing less than the full Common Market envisaged by Schuman, Monnet and other pioneers in the 1950s: the abolition by the end of 1992 of barriers and frontiers, creating a single, integrated market.

In Britain, helped by the 1992 publicity campaign launched by the Department of Trade and Industry, national awareness of the implications is rising fast. As more and more single market measures are passed, thanks to majority voting in the EC Council of Ministers, much of 1992 is taking place of its own accord, with business activity refusing to wait for the official deadline. Occasional indications (the issuing of Euro-passports, the European Commission's power to approve the Rover–British Aerospace deal, French takeovers of water companies or Hovis and HP sauce) have alerted the public to the fact that an historic shift is taking place. It is a two-way process. While British property and construction firms are becoming more active on the Continent, for example (especially as the Channel Tunnel nears completion), Dutch and other European property and financial institutions are already making inroads into British property markets. In all areas of commerce, from property to manufacturing industry and financial services, freer cross-border competition means that both Britain and its European partners and competitors in the EC will have to try harder—but the rewards will be much richer in an expanded market of over 320 million people.

This book sets out to explain what the single market will mean to us—managers, producers, consumers, professional people, employees, readers and viewers, businessmen and women—as the whole of Europe comes to be regarded as one home market. It also seeks to provide a handbook for specific areas of business and everyday life—the professions, transport, tourism, banking, local government, takeovers and so on—while also examining political and constitutional issues, such as the transfer of national sovereignty involved in the Single European Act.

Visionaries versus pragmatists

The question of whether 1992 is a target date for an integrated Europe or something more like a state of mind—a vehicle for free market principles, as Mrs Thatcher believes, or a step on the road to a European national identity, as Delors seems to hope—was highlighted in 1988 by the political row in Britain over the appointment of Leon Brittan to succeed Lord Cockfield as the senior British Commissioner in Brussels in January 1989. Lord Cockfield, critics said, had 'gone native', particularly in advocating VAT harmonization as part of the 1992 process, and Brittan would be expected to take a more obediently Thatcherite line. An earlier example of the dichotomy of views on 1992 was the political bombshell Delors dropped in the summer of 1988 as the European Parliament was preparing to go into recess, a bombshell whose shock waves are still reverberating.

With Parliament debating the outcome of the EC summit in Hanover, which had just ended with agreement to look into the idea of a European Central Bank, Chancellor Helmut Kohl of West Germany, who chaired the Hanover meeting, did his best to smooth over impending controversy. He knew that Mrs Thatcher was adamantly opposed to the concept, which implied further central EC control. He told Euro MPs that he hoped the special EC Committee on Monetary Union would recommend 'pragmatic steps' at the Madrid EC summit in June 1989. Delors, responding to Kohl's report on Hanover, offered a startling vision of what was really happening in Europe. Monetary union, he said, was just one aspect of the rapidly developing programme for the abolition of barriers to trade and mobility in the EC by the end of 1992. There would have to be 'the embryo of a European Government in one form or another' by the mid-1990s. Kohl, picking up the visionary theme, reinforced the Delors message by saying that the European Parliament would, sooner or later, exercise powers 'not far below those enjoyed at present by national parliaments'.

Delors' remarks were clearly an exaggeration, but they had a purpose —to alert European publics, including (perhaps above all) the British one, to the fact that, even though the EC is committed irrevocably to 1992, there are differing concepts of what 1992 is intended to bring about. Delors also wanted to remind national parliaments that they had already conceded a significant degree of sovereignty to the EC. Hence his observation that, within ten years, 80% of economic and social legislation would be passed at the European level.

In November 1989 Delors went further, proposing to MEPs at Strasbourg a permanent European prototype government or 'standing committee' of deputy prime ministers from the Twelve, with the Commission slimmed down into a leaner, more political body less involved in day-to-day management. Delors also backed a proposal put forward by Michael Heseltine in Brussels for a second chamber at the European Parliament made up of MPs seconded from national parliaments.

The debate took a bitter turn during the 1989 European election, with Edward Heath, the former Prime Minister, accusing Mrs Thatcher of 'talking absolute rubbish' by expressing fears of a 'European superstate'. Michael Heseltine, a former Cabinet minister and, like Heath, a staunch pro-European, also attacked 'blind' and 'grudging' attitudes to Europe. In Brussels, Heath accused Mrs Thatcher of breaking the EC treaties he had signed and taking a 'preposterous and insulting' attitude to the Community. In response, Mrs Thatcher told the Commons she was a 'European idealist' but would not permit the single European market to take away from Parliament the power to run Britain's economy and taxation system or to introduce 'a detailed bureaucracy of standardization and harmonization'.

The campaign was marked by a concerted Government attack on 'meddling' from Brussels. For many, such concerns were underlined by Britain's failure in May 1989 to prevent EC health ministers using majority voting to override British objections to a new law requiring detailed health warnings on cigarette packets by 1993. However, even some Conservative MPs felt the Thatcher line out of touch with public mood on Europe, and the *Sunday Telegraph* said on 18 June 1989 that the 'superficial judgement' that being anti-European won votes was 'a major blunder'. Lord Plumb, then President of the European Parliament, told the Royal Institute of International Affairs: 'Those who call for a Europe merely of sovereign states co-operating with each other where they wish misunderstand the nature of the Community. It has long since gone beyond that stage.' But the furore caused by the Conservatives' poor electoral performance forced John Major to try and convince critics the Government was not 'lukewarm on Europe.' In a keynote speech to the Economic Club in New York in September, Major said that it was 'ludicrous' to suggest that Britain was unenthusiastic about Europe, and insisted membership would remain a 'fixed point' in its future.

In fact, the phrase '1992' is already fast becoming as familiar in Britain as *quatre-vingt-douze* in France, *novanta due* in Italy or *der Binnenmarkt* (the internal market) in West Germany. However, confusion and conflict still arise over both the actual content of the internal market programme and its final goal. Mrs Thatcher is impatient with grand schemes, and insists that 1992 must mean less regulation, not more. She also wants 1992 to mean that British firms will have as much chance of taking over Continental companies as European firms have of doing the same to British concerns, with covert barriers to British merger bids removed. The visionaries are also preoccupied with practicalities—Schuman's 'concrete achievements' —but see the 1992 programme as a further, vital stage on the road to perfecting the vision of the EC's founding fathers, who, when framing the Treaty of Rome in 1957, had more than a mere customs union in mind. The Six wished to lay the foundations of a united Europe which, through economic and political integration, would render unthinkable the kind of war which had scarred and devastated Europe in the past.

'Nobody ever lost votes by being anti-EC'

On the other hand, in Britain, phrases or concepts with the prefix 'Euro' tend to arouse negative feelings, whatever personal or national regard we may have for the Dutch, Belgians, Italians or Danes. On the whole this is due not so much to outright hostility to the EC as such (although this certainly exists) as to a feeling that EC membership has not brought the British people many tangible benefits since accession in 1973. There is some resentment at 'harmonization' measures, with earlier moves such as the decimalization of currency and metrication of measurements (litres, metres and so on) seen as part of a general process of 'Europeanization'. The new Euro-passport is accepted, but, rather like other new facets of modern British life such as the new-look telephone boxes, arouses few warm feelings and is disliked by many (some compare the Euro-passport's appearance, disparagingly, to that of a building society paying-in book).

The Common Agricultural Policy (CAP), from which Britain benefits less than most other large EC states, has made the EC a laughing-stock in British eyes, and even the British budget rebate—agreed after much painful negotiation in 1984—has not changed this perception of the EC as the home of butter mountains and wine lakes. Visitors have been known to arrive in Brussels looking for them. Alas, EC surpluses are stored in the different twelve countries. The image of 'fat cat' bureaucrats in Brussels has not helped, nor has the tendency of the tabloid press to play on the image by seizing on lunatic-fringe proposals and conveying the impression that unhinged EC officials will not stop until they have harmonized everything, up to and including the British sausage or British ice cream. The European Commission often makes a useful 'whipping boy', and tends to be criticized even when what is really under fire are decisions taken by the Council of Ministers, in which all twelve nations are represented (see Chapter 2).

To meet such criticisms and perceptions (by no means confined to Britain) the Commission deliberately adopted a 'new approach' in 1985, continuing to press for harmonization where it believed it necessary but also relying on the mutual recognition of national standards (see Chapter 4). To meet the well-founded British complaint that the CAP was an intolerable and inefficient policy, the Brussels summit of February 1988 passed—in modified form—the Delors package of financial reforms, including farm cutbacks and ceilings on farm spending. Sceptics still claim that average British families spend an extra £10 a week on food because of the CAP system of guaranteed payments to farmers. One recent report (*Consumers and the Common Agricultural Policy*, from the National Consumer Council) put the figure as high as £13.50 a week.

The CAP has only been reformed, not abandoned, but the food mountains have begun to topple, and the 1988 reforms are beginning to take effect. The Commission, refuting the NCC argument, claims that a basket of foodstuffs costs less in Europe than it does in other parts of the world. Limited farm support will continue to be a feature of an integrated Europe to maintain rural livelihoods and ensure Europe's food supplies.

1992 hopes and fears

Britain, in other words, is in the EC to stay (even the Labour Party no longer regards withdrawal as an option), and had better adapt to the world of 1992 in order to shape it and take advantage of it. Present attitudes in business and the professions vary, with some welcoming the opportunities of 1992, some fearing the risks, and others still largely puzzled by it. The enthusiasts include companies already prepared for business with the Continent; banks and insurance companies; firms which have European subsidiaries or have merged with European companies; haulage companies and smaller airlines; and those in the computer and high-tech fields such as Roger Bellass, European Director for Customer Support at Tandem Computers, who argues that 'the computer industry is in a particularly good position to exploit the single market, since information technology will be one of the main tools other industries will use to compete in this new environment'. This, he said, in an interview with *The Times* (August 1988), is especially true of financial services and manufacturing industry, to the benefit of the consumer:

> After 1992 it will not be enough to pay lip service to customer
> service . . . customer expectations across Europe will rise to the
> highest common denominator. Just as the arrival of Japanese
> electronic goods in the West has given us higher expectations of
> what these goods should be like, and how reliable they should be,

the advent of the single market will mean customers will expect the same standards from all companies as they get from the best ones, whatever country they are from.

1992, in other words, will benefit those who get customer service right.

Others are more fearful, or believe that customer service will deteriorate. Michael Dobbs of Saatchi and Saatchi, the advertising agency, in an article in *The Times* the same month, thinks that 1992 has become 'too fashionable', a 'commercial virility symbol which is distracting and misleading trusting businessmen', who should be looking to markets elsewhere (for example, in the Far East). He points out that, with free cross-border competition, many companies (for example, in the car manufacturing business) will fail. The age of Europe Inc. and Euro-conglomerates leads to panic reactions, with 'partnerships sought in a hurry, often with confused motives and unsuitable partners'.

Others in the 'no' lobby include, at least until recently, television authorities, who oppose the Commission's plans for Euro-regulation of television and satellite broadcasting (see Chapter 13). Also hostile to 1992 are many of Britain's customs officers, who say that over half of the illegal drugs which enter Britain (for example, cocaine) do so from other EC countries. In the words of Mike King of the National Union of Civil and Public Servants: 'If we were to give up frontier controls we would become as weak as the weakest member state.' The European Police Union (EPU), which represents half a million police officers, is divided over the advisability of opening up frontiers. With 1992 in mind, European police forces have already stepped up their co-operation through sophisticated computer methods, and British police, for example, work closely together with their Spanish counterparts to prevent drugs entering the EC through Spain. The police forces of four European nations—Britain, the Netherlands, Belgium and West Germany—joined together in 1988 to hunt IRA terrorists who had caused mayhem through shootings and bombings aimed at British servicemen on the Continent. However, on balance, the EPU still fears that criminals of all kinds will find it easier to move around Europe after 1992 than the police seeking to catch them.

Somewhere in the middle between the optimists and the doubters are those business executives and professional people—probably the majority —who are not sure what 1992 will bring but are doing their best to prepare for it. Take the legal profession, for example. The Law Society has set up a working party on 1992, on the assumption that the mutual recognition of legal qualifications (subject to 'top-up' tests in the country concerned) will mean changes in the structure of the legal profession within Britain. The distinction between barristers and solicitors, for example, could become eroded, and restrictions in England and Wales against members of the Scottish Bar will look absurd in a frontier-free Europe. Meanwhile, lawyers in Britain could be in a good position to pick up Continental business, especially since a number of English law firms (mostly in the City) have already established themselves on the Continent: 17 have offices in Paris and eight have offices in Brussels. A report by chartered surveyors Fletcher King in May 1989 also predicted benefits for property investment in the City and Kent in 1992, because of the single market and the Channel Tunnel, and estate agents began advertising houses for 'EC commuters' close to air- and seaports with fast Continental links.

Language: no longer enough to shout louder

Behind these hopes and fears lies the problem of language. English tends to be the language of international business, and is even used at EC summits (it is said that Helmut Schmidt of West Germany and Giscard d'Estaing of France conversed in English in private when they were Chancellor and President). On the other hand, company and marketing executives will find after 1992 that it is a handicap not to be fairly conversant with at least one other major European language, and preferably two or three. North Europeans—the Dutch, West Germans and Danes—tend to speak very good (if not impeccable) English, as increasingly do South Europeans in business and the professions.

Some business executives think that the dangers are exaggerated. Malcolm Miller, sales director of the mass-market computer company Amstrad, maintains that 'you can always make yourself understood, or find someone to translate'. Dr Michael Wintle, Director of the Centre for Modern Dutch Studies at Hull University, points out (*The Times*, Letters, August 1988) that British trade with the Netherlands has not been inhibited by the fact that few Britons speak Dutch. The two nations exchange 10% of their imports and exports, there are close links between the City and Amsterdam, and Unilever and Royal Dutch Shell are jointly owned. Therefore 'The implication that to do business with the Dutch you must speak their language is empirically a false one,' he said. A further test of the significance of language skills will be the performance of French companies in the unified market, since, although the French expect others to learn their language, they are no more noted than the British for their mastery of other tongues—least of all, English.

Mastery of Continental languages will nonetheless be an important asset to both medium-sized businesses and the multinationals, and cassette tuition companies like Linguaphone, intensive language courses such as Berlitz and residential 'immersion' language schools like the Business Language Consultancy in Devon expect an increase in interest. The Government's contribution is new Language Export Centres, with London courses for businessmen (some arranged at City offices) organized by the Polytechnic of Central London and financed by the Government, industry and the language colleges themselves. Yet these still lag behind the more purposeful business-and-language programmes set up in, say, West Germany, with 1992 in mind. Even many multinationals in Britain still take the view that 'all you have to do is shout a little louder—in English'. In the single market this could be a costly piece of arrogance.

Conversely, English courses for European business executives offered at the City of London Polytechnic and elsewhere hope to tap 'the tremendous thirst for business English in Europe'. Similar schemes are under way at Bristol and Durham Universities. English tends to be the language of conferences and stock markets, and is the second language in most EC countries.

Time, weights and measures and retailing

Other practicalities need to be considered, such as the lack of 'harmonization' between British Summer Time, Greenwich Mean Time and the setting of clocks on the Continent. At present, when British executives telephone Amsterdam or Stuttgart just before lunchtime in London, or at the end of the afternoon, they are likely to find that their client has already left the office. Conversely, when the Continental contact telephones London, Birmingham or Glasgow first thing next morning from the office, the British business executive is still at home having breakfast or reading the paper on the train to work. In its report *Making the Most of Daylight Hours* the independent Policy Studies Institute argues that dispensing with GMT and bringing British time into line with the rest of Europe will save energy, increase tourism and lead to fewer road accidents. Others —notably farmers, builders and Scots—object.

Weights and measures are also due for 'harmonization' following a new EC draft directive on metrication, updating the 1979 directive— although the daily pint of milk appears safe. Under the new scheme imperial units such as gills, fluid ounces, inches and yards will go metric by 1994, although the therm and the fathom will be retained until 1999. Britain is seeking permanent exemptions for the pint when used for milk and beer; for the troy ounce, used in bullion trading; and for the mile, which, however, seems likely to give way eventually to the kilometre, just as pounds and ounces are being replaced in shops by kilos and grams.

This, in turn, will have an impact on retailing in 1992, as transfrontier store chains become more feasible. The Corporate Intelligence Group (51 Doughty Street, London WC1) warns in its report on *Retailing and 1992* that although the UK retailing and distribution sector is one of the most efficient in Europe, it is tempting territory for Continental predators, since profit margins are high while legal restrictions on shops are less severe than on the Continent.

Another broad area related to European integration—though not yet covered by an EC directive—is health. Arrangements already exist between EC states to provide basic health care for each other's citizens on a reciprocal basis, but travellers are still advised to take out private insurance, and the prospect of a Europe-wide health service seems remote. According to the Office of Health Economics: 'The priority must be cautious experiment.' The Commission has proposed an EC common format health card containing a citizen's medical details (such as blood group) as a first step.

1992: not a magic number

Therefore it is a mistake to suppose—in the words of one EC official involved in the 1992 project—that 'neon lights will flash in the sky' at midnight on 31 December 1992, and a voice from Heaven will proclaim an integrated Europe. In aspects of commerce and daily life the programme will continue after 1992, and the European Court will have to deal with continuing disputes over 1992 directives.

A further difficulty is that UK law is based entirely on traditions differing from Continental law, much of which derives from the Code Napoléon, and harmonizing legal practice and theory will prove to be an immense task—perhaps impossible in some areas.

However, industry and the professions are preparing for a major change in the way we do business. The trades unions are also getting ready: after a record of hostility towards the EC, the Trades Union Congress (TUC) and its European equivalent, the ETUC (which represents 44 million workers), accept the 1992 programme, and want it to include the protection of employee rights. There may even emerge European unions to represent shopfloor workers in amalgamated European companies—a development which would have an impact on some of the TUC's more old-fashioned policies such as its opposition to single-union deals.

Such resistance by the TGWU under Ron Todd led to the decision by Ford in 1988 to locate a new electronics components factory not in Dundee, where it would have created much-needed jobs, but at Cadiz in Spain. Unless union attitudes—as well as rhetoric—change, jobs could increasingly go to cheaper Southern countries in the single market.

Calls for a 'social dimension' have given rise to charges that, despite Delors' assurances that the Commission is 'not like Napoleon's Grand Army, it only intervenes when it must', 1992 is a vehicle for European corporate socialism and superstate interventionism. Such arguments, which threaten to politicize what is intended as a programme for frontier abolition, are examined in Chapter 10 and the Conclusion.

The public at large, however, is likely to see 1992 in terms not of Left–Right politics but of the risks and opportunities the single market programme presents for ordinary travellers and businessmen—and opinion polls suggest that British people are more enthusiastic, and more willing to surrender a degree of national sovereignty, than is commonly thought.

Above all, the growing number of business executives who commute as naturally to Amsterdam or Paris as to Swindon or Liverpool are already involved in the realities of the new Europe, and the rest are catching on fast. As Lord Plumb, President of the European Parliament, remarked:

British firms should not assume that the old habit of doing things late and by halves will work this time . . . Continental companies are not going to wait until we are ready. There will be an inevitable period of shake-out, and the time to begin the preparation is now—at the latest.

Similarly, the ordinary citizen is beginning to appreciate the extent to which decisions made in Europe affect their daily lives – from water supplies to freedom of speech. The attempt by Nicholas Ridley, the former Secretary of State for the Environment, to grant the English and Welsh water authorities exemptions from EC drinking-water purity laws was denounced as 'illegal' by the Commission in February 1989. Only then did the extent to which the quality of British drinking water lagged behind European standards become fully apparent. In September, the Commission decided to carry out its threat of court action, despite last ditch attempts by Britain to convince officials it was doing all it reasonably could to meet EC demands. Britain is by no means alone in failing to meet EC water purity standards. Indeed, some observers predict that almost all member states will find themselves in front of the court for failing to honour their legislative obligations. But the move introduced an unwelcome element of uncertainty in the Government's efforts to privatize the water industry. Carlo Ripa de Meana, the Environment Commissioner, also tabled a directive preventing the pumping of untreated waste into the sea, which has further complicated the Government's water-privatization plans, now in the hands of Chris Patten, Ridley's successor. The Commission is demanding that Britain, which should have complied with a 1980 drinking water purity directive by 1985, do so by 1993. Britain has objected that this would cost billions of pounds.

Faced by Ayatollah Khomeini's death threats against Salman Rushdie, the controversial author of *The Satanic Verses*, EC Foreign Ministers demonstrated in March 1989 how effective the Community could be in foreign affairs by rallying behind Britain and agreeing to temporarily withdraw their ambassadors from Tehran in protest at Iran's 'intolerable behaviour'.

British citizens, like their fellow Europeans, have finally realized that the Community is acquiring a say in many of the issues that were once regarded as the exclusive preserve of national governments.

1 THE IMPACT OF 1992
Ten ways the single market will change our lives

Imagine that you are John Armstrong, marketing manager for an office equipment company in Manchester. Shortly after the completion of the single European market on 31 December 1992 you put in a bid with the City Council for a contract to supply high-tech office equipment. However, West German, Italian and French firms are competing with you on an equal basis—and the West German bid is accepted. On the other hand, you have just got back from Ghent, where, to the chagrin of the local Belgian firms, your bid for a major contract was successful. You also have high hopes of a supply contract at Lyons in France. You are learning to operate within a home market of twelve countries.

To relax from business pressures, you take your family off for a break through France to Spain, using your new burgundy-coloured Euro-passports and putting your car—with EC-controlled exhaust emissions —on the new Channel Tunnel rail link with the Continent. While in Spain, you interrupt your holiday at an EC-approved pollution-free beach to call on your brother, an accountant who now works for a newly integrated Euro-telecommunications company near Madrid. On the way back to Calais you stop at a Barclays–Crédit Lyonnais Euro-bank and use your 'smart' electronic Euro-card to draw Danish kroner for your next trip to Copenhagen—thinking to yourself how much easier it will be when the ECU is finally introduced as a common currency, controlled from the newly established European Central Bank based in London and Frankfurt.

Back home in the UK, you tune in to a variety of television satellite channels to watch the Euro-weather forecast and business news. Next morning, your managing director contacts you on your EC-compatible carphone to warn you that you might have to go to Brussels to seek permission for the proposed merger with your firm's Dutch subsidiary —unless the Dutch take the firm over first. The prospect does not arouse any particular anxiety, beyond the economic viability of the deal. You think of yourself automatically as a Mancunian, an Englishman—and a European.

Ten benefits of the single market

This, or something like it, is what the world of post-1992 integrated Europe is supposed to be like. The aim of 1992, as enshrined in the Single European Act—a legally binding document amending the Treaty of Rome —is to fulfil the original EC vision of a common market without obstacles to the free movement of goods, services, capital and people. Not all of the

Euro-developments projected in the imaginary John Armstrong's life will come about, but 1992 will have a major impact on the way we live and do business. Among other things, it will mean:

- **EASIER TRAVEL.** Frontier controls will be all but abolished at the EC's internal frontiers, although not at its external points of entry (if anything, external controls will be increased to ensure that non-EC citizens do not find 'soft' entry points and then go on to exploit the benefits of the single market). Computer-read, single-format EC passports will cut down delays, and police and immigration forces will tackle crime more through behind-the-scenes co-ordination than through frontier controls. Duty-free sales will disappear, and by way of compensation ferry companies—which stand to lose over £160 million from the abolition of duty-frees—are planning floating offshore superstores, using converted roll-on–roll-off ferries.

- **A BUSINESS BOOM.** 320 million customers await the efforts of EC business, from Britain to Denmark to Greece and Portugal, with all firms competing on equal terms in a huge open market. One of the key provisions obliges public authorities to give enterprises from any EC nation an equal opportunity to win high-value contracts.

- **BORDER SAVINGS.** Frontier delays for goods vehicles (many trucks and lorries now wait at borders for eight hours or more) cost an estimated £17 billion, according to the European Parliament. Restrictions on tendering for public contracts cost a further £60 billion. The simplified customs procedures of the Single Administrative Document—which Britain was one of the first EC countries to introduce—will save costs. However, the Kangaroo Group (an EC 1992 pressure group founded by the late Basil de Ferranti, Conservative MEP and a determined campaigner for border abolition) says that hold-ups at borders still cost British and European consumers 80p for every £10 they spend.

- **JOB RECOGNITION.** A teacher from Glasgow will be able to teach in Lyons or Copenhagen, and an accountant from Brighton could go and work in Naples or Frankfurt, all on the basis of mutually recognized qualifications and diplomas. Linguistic barriers will still cause problems—and will work against the British, since, as a nation, our grasp of Continental languages is still poor.

- **FINANCIAL SERVICES.** Restrictions on capital movements are to be lifted in 1990. EC citizens will be able to open bank accounts in due course or take out mortgages anywhere in the Community, with some exceptions in Southern Europe. There is a long-term plan (still under discussion) for a European Central Bank.

● **CONSUMER PROTECTION.** EC states will no longer be able to block imports of foodstuffs or toys because they do not meet national labelling, health or safety standards. Broad criteria and common standards are being devised.

● **FREE COMPETITION.** Protectionist practices preventing free competition—including competition in transport by road, sea and air—will become illegal. The first stages of liberalization in aviation and road haulage are already in effect, preventing cartels and quotas and allowing smaller operators increased market access.

● **VAT AND INDIRECT TAXES HARMONIZED.** This is a controversial area because of the Government's electoral commitment not to allow the abolition of VAT zero rating on basic goods such as food and children's clothes. However, the basic principle of the 1992 programme is that, once border controls have gone, trade in the integrated market will be distorted if there are large differentials between VAT rates.

● **TELEVISION AND BROADCASTING.** Technical standards for television and satellite technology are to be harmonized in conjunction with the 1992 programme to ensure that the twelve EC nations do not have incompatible systems, obstructing sales and communication. To prevent European television being dominated by American or Australian soap operas, a majority of programmes 'where practicable' will have to be of EC origin.

● **THE TELECOMMUNICATIONS MARKET.** This is being opened up, under a plan (tabled by the Commission in June 1987) for ending the monopoly supply of customer terminal equipment and telecommunications services, including databases and electronic mailboxes. Eventually, electrical plugs and sockets may also be standardized so that travellers do not have to carry adaptors or change plugs—but at the moment this seems unlikely.

More detailed lists of changes are given at the ends of relevant chapters.

Lord Cockfield and the 1985 White Paper

The momentum which produced this blueprint for change is partly political, partly economic. Much of the drive came from Lord Cockfield, for four years Britain's senior Commissioner in Brussels, with responsibility for the internal market. As he told us: 'Only on a European rather than a national basis can we hold our own in the world.' Formally speaking, the Single European Act and 1992 have their origins in a series of declarations by EC summits on the way forward, notably the Copenhagen summit of December 1982 ('We instruct the Council to decide . . . on priority measures to reinforce the internal market') and the Brussels summit of March 1985 ('We lay particular emphasis on . . . action to achieve a large single market by 1992, thereby creating a more favourable environment for stimulating enterprise, competition and trade'). The programme really began in 1985, with a European Commission's White Paper, followed by the Single European Act agreed at Luxembourg in December the same year.

The White Paper was Lord Cockfield's brainchild. A former Conservative Cabinet Minister and tax expert, and previously chairman of Boots the chemists, Lord Cockfield (then 68) had a ponderous, lawyer's manner calculated to convey tedium rather than vision. However, Cockfield, it turned out, believed passionately in a Europe in which crossing from one country to another—from France to West Germany, say, or from England to the Netherlands—would entail no more formality for a traveller or lorry driver than passing from England to Scotland. The burgundy-coloured Euro-passports which are gradually replacing the blue, stiff-backed British ones of old are part of this drive for a frontier-free Europe.

It was Lord Cockfield's determination and drive which brought the 1985 White Paper to life, also bringing the Commissioner into frequent conflict with Mrs Thatcher in the process. However, beneath the vision lay a simple and highly practical stratagem: to define the internal market programme by dividing it into approximately 300 specific proposals, or groups of proposals, which would then be presented to the Council of Ministers in a timetable geared to completion by 31 December 1992. The Commission was aided, moreover, by a provision in the Single European Act laying down majority voting procedures in the Council of Ministers for internal market measures, thus effectively robbing individual nations of the power to veto proposals they found unpalatable (see Chapter 3).

1992 measures already in force

In the four years since 1992 became more than a gleam in the eyes of Cockfield and Delors, the programme has gone steadily forward. Despite 'slippage', over a third of the 1992 measures have been passed into law—and EC law takes precedence over national law—with most of the remaining directives tabled and awaiting approval.

We are already, in other words, being governed by 1992 directives in all four of the areas covered by the 1992 concept: people, goods, services and capital. Technical standards are being harmonized, with common standards for products from lawnmowers (and the noise they emit) to forklift trucks (including their forward and reverse gears). The idea of an integrated Europe seems somewhat farfetched if one is, say, an Englishman encountering obstacles when trying to buy a house in Italy, a Dutchman trying in vain to settle a garage bill in France with a Eurocheque or a West German infuriated at having to pay a motorway tax in Belgium, but under the 1992 process such irritations are beginning to disappear. The process will be a long one, with many countries facing prosecution against outmoded protectionist practices in the European Court of Justice in Luxembourg. However, it is under way, and has already begun to take effect, with national governments often doing their best to disguise it by presenting new EC laws as national legislation.

Let us take the problem of moving goods around the EC by road. In June 1988, after months of prevarication, EC Transport Ministers agreed to abolish all EC, bilateral and transit road haulage quotas by 1 January 1993, with a rider stating that, by June 1991, the Council of Ministers must specify the harmonization measures required to ensure free cross-border competition. Ironically, this measure (a regulation, not a directive) was passed under West German chairmanship, even though the West Germans had been among the most vociferous opponents of free competition in road transport, fearing that their haulage companies would lose out to more efficient Dutch or Belgian ones—as indeed they may after 1992. To allay West German fears, the Commission, playing a role which is becoming increasingly common in controversial 1992 measures, agreed to undertake an informal review of lorry drivers' hours of work and rest and to make tachograph inspections more strict. But the measure was passed, and it is vital to the 1992 objective, given that over half of all internally traded EC goods go by road.

Equally, 1992 involves the liberalization of air transport, the second phase of which is due to begin in 1990, inaugurating an era of greater competition and cheaper air fares.

As another example, take the freedom of professional people to move around the EC as if it were one country. Shortly after the road haulage agreement by Transport Ministers, Trade Ministers met in Luxembourg to draw up common principles for the mutual recognition of diplomas by all twelve EC states. What this means is that, after 1992, a surveyor from Birmingham will be able to practise in Barcelona without retaking surveyor examinations, and a lawyer from Leeds will be able to find employment in Frankfurt if he or she so wishes without resitting Bar finals (although in some cases, such as lawyers and accountants, a local 'top-up' test may be required to prove adequate knowledge of local law). The same, of course, applies in reverse—and it remains to be seen whether Continental Europeans will benefit more than Britons or vice versa.

A third vital 1992 directive, on 'public procurement', obliges public authorities, including local government, to open up major public supply contracts to tender from any EC firm. If an Italian or Dutch company makes the best offer—as our imaginary office equipment supplier from Manchester found—it must be accepted, and it is hard luck for the home-based British bidder. After 1992 there will also be great competition

between EC ports, especially once the Channel Tunnel is in place. Liverpool, for example, hopes to gain extra global (especially transatlantic)
container trade, becoming once again Europe's premier trading port and
taking business from Rotterdam. The Dutch, for their part, believe that
Rotterdam will hold its own, if only because Britain has failed to plan for
the necessary fast road and rail links needed to attract business to the
Mersey after 1992.

The challenge to Britain

Much, in other words, will depend on the confidence, energy and ability of
British companies and professionals, and their willingness to meet the
1992 challenge both by facing competition from other EC nationals on their
home ground and by trying to make inroads into domestic markets in the
other eleven EC states.

As Neil Hartley of National Westminster's 1992 Policy Unit points out,
1992 will mean job losses as well as job creation, through mergers and
market penetration. Professor Peter Herriot of Birkbeck College, London,
warns that Britain risks an 'exodus' of skilled graduates to Europe ('design-
ers to Dusseldorf, physicists to Freiburg, engineers to Essen'), a finding
supported by the Institute of Manpower Studies at Sussex University in its
1989 report *The Graduate Labour Market in the 1990s*. Others caution that
high salaries for, say, working in telecommunications in Frankfurt are
offset by high taxes and cultural dislocation. Headhunters Saxton Bamp-
fylde, who recently surveyed managers responsible for 1992 in 130 large
companies, say the successful Euro executive will be the man or woman
who knows the local culture well, rather than the 'Euro yuppie', who stays
in bland business hotels and is 'dressed out of the contents of a duty-free
shop'.

Britain is perhaps best placed in a fourth area: financial services. In 1988
EC Finance Ministers agreed to liberalize capital movements across EC
borders by July 1990, despite strong reservations on the part of the socialist
government in France, which argued that allowing EC citizens to move
cash around the Community could only encourage tax evasion. In its
now-familiar role as honest broker, the Commission agreed to study ways
of increasing tax inspection, thus overcoming French doubts and allowing
the directive to go forward.

Coupled with a new 1992 banking directive allowing High Street banks
to operate anywhere in the EC under a single licensing system, the capital
movements directive will mean that EC citizens—including Britons—can
deposit or borrow money anywhere in the Community, with exchange
controls abolished (except, for a provisional period, in Greece, Spain,
Portugal and Ireland). Whether NatWest and Barclays make more of an
inroad in France than the Crédit Lyonnais or the Deutsche Bank achieve in
Britain will depend on the drive of the banks concerned. The same applies
to insurance, where Britain also has a strong reputation.

There are, of course, drawbacks to these schemes. The sceptics who argue that 1992 'will never happen' are not totally wrong. Before leaving office at the end of 1988 and handing over as senior British Commissioner to Leon Brittan, Lord Cockfield repeatedly warned of 'slippage' in the 1992 programme, indicating that some of the directives might have to be implemented after 1992. The Commission's 'progress report' on the internal market, issued in the autumn of 1988 as the first Delors Commission was coming to an end, stated that despite some persistent difficulties, the EC was on target for the completion of the European internal market by 1992. Announcing the adoption of the Commission's mid-term review in November, Lord Cockfield said there was 'considerable cause for satisfaction in what has been achieved in the 3½ years since the White Paper was adopted'. However, the report could not disguise the fact that much of the Community's progress has been limited to the removal of technical barriers to trade, leaving the balance sheet on the removal of physical and fiscal barriers distinctly 'less healthy'.

The report presented to the EC summit meeting in Rhodes in December 1988 highlighted the failure of Council to cope effectively with the problems presented by the Commission's call for fiscal approximation, the free movement of people across frontiers and the introduction of controls on plants and animals. It was also to be accompanied by a subsidiary report dealing with progress in the more controversial areas of monetary and social policy, as well as regional development, research and technology, and environmental issues. Lord Cockfield insisted that both reports were necessary in order to reinforce the general impression that the internal market had become 'the key that opens the door to Europe's future', and to remind member states of the importance of dealing with the wider policy issues raised by the movement towards economic integration. However, the subsidiary report was discreetly removed from the agenda in an attempt to avoid controversy between member states.

The mid-term review noted that of the original 300 White Paper legislative proposals (now reduced to 279) the Commission had placed 90% in front of Council by December. However, Council had adopted or agreed to adopt little more than 40% (about 107 out of the 279), and had fallen seriously behind schedule. Although there had been significant progress in areas as varied as the liberalization of financial services, opening up the Community's large public procurement sector to cross-border competition and the creation of an internal market for air and road transport, the persistent inability to reach a compromise on fiscal approximation and the abolition of internal frontier controls cast a potentially ominous shadow over the future of the Commission's timetable.

In an updated report in June 1989, the Commission said that 134 of the proposals had been agreed fully or partially, with 97 still awaiting approval and 48 to be tabled. It added that a further cause of concern was member states' tardiness in incorporating internal market directives into their national legislation.

Expanding 1992 horizons

Yet in a sense, the question of whether all directives are in place by New Year's Day 1993 is immaterial. 1992 is a complex of directives, regulations and other measures which, added together, are a shift in the way the EC is organized—and the way we are governed. Whether we like it or not, 1992 is developing beyond the confines of the 1985 White Paper and taking on a life of its own. Almost any European-wide scheme, in fact, can now be related to 1992.

Broadcasting offers one example. Many governments and broadcasting authorities argue that harmonizing television standards and encouraging a 'European' culture in the media are not part of 1992. However, the White Paper refers to the need for 'a single Community-wide broadcasting area' on the grounds that the Treaty of Rome provides for 'a common market in services'. The Commission has therefore drawn up plans for common standards in advertising and the co-ordination of satellite technology and cable television, arguing that television constitutes an economic service within the meaning of the Treaty, and that, because of the rapid development of satellite technology, there must be a framework to guide broadcasters and television authorities in the integrated European market.

European policies directly affect products from shoes (the British Footwear Manufacturers Federation is appealing to the EC to act against a flood of foreign—i.e. non-EC—exports to the UK) to cigarettes (from 1 January 1993 cigarette packets must carry prominent, bluntly worded health warnings). EC regulations on blood alcohol levels to reduce drink driving are planned. Even horse racing and field sports are affected: Ladbrokes has protested to Brussels that Paris Mutuel Urbain, the French offtrack betting organization, is expanding into the EC with government help, while British landowners have joined forces with boar hunters in West Germany and partridge shooters in Spain to oppose a new meat hygiene directive restricting game hunting, which, some would argue, is not an internal market matter.

The air-liberalization package does not include the question of air traffic control: yet as Europe's skies become more congested, causing inconvenience and delays for air passengers (not least for those who have saved up for package tours), logic seems to demand a greater role for Eurocontrol, the underused European air traffic control centre at Maastricht in Holland, even though Eurocontrol is not an EC body and has nothing to do with 1992.

Equally, there is no mention of defence in the 1992 White Paper. Yet it is increasingly assumed that at some point an integrated Europe will need some form of military integration—or at least military co-operation—to defend it. The Single European Act, which stipulated 1992 as the target date for completion of the internal market and laid down the principle of qualified majority voting, also made provision for co-operation between EC states on 'the economic and political aspects of security'. Whether the framers of the Act had a specific aim seems doubtful. The phrase has given rise to varying interpretations, with the French and West Germans inclined to translate 'security' as 'defence', while the British prefer a far vaguer interpretation, implying only consultation on wider European security interests (see Chapter 16). In practice, France and West Germany have moved towards closer military co-operation, and the Western European Union (WEU), at present based in Paris and London, has been re-activated as the forum for discussion of a joint European defence effort, perhaps as the European pillar of the North Atlantic Treaty Organization (NATO).

VAT, the ECU and national sovereignty

The 1992 momentum raises other difficulties and challenges which—like defence—are related to the central problem of national sovereignty in an integrated Europe. Moves towards the harmonization of financial services and freedom of capital movements automatically raise the question of economic and monetary union, with a European Central Bank and—in the long run—a single currency based on the European Currency Unit, or ECU. Quite apart from the fact that the ECU has close associations with the French medieval coin, the *Ecu* (and therefore raises non-French hackles), there are fundamental objections to the formation of a European Bank to control the money supply in an integrated market.

Similar objections arise—and not only in Britain—to the approximation of VAT rates. For Britain, unless compromise proposals for retaining some zero rating are accepted (see Chapter 11), the harmonization of indirect taxation would necessarily involve the abolition of VAT zero rating for basic goods, a politically sensitive move which no government could consider with equanimity. Lord Cockfield has pointed out that, in framing the VAT directive, he deliberately left open a loophole for Britain by suggesting that, for a limited period, zero rating could be retained in cases where its abolition would cause undue hardship for low-income groups. However, beyond the argument about the immediate political and economic impact of VAT harmonization or approximation lies the objection (most strongly voiced in the Treasury but also felt in other government departments) that to concede further control of fiscal policy to Brussels would be to surrender one of the traditional instruments of government policy, altering a basic constitutional relationship between the government and the governed in the traditional nation-state.

It is unlikely that all the internal market directives (let alone measures associated with 1992 but not part of the core programme) will be tabled and approved by 31 December 1992, but the programme, once launched, has become unstoppable. The Hanover summit of June 1988 recognized this by declaring that the 1992 programme was 'irreversible'. The eventual goal of European union is a long way off, and there is much room for argument about what union means. But the 1992 concept has taken root, and the argument is about the details and the extent.

In at least one area there is little resistance to pooling sovereignty: the battle against environmental pollution, which obviously transcends national barriers. On 2 March 1989 EC environment ministers agreed on a 100% phasing out of all chlorofluorocarbons (CFCs), chemicals used in aerosols which harm the ozone layer, by the year 2000 (Britain had wanted a more modest target). On 9 June they set new standards for small cars (below 1400 cc), cutting noxious emissions by 60% through the use of catalytic converters with effect from 1 January 1993. Britain, often criticized for a poor record on the environment (including such issues as power station emissions), has attempted to reverse its image following Mrs Thatcher's 1989 espousal of the Green cause.

The arts and education

No corner of life, commerce or even the arts seems likely to escape the long arm of Brussels. Even art dealers and auction houses, which might have thought themselves remote from arguments about harmonization and integration, face the prospect of a 1992 directive under which British dealers would have to impose VAT on works of art and antiques, thus risking (according to objectors) the loss of their current competitive edge and the transfer of international auction business to Geneva (Switzerland being outside the EC) or New York.

In education, traditionally regarded as a national prerogative and not an EC responsibility, the International Baccalaureat could challenge the A-level as a certificate of higher school education. The IB system, taught in 400 schools around the world at present, requires students to study three subjects in depth to the equivalent of A-level standard, but also to take three other subjects to a less exacting level, with a deliberate mix of science and humanities. Seventeen British schools and colleges teach the IB at present, with the examination board based at Bath University.

In higher education, the polytechnics have the edge in European business studies, with courses at Humberside College of Education, Kingston Polytechnic, Lancashire Polytechnic, Middlesex Polytechnic and Trent Polytechnic in Nottingham, which links up with the University of Paderborn in West Germany and the Groupe Ecole Supérieure de Commerce in Toulouse. Such links are supported by the EC's Erasmus fund.

Dutch and French Socialist MEPs have proposed a European history book, in which national viewpoints on Waterloo, the Franco-Prussian war or the Second World War would be counterbalanced by other viewpoints and 'descriptions of events which occurred simultaneously in all member states, to stimulate an awareness of belonging to a single political entity'.

Hugh McMahon, a former history teacher and now Labour MEP for Strathclyde West, dismisses this as 'Euro-culture gone berserk': the EC cannot produce 'a sanitized version of the conflicts and wars which took place in Europe in previous centuries'.

There is nonetheless a detectable shift in arts syllabuses, and hence reading habits, towards European literature. Obviously, people will continue to read American blockbusters, or any novel they like. But publishers at the 1988 Frankfurt Book Fair reported 'the search for the big European novel rather than the big American novel'. One Collins executive said that British publishers 'now spend more time at Frankfurt with the Europeans than we do with the Americans'. The trend began with the success of Umberto Eco's *The Name of the Rose*, and continued with Patrick Süsskind's *Perfume*. According to the *Sunday Times* of 23 October 1988:

> By 1992 British publishers will be buying European rights instead of UK rights in British novels, in order to protect themselves from American editions imported into this country across the unrestricted frontiers of Europe . . . Publishers will have more of a sense of themselves as Europeans.

A conference on the European film and television industry and 1992 was held in London in May 1989, as part of the Commission's 'Media 92' campaign for integration of European audiovisual industries. The advertising industry is also preparing for the single market, focusing on the potential of a 'European High Street'—although according to Ross Harvey of Admap, who organized the first conference on advertising in 1992 at Deauville in April 1989: 'The UK advertising industry has been backward about trying to build advance ties and reduce barriers with European counterparts.'

The cost of twelve separate markets

The drive for integration, in other words, is as much political as economic. It stems not only from Euro-idealism (and an impulse to complete the work of the EC's founders) but also from a fear that, unless the EC works more closely together, not least in industry and technology, it will prove unable to compete effectively with other giant trading blocs, notably Japan/Asia and the United States.

The official Cecchini report on the benefits of the internal market (*The European Challenge 1992*) estimates that the integration of twelve national markets will save the EC £140 billion (about 5% of the Community's gross national product), create millions of jobs and stimulate enough growth to 'put Europe on an upward trajectory of economic growth lasting into the next century'. This, the report declares, is 'a firm prospect, not a tantalizing chimera'.

The Cecchini report can be criticized for biasing the evidence in a way which suits EC officials who wish the single market plan to succeed. But, even allowing for an element of Euro-wishful thinking on the part of the Commission, these are impressive claims. Cecchini could also have added that the countries which will benefit most from 1992 will be those which are best prepared for it. Unfortunately, despite the DTI campaign, awareness in Britain of how power in the EC works, and of the implications of 1992, is still at a low level compared to our Continental partners. In the following chapters we look at the decision-making structure of the EC and at how the Single European Act which is changing our lives came about.

2 THE LONG ARM OF BRUSSELS
Who wields power in the New Europe

In framing the Treaty of Rome, which establishes the EC's institutions and defines their roles, the founders dealt with the most obvious political fact of life in the new European venture: that decisions taken in the name of the member governments (six in the beginning, and now twelve) would have to have the consent of all. Thus arose the Council of Ministers, which often puzzles outside observers since it does not exist in permanent session. It does, however, have a permanent secretariat and EC ambassadors in Brussels (known as Permanent Representatives), who take day-to-day decisions when the Council is not in session.

The Council, which has the last word in EC legislation, is simply made up of those ministers from the twelve governments with responsibility for the subject in question. Thus farm prices are settled (or not settled) by Agriculture Ministers, who then disperse back to their respective capitals and are replaced by their ministerial colleagues who deal with steel (Industry Ministers) or currencies (Finance Ministers) or pollution (Environment Ministers). 1992 internal market directives are dealt with by Trade Ministers, unless they obviously fall within the purview of another set of ministers (financial services directives, for example, usually go to Finance Ministers).

One side-effect is that ministers from the twelve nations get to know each other intimately, and act almost as a European government. On the other hand, all ministers feel that they owe their first obligation to their national electorates. Once back home from a Brussels or Luxembourg meeting, they tend to disguise the extent to which they co-operate in the European cause and choose to emphasize instead the role they play (imagined or real) in defending national interests in an EC context.

The task of representing Europe as a whole, at least in the public eye, falls to the European Parliament in Strasbourg, with Euro MPs drawn from all twelve states, and to the European Commission, with its headquarters in Brussels. The European Parliament, however, was set up under the Treaty of Rome as a largely consultative body, initially called the European Assembly. It is only since direct elections in 1979 (and more recently since the advent of the Single European Act) that it has begun to acquire a more decisive role in EC affairs. Rightly or wrongly, therefore, the European Commission has come to appear in the public mind as the central EC institution, and the one people regard as imposing its will on EC citizens as

'Brussels'. The more the Commission tries to avoid this image, carefully pointing out that it is an executive body and that there is a constitutional balance to be observed between the Commission, the Council and the Parliament, the more power and influence seems to flow towards the Berlaymont, the Commission's star-shaped plate-glass headquarters in Brussels.

The European Commission

Despite its power and importance, the Commission is appointed, not elected. It is often described as the EC's executive branch or central bureaucracy. However, its function is more wide-ranging than this might suggest. It was established under Article 155 of the Treaty as the body which would originate draft legislation to put before the Council of Ministers and Assembly (Parliament), and which would then implement the resulting directives. However, Article 155 also gives the Commission the right to 'have its own power of decision and participate in the shaping of measures taken by the Council and the European Parliament'. The Commission can issue regulations of its own accord, without reference to the two legislative bodies—as it did, for example, after the Chernobyl nuclear accident, by imposing a *cordon sanitaire* around the EC against the importation of goods contaminated by radiation. However, the Commission also has the power 'to participate in the shaping of measures' which do pass through the Council and Parliament. It does this by sitting in on Council sessions, and by meeting at the Parliament building in Strasbourg once a month, when Euro MPs are in plenary session. Commissioners are therefore present—and active—at all three stages of the decision-making process: initiation of draft proposals, debate and implementation.

This is of particular importance where 1992 is concerned. Quite apart from powers given to it under the Single European Act, the Commission has been able to originate 1992 legislation; take part in, and even guide the modification process as 1992 directives pass through the Council and Parliament; and then implement the resulting laws. The key role in the first phase of the 1992 programme (1985–8) fell to Lord Cockfield, as Internal Market Commissioner: it now rests with Martin Bangemann of West Germany, under the direction of President Delors. The Council and Parliament can overturn draft 1992 legislation if they are so minded, since they have the final say. However, in practice, the discussion of 1992 takes place within a framework defined by the Commission, and on the basis of proposals devised within the Berlaymont. This makes Delors and his 16 Commissioners potentially powerful figures. In the first Delors administration, for example, Peter Sutherland, the Irish Commissioner, matched Lord Cockfield's 1992 crusade with a forceful campaign of his own to exploit to the full the powers given to the Commission by the Treaty to intervene in mergers and takeovers if they distort competition.

The Commission is not, on the other hand, a 'foreign junta', as one peer memorably claimed in July 1988 during the debate in the House of Lords on the Rover–British Aerospace merger. Its national composition is carefully balanced, and Britain plays a full part in it—as in the Council of Ministers. In the present Community of Twelve there are 17 Commissioners—two each from Britain, France, West Germany, Italy and Spain, and one each from Belgium, Denmark, Greece, Ireland, Luxembourg, the Netherlands and Portugal. The 17 Commission members are appointed by their national governments—in practice, their respective prime ministers, who discuss the appointments at the EC summit preceding the four-yearly change of staff at the Berlaymont. Heads of government naturally seek to appoint Commissioners who will represent the national interest.

By some unwritten law, however, Commissioners almost always 'go native'—the charge most often levelled at Lord Cockfield before his replacement by Leon Brittan—leading to perpetual tension between Brussels and the national capitals. The contradiction is built into the solemn oath Commissioners take on arriving in Brussels, which commits them 'to perform my duties in complete independence, in the general interest of the Communities'. Commissioners also vow 'in carrying out my duties neither to seek nor to take instructions from any Government or body'. The oath adds pointedly that all member states of the EC have undertaken to respect this principle and 'not to seek to influence Members of the Commission in the performance of their task'—a promise sometimes more honoured, as Hamlet said of the Danish King's pledges, in the breach than the observance.

Each Commissioner is given one or more portfolios dealing with specific areas of policy (a list of the current Commission portfolios is given at the end of this book), with portfolios traditionally allotted by the Commission President over dinner at a chateau on the outskirts of Brussels, in a 'night of the long knives'. For Britain the most significant move in the Delors reshuffle of December 1988 was the allocation of the internal market portfolio, previously held by Lord Cockfield, to Martin Bangemann of West Germany—albeit divested of responsibility for financial services and fiscal approximation. But the two British Commissioners were nevertheless given key portfolios. Leon Brittan takes over from Peter Sutherland as Competition Commissioner, with responsibility for relations with the European Parliament and financial services, while Bruce Millan was put in charge of the Community's regional development funds. The controversial issue of fiscal approximation was given to the junior French Commissioner, Mme Christiane Scrivener, who is known to be sympathetic to the problems faced by Britain and Ireland over the proposed abolition of value added tax zero-rating. The powers of the European Commission President should not be exaggerated: he is not 'President of Europe', since power is shared with the other EC institutions, nor is he equivalent to a national prime minister, since Commission decisions are taken collectively, usually by majority vote. However, the President adopts an increasingly high profile, and attends Western economic summits alongside other Western leaders on behalf of the EC as a whole.

Each Commissioner has a staff or cabinet. The Commission bureaucracy is not as large as is sometimes imagined: including its 23 Directorates General, which report to Commissioners, it has about 15,000 staff (including interpreters and translators), less than the administration of Edinburgh—although the Eurocrats' high tax-free salaries and perks help to create the popular image of a bloated bureaucracy. It is also regarded as one of the most open bureaucracies in the world. The Council has a staff of 2000 and the European Parliament 3200.

The Commission meets on Wednesdays to review draft legislation, take legal action against recalcitrant states through the European Court of Justice, issue regulations and so on. A regulation differs from a directive in that it applies in detail to all member states. A directive, by contrast, lays down the aim and principle of a measure but leaves it up to national parliaments to put the new law into national form. In addition, the Commission administers EC funds, such as the regional fund or the farm support budget, and negotiates trade agreements on behalf of the EC.

The Council of Ministers

The Council represents the governments of the Twelve, and thus acts as a counterweight to the Commission, whose main focus is EC-wide rather than national. On the other hand, the Council also has to bear in mind the wider European interest. This is especially true of the twice-yearly EC summit, or European Council, which takes fundamental decisions about the Community's future direction.

As noted earlier, the Council does not meet continuously but is an *ad hoc* body made up of national ministers with responsibility for the policy area under discussion—Foreign Affairs, Agriculture, Transport, Industry and so on. The supreme body, therefore (the summit), is made up of prime ministers, or in one case (France) the president (hence the formal reference to 'the heads of state and government' at European Councils). Summits were not formally provided for in the Treaty of Rome, and only began in 1975. The institution of the twice-yearly (formerly thrice-yearly) European Council is now laid down in the Single European Act, and therefore in the Treaty. There is a growing tendency for the summit to deal with complex 1992 issues which in theory should have been sorted out at a lower level but which have proved intractable.

Unlike the Commission, which has a President appointed for two years (usually renewed, making a four-year term), the Council is chaired by each member state in turn for a period of six months. This rotating chairmanship is referred to—rather confusingly—as the Presidency of the Council of Ministers, in addition to which the European Parliament has its own President (Lord Plumb). The three EC Presidents sometimes hold joint meetings (for example, to sort out a dispute over the budget).

The President of the Council is the prime minister of whichever country holds the six-month rotating Presidency. In the first half of 1989 this is Felipe Gonzalez of Spain, in the second half of 1989 President Mitterrand of France (because France follows España in the alphabet of the country concerned). In 1990 the Council Presidents will be the leaders of Ireland and Italy, followed by Luxembourg and the Netherlands in 1991, and in 1992 Portugal and Britain (United Kingdom). It will therefore fall to Britain to preside over the celebrations on 31 December 1992, handing on the Presidencies of the single market to Denmark and Belgium in 1993. Since the Foreign Ministers meet regularly to deal with day-to-day Council business (when they become known as the General Affairs Council, rather than the Foreign Affairs Council), in practice the Foreign Minister of the Presidency nation is in the chair most often, and is therefore also referred to as President of the Council.

If the function of the Commission is to draw up draft legislation, including the draft EC budget, the task of the Council, in its various ministerial forms, is to examine the draft measures in conjunction with the European Parliament and in due course to amend, accept or reject them. Measures are usually examined first—and comprehensively—by EC Ambassadors in Brussels, the Committee of Permanent Representatives, known collectively by the French acronym COREPER. When COREPER agrees unanimously on a measure (usually an uncontroversial one) it passes through the full ministerial Council on the nod, appearing on the agenda as what is called in the jargon an 'A Point'. Otherwise a directive can only become EC law when it has been passed by the ministers of the Twelve in the Council, sometimes by unanimity, sometimes by majority vote. The question of majority voting (strictly speaking, qualified majority voting, based on a complex mathematical formula) is crucial to the 1992 process, since under the Single European Act internal market measures can be passed by majority vote.

The system of rotating Council Presidencies is also relevant to the 1992 programme, for the simple reason that each EC nation has different attitudes and priorities. Under the West German Presidency in the first half of 1988, for example, EC–Comecon *rapprochement* moved forward, and a large number of single-market measures were approved. Greece, which took over from Bonn for the second half of 1988, also pursued 1992 objectives, despite fears that the abolition of borders would expose the relatively weak Greek economy to cross-frontier competition. However, Council President Andreas Papandreou, the Greek prime minister, put the 1992 stress on social issues such as health and safety at work and (more controversially) worker participation in industry, a trend opposed by Mrs Thatcher, notably at the Rhodes EC summit (European Council) in December 1988, just before Greece handed over the Presidency to Spain. Since

Spain and France, which inherited the rotating Presidency in the second half of 1989 (after the EC summit in Madrid on monetary union), broadly share the Greek outlook and also have left-wing administrations, social issues have come to the fore alongside 1992 economic and political ones.

Like Commission meetings, sessions of the Council are held behind closed doors, a practice which has increasingly led to the charge that EC decision making is unacceptably secretive. Ministers retort that—unlike Commissioners—they are elected in their home countries and are therefore accountable. Equally, there is a large Brussels press corps which is regularly briefed by national spokesmen, both during and between Council meetings, and which reports what goes on behind the scenes through contacts with officials. Nonetheless, concern is growing over what is known in EC jargon as the 'democratic deficit' or lack of democratic control over EC decision making, and there is pressure for the Council to open at least some of its proceedings to the public, with a press gallery at the Charlemagne building (the Council's headquarters, opposite the Berlaymont) on the lines of the press galleries at Westminster and other EC parliaments.

Ministers continue to argue that their deliberations are too sensitive to be exposed to the public gaze, partly because Council debates involve a great deal of bargaining between nations as ministers try to find a balance between national interests and the wider interests of the EC as a whole. Once back home, ministers sometimes find it convenient to blame an unpopular measure on 'Brussels'—but, in the last analysis, 'Brussels' means the Council, in which all twelve nations take an equal part.

For three months in the year (April, June and October) Council meetings are held not in Brussels but in Luxembourg. This practice is jealously guarded by the Luxembourgers, who have built a large European Conference Centre in the Grand Duchy, but it is a constant source of irritation to the large numbers of officials and journalists who have to make the 2½-hour journey to Luxembourg from Brussels. Moving documents and staff between the three EC centres (Brussels, Luxembourg and Strasbourg) is also estimated to cost the EC taxpayer up to £100 million a year. There is growing pressure to move the European Parliament from Strasbourg to Brussels as part of a campaign to centralize most EC functions, making Brussels the administrative and legislative centre for the single market and making good its claim to be 'the capital of Europe'.

Qualified majority voting

Since qualified majority voting in the Council is so central to 1992—and so strongly criticized by those who think that power is shifting to Brussels too far, too fast—it is perhaps worth looking at it in detail. Under the Single European Act, 1992 issues can be (and in practice are) decided by a system of voting under which each member state is given a number of votes more or less consonant with its size and importance in the EC. Thus Britain wields ten votes, together with West Germany, France and Italy; Spain has eight; Belgium, Greece, Holland and Portugal have five each; both Denmark and Ireland have three; and tiny Luxembourg has only two. A qualified majority simply means 54 votes out of the total 76 from at least eight member states—meaning, in reality, that even two of the 'big boys' (for example, Britain and West Germany) acting together cannot block a decision. It takes three of the larger countries (or two of them plus one or two smaller states) to muster enough votes to stop a 1992 decision going through. But qualified majority voting does not apply to fiscal issues, which remain subject to the national veto.

The question of majority voting is a sensitive one, since it strikes at the heart of the national veto—that is, the right of any member state to veto legislation it does not like. Originally, most EC laws had to be passed by unanimous vote, but in the 1960s pressure built up for a switch to majority voting. When this ran into difficulties (mainly because of French opposition) the Six (as they then were) agreed on an informal arrangement known as the Luxembourg Compromise. This said that majority voting would be gradually introduced, but that the right of national veto would be retained where 'very important interests of one or more partners are at stake'. In practice, this proved unworkable. The advent of qualified majority voting under the Single European Act seems to have ended the Luxembourg Compromise, at least for 1992 issues, although this will only really become clear in the course of time, as qualified majority voting is tested in practice (it is already being used increasingly). On non-1992 issues the right of veto is unaffected: on the other hand, the dividing line between 1992 issues and non-1992 issues is not always obvious. (For a discussion of whether the European Central Bank proposal can be vetoed, see Chapter 8.)

The Commission has come under fire for categorizing controversial proposals such as the European Company Statute as internal market legislation requiring only a majority vote. Similarly, the Commission has invoked Article 90 of the Treaty of Rome to bring in new directives liberalizing the telecommunications equipment market, a move contested by France in the European Court of Justice. The Commission also drew criticism in 1989 for alleged corruption and excessive perks within its bureaucracy. Delors replied that such accusations amounted to a 'phoney war' to divert attention from key 1992 issues.

The European Parliament

It is sometimes supposed that Euro MPs are the decision makers in the EC, by analogy with Westminster. This is a misconception. The other widely held view of Euro MPs—that they enjoy a comfortable lifestyle with many perks—is less inaccurate, although MEPs can point to the arduous journeys they are obliged to make between their home constituencies and the Parliament's premises in Brussels and Strasbourg, or to conferences outside Europe (for example, for meetings with representatives of the ACP countries).

The Parliament has its origins in the European Assembly (initially the Assembly of the European Coal and Steel Community, before the EC proper was formed), to which national MPs were seconded. At first, the Assembly had 142 members; this was increased to 198 when Britain joined the EC in 1973 together with Denmark and Ireland, making an EC of Nine. However, the major change in the Parliament's fortunes came in 1979, when the first direct elections were held to a body of 410 seats, expanded to 434 seats for the next Euro elections in 1984, by which time Greece had joined the Community. The present Parliament has 518 seats, because of the entry of Spain and Portugal in 1986. The last elections, in June 1989, saw victories for the Socialists and Greens and losses for the centre and right-wing parties which had dominated the previous Parliament. Voter turnout was 56% for the EC as a whole and 37% in the UK (higher than the 32% turnout of 1979 and 1984). The British Labour Party won 13 extra seats at the expense of the Conservatives, whose electoral campaign was described by Sir Leon Brittan as 'negative, damaging and confusing'. Even before the vote, the Spanish Partido Popular abandoned the Conservatives for the Christian Democrats.

The voting pattern throughout the EC was one of protest against ruling parties, with startling gains for the Greens in the UK and for the far right in France and West Germany. However, because of the lack of a common electoral system, despite provision for one in the Treaty of Rome, the success of the Greens in the UK—with 2.3 million votes, or 15% of the vote, compared to the Conservatives' 34% and Labour's 40%—was not reflected in seats. Britain uses the first past the post system, whereas most other EC nations have some form of proportional representation (Ireland uses the single transferable vote). The Euro MPs, who sit in political groupings rather than national blocs, re-assembled in July 1989 with renewed confidence in their status as Europe's legislature. Lord Plumb (Conservative) was replaced as President by Enrique Barón Crespo, a Spanish Socialist, reflecting the new left-wing dominance of the chamber (260 seats, a narrow majority). On many 1992 issues, from the environment to workers' control, the Left and the Christian Democrats have informal understandings, giving the Parliament a potential consensus to push through measures disliked by Mrs Thatcher.

On the other hand, the Parliament did not become a true legislature even in 1979, and it took the Single European Act to give Euro MPs greater powers, especially with regard to 1992. Until this Act the Parliament was an almost exclusively advisory body in nearly all policy areas; Article 137 of the Treaty refers to its 'advisory and supervisory powers'. It offers 'opinions' which the Council can (and does) ignore, with one notable exception: the budget, where Euro MPs exercise joint control with the Council of Ministers in non-obligatory expenditure—that is, all spending except for farm support ('obligatory' in the sense that farm spending is a legal obligation laid down in the CAP).

Even here, however, the Parliament's powers are limited: farm spending, over which it has little or no control, still accounts for some two thirds of the budget, even after the Delors reforms, so that Euro MPs can only really influence one third of EC expenditure. They do so through a series of readings of the draft budget, which, after being drawn up by the Commission, goes back and forth between the Council and Parliament. However, the Parliament cannot increase expenditure beyond a 'maximum rate', which is set by the Council. This gives the Council the upper hand, and has in the past led to a wearisome annual tussle between the two institutions, often resulting in failure to adopt a budget at all and forcing the EC to resort to emergency monthly funding based on the previous year's budget (a system known as 'provisional twelfths') until a compromise is reached.

The Delors reforms, designed to prepare for 1992 by ridding the EC of budgetary wrangles, have greatly eased this problem, and annual budget crises no longer arise.

The Single European Act, moreover, gives the Parliament two further important roles in addition to its budgetary powers. Under the new 'co-operation' procedure (in effect, a second reading of 1992 legislation) the Council adopts a common position on a bill, taking into account the Parliament's opinion, and the Parliament then has three months to accept the proposal. If it does so, or takes no action, the proposal passes into law: but if MEPs propose amendments, or reject the bill, on its second reading by the Parliament the Council can only pass its original version by unanimous vote. Otherwise it must accept Parliament's version, or drop the bill altogether. Second, a new 'assent' procedure gives the Parliament a final say in commercial agreements negotiated between EC and non-EC countries (and indeed in the admission of new member states to the Community).

In the European Parliament debates on the Single European Act after it was signed at the Luxembourg summit of December 1985 many Euro MPs argued vehemently that the Act should be rejected, on the grounds that the new powers it gave to Strasbourg were inadequate, even insulting. The majority view, however, was that the Act's powers could be used as a basis for Parliament's campaign to transform itself into a true EC legislature. Euro MPs have indeed made effective use of both the 1992 'second reading' and their power to accept or reject trade agreements (in the latter case, for example, by repeatedly holding up three trade protocols with Israel because of Israeli behaviour towards Palestinian Arabs). According to a study by James Elles, MEP, until the Single European Act the Commission took up wholly or in part about 85% of the Parliament's amendments to proposals—but the Council accepted far fewer.

Will the European Parliament ever become a true EC legislature? The weight of the EC's institutional structure, even as amended by the Single European Act, is probably against it. MEPs can put written questions to EC Commissioners and insist on a published answer (at an estimated administrative cost of £500–1000 per answer); ministers from the country which is in the EC chair must appear before Euro MPs to report on current EC issues and answer questions; and, in theory, Euro MPs can even dismiss the entire Commission—a power never so far used in practice. However, many Euro MPs themselves feel that the Parliament will not become the voice of the peoples of Europe until it has greater legislative powers and until its activities are centred in one place, preferably Brussels. At present, Euro MPs hold their plenary debates at their chamber in Strasbourg, in the Palace of Europe, and their committee and group meetings in Brussels, at the parliament building not far from the Commission and Council, while the Parliament's Secretariat is located in Luxembourg.

As part of the current rebuilding of the Brussels EC quarter to make a vast 'Euro City' for 1992 and after, a new debating chamber (described as a conference centre) is being built behind the Parliament's committee rooms. The Treaty of Rome, in fact, does not fix any seat for the Parliament, and in September 1988 the European Court overruled French objections to plans for holding plenary sessions in Brussels.

In time, the pressures of the integrated market may force the Parliament to re-organize its work to resemble more closely that of a national parliament, with debates held continuously rather than for one week in four and increasing liaison between the European Parliament and national MPs. One estimate is that the Single European Act has increased the Parliament's workload by 30%. In Britain the House of Commons Select Committee on European Legislation sometimes scrutinizes EC laws only after they have been passed, because of the sheer volume. Options for increasing Westminster's scrutiny include a special question time on EC matters and allowing the Commons committee to see draft EC directives. (See also Chapter 10.)

The European Court of Justice

The 13 judges and six advocates-general of the European Court are nominated by member states and serve for a six-year term. They are required to be persons of the highest legal qualification 'whose independence is beyond doubt'. The Court, situated in Luxembourg, is the guardian of the Treaty and the EC's supreme legal body. It is not to be confused (but often is) with the European Court of Human Rights in Strasbourg, which is a Council of Europe body. (Still less is the European Court to be confused with the International Court of Justice in The Hague, as happened in one quality newspaper.)

EC law takes precedence over national law. Thus one function of the European Court is to give preliminary rulings on cases referred to it by national courts when a point of EC law is at issue. The national court then has to apply the ruling. However, cases can also be brought directly to the Court by individuals, companies or governments. In many cases it is the Commission which brings cases against both companies and member states for infringement of EC rules—including 1992 legislation. The first stage involves a written complaint and defence: there is then an oral hearing, in which both sides present their cases to the judges; in the third stage, the advocate-general gives an opinion; and finally, the judges deliver a verdict, arrived at by majority vote. The verdict usually (though not invariably) follows the advocate-general's opinion, as it did, for example, in rulings in 1988 against Britain over VAT exemptions.

The Court, like the Commission, is not an alien body but draws its members from all twelve states. Until recently, its President was a senior British judge. However, as 1992 approaches, its workload is becoming intolerable (it has only 500 employees), and in July 1988 the Council of Ministers agreed to the setting up of a lower-level EC Court of First Instance to sift cases before they reach the European Court proper. The new lower-level court should reduce the time taken to produce judgments in Luxembourg (currently anywhere between eighteen months and three years). However, there is no prospect of the Court's workload decreasing. On the contrary, as more and more 1992 directives are passed, an increasing number of test cases will be brought as the limits of single market legislation are probed—and as those who failed to stop 1992 laws passing through the Commission, Council and Parliament use the European Court as a last resort.

The Economic and Social Committee

This is an advisory body which brings together trades unionists, industrialists and other sectors of EC opinion to provide a sounding-board for ideas and to exchange news on current EC policies and proposals.

3 AMENDING THE TREATY

How the Single European Act was passed and what it contains

The Single European Act entered the world with a bang—literally. As European leaders gathered for the EC summit in Luxembourg in December 1985 a small bomb was thrown from a passing car onto the roadside near the Euro-Conference Centre on the Kirchberg. No motive was ever discovered: there had been a number of isolated, small-scale bombings in the Grand Duchy during the previous year, for no apparent reason, and this was assumed to be another such attack. Mrs Thatcher, who had survived the Grand Hotel bomb at Brighton the previous year, remarked calmly that bombs always caused anxiety but that the EC leaders had continued their deliberations unchecked.

Nonetheless the incident was perhaps symbolic, for the Single European Act, largely misunderstood or underestimated at the time, was itself a time-bomb. It was the culmination of 30 years of EC post-war history, and had given rise to a 'volcanic' display of opposition from Mrs Thatcher only six months before, at the Milan EC summit in June 1985, at the end of Italy's Presidency. The Act marked the first real attempt to bring the original Treaty of Rome up to date and shape the EC of the future. To understand its explosive content, it is necessary to go back to the Treaty of Rome itself and the beginnings of the Community.

The origins of European union

The idea of a European-wide system of government can be traced to medieval times, when the concept was one of a united Christendom. Scholars such as Aquinas or Erasmus thought of themselves as European, and moved freely from one university to another. In the seventeenth century William Penn, the Quaker, even proposed a European Parliament. In practice, however, European unification for the most part meant unification by force, through empires, from Charlemagne to Napoleon and Hitler. The rise of the nation-states in the eighteenth and nineteenth centuries, moreover, militated against the concept of unification, with notions of pan-European identity replaced by a balance of power between states, as at the Congress of Vienna in 1814–15. The First World War destroyed the old order but left Europe in a confused and disorganized state, prey to Fascist and Communist dictators.

It was the Second World War and its aftermath which produced a desire for union based on a determination to pool resources and make Europe into a peaceful force on the world stage. Hitler, it has been said, was the unwitting catalyst for democratic European unification. The apparently eternal problem posed by German power would be solved by bringing Germany (or at least West Germany) into a closely enmeshed, democratic Europe. The post-war enterprise had its roots in the 1948 Benelux Union between Belgium, the Netherlands and Luxembourg, and grew over a period of six years into the EC of Six, with Benelux joined by France, Italy and West Germany. This post-war process of integration was given added impetus by the two emerging superpowers—from the United States in the form of Marshall Aid and American support for European reconstruction and from the Soviet Union (less benevolently), in the form of an armed menace to Western Europe which had the effect of pushing the Europeans closer together for common protection. Britain, despite Churchill's rhetoric about the need for a United Europe, remained aloof.

In the early post-war years the impetus towards European union was simple and direct. As early as 1948 there was a defence dimension to the process in the form of the Treaty of Brussels establishing the Western European Union (WEU), which included Britain. In the 1950s the WEU became moribund, partly because of the formation of NATO, and attempts to form a European Defence Community (EDC) also foundered in 1954 —because of a French veto. Instead, the emphasis was on economic union as a first step. However, it was always understood that the eventual aim was a union which had political and even defence implications as well as economic ones.

Monnet and the Franco-German Axis

The main driving force came (as much of the 1992 impetus was later to come) from a Frenchman: Jean Monnet. Originally from a family cognac firm (and its pre-war salesman in Britain), Monnet helped to co-ordinate the economies of the Allies against Hitler, and became a passionate advocate of Anglo-French integration after the war. However, the fulcrum of European union was, in the end, Franco-German, with Britain still standing on one side. The French fear was that after two world wars, and centuries of Franco-German conflict before that, Germany would once again dominate Europe, through its possession of key coal and iron industries in the Saarland, a border region like Alsace, which had often caused bitter rivalry in the past. Together with Robert Schuman, the French Foreign Minister, who came from Alsace and who was also an ardent proponent of European integration, Monnet put forward a plan —which bore Schuman's name—for a European Coal and Steel Community (ECSC) to oversee the industries in a common supranational interest. This duly came about in August 1952, under Monnet's chairmanship, with the Benelux nations and Italy joining France and West Germany.

Three years later the same Six, under the influence of Monnet's Action Committee for a United States of Europe, began work on the Treaty of Rome, founding a European Economic Community with much wider powers than the ECSC. The 1955 meeting of the Foreign Ministers of the Six at Messina, in Italy, on the legal basis for a Common Market led two years later to the signing of the completed Treaty in Rome, on 25 March 1957. Euratom, the European Atomic Energy Community, was also established in Rome on the same day as the EEC. In 1967 the three 'Communities'—the ECSC, Euratom and the EEC itself—were merged. It is therefore technically correct to refer to the 'European Communities'—but in practice the EEC is the one that matters. The phrase 'European Economic Community' is increasingly being shortened to 'European Community' as integration develops and the Community acquires a political as well as an economic character.

Largely due to continuing Franco-German *rapprochement*, helped by the personal relationship between de Gaulle and Adenauer, the EC made rapid progress towards its first goal: the removal of internal tariffs and quotas. As in the later case of 1992, the founding fathers laid down a target date for this customs union: 31 December 1969, 12 years after the signing of the Treaty. In the event, the removal of internal tariffs was completed over a year early, in July 1968, accompanied by the erection of a common external tariff to protect the new common market. The EC also fulfilled the Treaty's provision for a Common Agricultural Policy involving farm subsidies—a measure which was intended to support Europe's farmers and ensure food supplies but which was to consume a growing proportion of the EC's limited budget.

An ever-closer union

It swiftly became apparent, however, that the drive for integration went beyond a customs union and farm support. The subsequent history of the EC is a history of lurches towards the original goals of the Treaty preamble: 'To lay the foundations of an ever-closer union among the peoples of Europe . . . to ensure economic and social progress by common action to eliminate the barriers which divide Europe.' One early effort to fulfil this goal by creating a political as well as economic union was the Fouchet Plan (Marks I and II) of 1961, which proposed a joint foreign policy. However, this, like many other such plans, foundered on the objection—put forward most vehemently by de Gaulle—that foreign policy was a national prerogative not a supranational one. Similar objections ended the 1970 Werner Plan for Economic and Monetary Union by 1980; once again, governments declared that handing over control of monetary questions to the EC would be an unacceptable surrender of national sovereignty. The plan for European Union developed in 1976 by Leo Tindemans, then Belgian Prime Minister (and now Belgian Foreign Minister), also failed —not surprisingly, perhaps, since the Tindemans Plan not only combined the two earlier failed Plans for a joint foreign policy and monetary union but added schemes for common regional and social policies, a common industrial policy and a programme for a Citizens' Europe.

Yet Euro-Plans have a way of lingering on EC shelves rather than disappearing. There is now a social and regional policy, co-ordination of foreign policy ('political co-operation') and a plan for a Citizens' Europe, while monetary union is obstinately back on the agenda. It became clear as early as 1959, when both Greece and Turkey applied for associate membership status, that the EC had a centripetal pull which would lead to its further expansion. The key development was Britain's decision—under Harold Macmillan's premiership—to apply for full membership, beginning in 1961 (barely a year, paradoxically, after Britain had been instrumental in setting up the rival EFTA, the European Free Trade Association). The British application was vetoed by de Gaulle—the first French 'non'—in 1963, on the grounds that Britain's ties were transatlantic rather than European. It was renewed by Harold Wilson in 1966, and again vetoed by de Gaulle. However, de Gaulle's nationalism and Gallic disdain were at odds with Community philosophy. He clashed frequently not only with Britain but also with leading statesmen such as Dr Walter Hallstein, the West German President of the European Commission, who favoured a switch to majority voting in the Council of Ministers.

Enlargement: Britain joins the Community

In 1969 de Gaulle resigned, and a year later he died. With Pompidou and Brandt leading France and West Germany, respectively, the British application was again renewed under the premiership of the pro-European Edward Heath, amid tough bargaining over the accession terms. Denmark, Ireland and Norway (which had submitted and withdrawn applications in accordance with Britain's applications and rejections) also applied. Britain, Denmark and Ireland finally became EC members in 1973, bringing the total from Six to Nine. All three ratified the decision in popular referendums—in the British case in 1975, after the new Wilson government had renegotiated entry terms to ensure a British budget rebate. A Norwegian referendum on EC membership in 1972, by contrast, produced a narrow majority against, with the result that Norway stayed out—although the 1992 process has brought renewed signs of interest in Oslo in full membership.

In 1975, the year of the British EC referendum, Greece put in its membership application, followed by Spain and Portugal two years later. Greece duly entered the Community in 1981, bringing the membership from Nine to Ten, and the entry of Spain and Portugal in 1986 completed the enlargement process for the foreseeable future, producing a Community of Twelve and providing further pressure for economic and institutional reforms as part of the 1992 process.

However, the development of the Community has been far from easy, and more a matter of 'two steps forward, one step back' than of smooth progress towards the dream of Monnet and Schuman. In the 1970s the CAP began to become unmanageable as the subsidies system for both production and storage gave rise to surpluses—the beginnings of the notorious food mountains. On the plus side, moves towards a common foreign policy took on new life, with the agreed Davignon Plan of 1970 on regular contact between EC Foreign Ministers in 'political co-operation', or POCO for short. Enlargement to Nine and then Ten failed to produce the expected economic benefits, partly because of the global oil crisis of 1973 and partly because of the lack of a coherent plan for EC growth. On the other hand, in 1974–5 the Regional Development Fund was set up to close the gap between prosperous and less-prosperous regions of the EC, and it was agreed that the European Parliament should be directly elected. In 1979, through the joint efforts of Helmut Schmidt, the West German Chancellor, Valéry Giscard d'Estaing, the French President, and Roy Jenkins, President of the European Commission, the European Monetary System (EMS) was founded, with an exchange rate mechanism designed to limit currency fluctuations by linking member currencies to a newly devised European Currency Unit—the ECU.

The 1980s thus found the EC advancing unevenly towards the vision of the founding fathers, facing institutional and budgetary problems inherited from the 1950s and 1960s, and suffering—after the de Gaulle–Adenauer and Giscard–Schmidt years—from lack of overall direction, guidance and leadership. Of the major EC statesmen, Mitterrand and Kohl lacked strong personal rapport and did not, on the whole, lend new dynamism to the Franco-German axis, the traditional motor of EC progress. Mrs Thatcher, continuing the British tradition of standing aloof (indeed, reinforcing it) did not appear to regard the European cause with any enthusiasm, to put it mildly. If anything, her instincts lay in another direction—the Anglo-American transatlantic relationship so feared in earlier times by de Gaulle. Mrs Thatcher's rapport was with President Reagan of the United States rather than with her Continental counterparts.

The early 1980s were dominated not by visions of the future but by Mrs Thatcher's determined—and justified—campaign to persuade Britain's EC partners that Britain's contribution to EC coffers was unacceptably high (Harold Wilson's renegotiated terms not having been fulfilled). With the help of President Mitterand, the campaign eventually led at the Fontaine-bleau summit of 1984 to a compromise involving a rebate to Britain of 66% of the difference between its VAT contributions to EC funds and its share of EC benefits—in other words, the difference between what Britain put into the EC and what it got out of it (less than France or West Germany, which gained more in farm support). The Fontainebleau settlement also involved an increase in the limit on overall VAT contributions to the budget from 1% to 1.4%, with further rises to be discussed at a later stage.

All this had the merit of focusing attention on the chronic budgetary crisis and on the fact that the EC's 'own resources' were being outstripped by the cost of running a Community of Twelve. Reform was needed, but the shrill tone of Mrs Thatcher's campaign (and resulting anti-Common Market feeling in Britain) did not augur well for the reform effort. In the absence of convincing leadership from London, Paris or Bonn, much would depend on the new European Commission, led at the beginning of 1985 by a quiet, dapper Frenchman: Jacques Delors.

The Delors reform package

At the beginning of 1985 Delors made a tour of European capitals to introduce himself and to sound out opinion on four ways of moving the EC closer to the founders' goals:

1 Revival of the idea of a defence union;
2 Revival of the idea of monetary union;
3 Reform of the EC's institutional structure of Council, Commission and Parliament; or
4 Completion of the internal market through the complete dismantling of obstacles to trade (in other words, further development of the customs union).

In the end, the 1992 concept has come to embrace all four, either formally or informally, but in 1985 it was the proposal for completing the market which most appealed to EC leaders (Mrs Thatcher included), because it implied deregulation and freer competition. The difficulties began when Delors went on to argue that completing the internal market involved a mass of new legislation and that the Treaty of Rome would have to be amended—the birth of the Single European Act.

The practical basis of the Delors concept was simple: moves to harmonize EC standards and practices since the completion of the customs union in 1968 had come up against the obstacle of national protectionism. No state wanted to give up long-cherished practices in the wider interest. Therefore some supranational way would have to be found of persuading them to 'harmonize' or (as a first step, referred to as 'the new approach') mutually to recognize each other's standards. This became known in EC jargon as the 'Cassis de Dijon' ruling, after a celebrated case at the European Court of Justice in 1979. This arose when a West German firm found that it was prevented from importing Cassis de Dijon because it allegedly did not conform to exacting West German standards for liqueurs. The Court ruled that Bonn could only prevent the import of a French drink if it could prove that the liquid was harmful to health or contravened tax or consumer protection laws—which cassis (the basis of a popular aperitif called kir) did not.

In formulating their new plan for the internal market Delors and the Commission seized on the 'Cassis Principle' that, for goods to move around the integrated market unhindered, they need only conform to commonly agreed standards. Lord Cockfield, the Internal Market Commissioner, devised 300 measures to eliminate the technical, physical and fiscal barriers to intra-Community trade. In addition, the Commission took up earlier, unsuccessful ideas for institutional reform, monetary union and a common foreign policy. The last in this long line of failed visions was the Draft Treaty of European Union, devised by Altiero Spinelli, a veteran Italian Communist Euro MP, and adopted by the European Parliament.

The Milan summit: partial failure

The 1992 process which resulted is a diluted version of what union visionaries like Spinelli had wanted. On the other hand, the Single European Act goes further than sceptics had wished. When the EC Milan summit convened in June 1985 to take a first look at what was to become the Single European Act, Mrs Thatcher was highly suspicious of anything which went beyond the opening up of internal frontiers to facilitate movement and trade. Britain led the way in proposing a common foreign policy, going so far as to suggest a joint EC approach at the United Nations—which does not appear in the Single European Act as eventually agreed. However, Mrs Thatcher set her face firmly against changes to the Treaty of Rome, and—with the backing of Denmark—said that she saw no need for a special inter-governmental conference to agree such changes. Increased use of majority voting, the Prime Minister declared, could be covered by a 'gentleman's agreement' along the lines of the Luxembourg Compromise, with the national veto retained. Talk of European union was 'airy-fairy'.

The Milan summit was marked by bad feeling, caused by British anger over a Franco-German draft declaration on European Union which drew heavily on British proposals, and then went beyond them. However, at the end of the summit Mrs Thatcher was outvoted over the setting up of the Inter-Governmental Conference (IGC). President Mitterrand remarked tartly that the summit had sorted out 'those who favour a strong, united Europe from those who are hanging back'. The Milan summit communiqué (or rather, the Presidency's conclusions, since not all points were accepted unanimously) was the first mention of 1992 as a target date. It confirmed 'the need to improve the operation of the Community in order to give concrete form to the objectives it has set itself, in particular as regards the completion of the internal market by 1992 and measures to promote a technological Europe'. It also noted the need to improve decision-making procedures, partly by revising the powers of the Commission and the Parliament. The key section concluded:

> The summit discussed in detail the convening of a conference to work out the following with a view to achieving concrete progress on European Union: a treaty on a common foreign and security

policy on the basis of Franco-German and United Kingdom drafts: and amendments to the Treaty of Rome . . . The required majority has been obtained for the convening of such a conference.

Amid the row over amending the Treaty it almost went unnoticed that the Milan summit had instructed the Council of Ministers 'to initiate a precise programme of action, based on the White Paper . . . with a view to achieving completely and effectively the conditions for a single market in the Community by 1992 at the latest, in accordance with stages fixed in relationship to previously determined priorities and a binding timetable'. The Milan meeting, in other words, was not as disastrous for EC unity as it appeared at the time. The only question was whether, when the EC leaders re-assembled in Luxembourg at the end of the six-month Luxembourg Presidency, Mrs Thatcher would still be as adamantly opposed to Treaty changes.

The Luxembourg summit: Mrs Thatcher signs the Act

The Luxembourg summit began more auspiciously. The IGC Mrs Thatcher had so fiercely opposed at Milan took the modest form of a series of Foreign Ministers' meetings in autumn 1985. By the time the Luxembourg meeting convened, many of the basic issues had been agreed. The leaders were anxious to avoid a further display of disunity, and began by agreeing that Mrs Thatcher was right to put the 1992 emphasis on deregulation. Completion of the internal market would be designed to give a great impetus to the European economy, with special help for small and medium-sized enterprises. There was also initial agreement on giving the European Parliament a second reading of internal market legislation. However, France and Italy, with support from the Benelux nations, still wanted to turn the proposed Treaty amendments into an Act of European Union, creating a 'European space'—a phrase dismissed by the British as imprecise. They also wanted an expanded EC secretariat with power to co-ordinate EC foreign policy.

For Britain, again with support from Denmark, the priority was to make the existing EC institutions and mechanisms function more efficiently (for example, by revising the CAP) and to ensure that the move towards a frontier-free Europe did not imperil Britain's control as an island over drugs, immigration and plant and animal health. The summit eventually produced a compromise, but the tension between these two visions of 1992 has resurfaced in various guises ever since.

There was alarm on the second day of the summit when Denmark and Italy both threatened to walk out—the Danes because for them the draft agreement on 1992 went too far and the Italians because it did not go far enough. In a vivid if gory image, a distraught Delors protested that the changes insisted on by Britain amounted to a 'Texas chainsaw massacre'. However, in the end, late at night, the Single European Act was born, and the history of the EC had taken a major step. 'We decided to sit it out until we had a clear and decisive position,' a tired Mrs Thatcher told reporters after she had reversed her earlier opposition to Treaty changes—provided that they met British concerns. She still regarded amending the Treaty as unnecessary, 'but if they wanted it to be this way, so be it'.

Main points of the Single European Act

The Act laid down eight basic points:

1 1992. 'The Community shall adopt measures with the aim of progressively establishing the internal market over a period expiring on December 31 1992 . . . The internal market shall comprise an area without internal frontiers in which the free movement of goods, persons, services and capital is ensured in accordance with the provisions of this Treaty.' States could apply for exemptions, and the Act included a 'General Declaration' as follows: 'Nothing in these provisions shall affect the right of member states to take such measures as they consider necessary for the purpose of controlling immigration from third countries, and to combat terrorism, crime, the traffic in drugs and illicit trading in works of art and antiques.' On the other hand, the EC leaders agreed to avoid such continued national controls by introducing 'common measures' on police co-operation, visas, extradition and immigration. The Act also empowered states to take fellow states to the European Court if exemptions were 'improperly used' to restrict trade.

2 Practical steps to reduce the administrative and legal constraints on small and medium-sized businesses, with a Commission task force to oversee this deregulatory process.

3 In a concession by both Britain and West Germany, which had the strongest doubts about monetary union, the Act's preamble referred specifically to monetary union as an EC goal, to be 'progressively realized'. However, monetary union was not among the 1992 priorities laid down by the Act as legally binding, and Mrs Thatcher argued that the wording went no further than that of the Paris summit in 1972.

4 Disparities between richer and poorer regions of the EC were to be reduced (the policy known as 'cohesion') through the more efficient use of the structural funds or regional and social funds. To avoid a 'two-speed Europe', states would use their economic policies to promote 'harmonious development in the EC' and overcome 'the backwardness of the least favoured regions'. On Britain's insistence, this embraced 'declining industrial regions' in the north as well as

rural areas in the south. The Act authorized the Commission to recommend 'amendments' to the structural funds—and at the Brussels summit of February 1988, the leaders agreed to Delors' proposals for the funds to be doubled by 1992.

5 The European Parliament was given a new 'co-operation' procedure, enabling it to amend legislation through a second reading and in some cases—notably commercial agreements—to have the final say. On most issues, if the Parliament rejected a bill on its second reading the Council could still have the last word by passing the measure unanimously.

6 Technological research to be encouraged within an agreed framework. Britain held up the resulting five-year (1987–91) research framework programme—eventually reduced to £4 billion (5.3 billion ECUs)—on the grounds that the technology projects involved had not been properly approved and there was too much research duplication among the EC nations. However, the programme—including information technology (ESPRIT), advanced telecommunications research (RACE) and industrial technology (BRITE)—eventually went ahead, albeit with a smaller budget than the 7.7 billion ECUs the Commission had wanted.

7 The environment. The EC was to take action to improve the environment, contribute towards the protection of human health and ensure 'a prudent and rational utilization of natural resources' on the principle 'that environmental damage should be rectified at source and that the polluter should pay'. Denmark's objections that its own standards were higher than those of the EC were met by a clause stating that the Act need not prevent member states taking 'more stringent measures' than the EC norm.

8 A separate Title provided for 'European co-operation in the sphere of foreign policy'—as distinct from external or trade policy, which is handled by the Commission, although it also impinges on foreign policy. The leaders undertook to formulate and implement a European foreign policy by consulting one another 'so as to ensure that their combined influence is exercised as effectively as possible through co-ordination, the convergence of their positions and the implementation of joint action', with Foreign Ministers meeting at least four times a year on political co-operation issues. Most controversial was paragraph 6a: 'The High contracting Parties consider that closer co-operation on questions of European security would contribute in an essential way to the development of a European identity . . . They are ready to co-ordinate their positions

more closely on the political and economic aspects of security.' This should not conflict with the competence of either NATO or the WEU, the new Article said. A new foreign policy secretariat would be set up in Brussels (and duly was) but with purely administrative functions.

Ratification of the Act

The day after the Luxembourg summit, Delors declared that the EC could now undertake 'the adventure of progress towards union'. In fact, every EC summit since December 1985 had grappled in one form or another with the consequences of the Single European Act and of its inbuilt contradictions. Nonetheless, the Act is in force, and the arguments are about interpretation, not about repealing it—which is impossible. In the course of 1987 the Act was ratified by every national parliament, including Westminster, where the Lords almost staged a rebellion but in the end consented. Every ratification debate revolved around the degree to which the Single European Act involved a partial surrender of national sovereignty to the EC. In the case of two countries—Denmark and Ireland—it took popular referendums to resolve the question of the Act's constitutionality—in Denmark in March 1986 (56.2% in favour) and in Ireland in May 1987 (70.2% in favour).

The Act was passed, the Treaty was altered and with it the nature of the EC, even if some of the 1992 goals—such as monetary union—were put off to the distant future and others—such as foreign and defence policy co-ordination—were diluted or left ambiguous. The heart of the matter was the commitment to a single European market by 31 December 1992, and the agreement that the EC had the right to lay down policy throughout the Community in areas from taxation to tourism.

4 STANDARDIZING EUROPE

Technical harmonization from telecommunications to pharmaceuticals

Suppose European business executives were required to change the colour of their shirts at every EC frontier crossing in order to satisfy the national regulations of individual member states. This kind of absurdity is not so far removed from the obstacles faced by EC manufacturers trying to export their products, whether cars, telecommunications equipment or foodstuffs, to other EC member states.

In June 1985 the European Commission published what has perhaps become its most widely known White Paper, *Completing The Internal Market*, which outlined an ambitious strategy and timetable for the task of removing the Community's internal barriers to trade and merging twelve disparate economies into one by 31 December 1992. It defined three separate categories of internal barriers to the free movement of capital, goods, labour and services, the fiscal, physical and technical barriers to trade, whose existence had been identified by the Delors Commission as being responsible for the 'economic balkanization' of the Community.

The White Paper argues forcibly for the complete and effective removal of all three categories of barrier. But it is the removal of the technical barriers to trade, the plethora of different technical standards for individual products drawn up by each member state (ostensibly for health, safety and environmental reasons) which holds out the prospect of creating a single industrial market of continental proportions, thereby enabling Europe to compete more effectively with its competitors in Japan and the United States.

Along with the creation of the Common Agricultural Policy, setting up a Common Market, as specified under Article 100 of the Treaty of Rome, was one of the fundamental objectives inspiring the foundation of the EC. However, despite a promising start, the Community soon lost its way. The first step towards the creation of the Common Market was the establishment of a common customs tariff, completed well ahead of schedule in 1968. It was followed ten years later by the adoption of the Sixth VAT Directive, which formed the basis of the Community's indirect taxation system and provided a common method for allocating revenues from national VAT receipts to the Community budget.

However, the impact of the two oil crises of the 1970s, and the unprecedented combination of inflation and recession that resulted, brought the promising progress of the Community's first 20 years to an abrupt halt. The impetus towards economic integration rapidly dissipated, and in many respects the Community began to move backwards. Member states, although required by the Treaty of Rome to dismantle all tariff barriers between them, showed a polite respect for the letter of the Treaty and systematically set about undermining its spirit by erecting a large network of non-tariff barriers, epitomized by divergent technical standards, in a forlorn endeavour to protect themselves from intra-EC competition.

The Community's preoccupation with the accession of new members during the 1970s and 1980s effectively ruled out any serious attempt to rectify this deteriorating situation. In this context, the Commission's efforts to harmonize every technical standard on a product-by-product basis were reminiscent of the labour of Sisyphus. In the mid-1980s the European Commission and the Council of Ministers launched a long-overdue resuscitation package for the ideals expressed by the founders of the EC.

A new approach to technical harmonization

Following recognition by the Council of Ministers that, in the field of technical standards and regulations, the goals of all national legislation were more or less identical, the European Commission was granted a licence to abandon its traditional one-dimensional approach to technical harmonization in favour of a new multi-dimensional strategy based on selective harmonization and mutual recognition.

The traditional approach, which required years of tortuous negotiations to arrive at a common position for a single product standard, was inherently bureaucratic, extremely unpopular and very time consuming. In many cases it had proved to be completely futile. By the time the new product standard had emerged from the bureaucrat's briefcase and onto the shopfloor it had often been made redundant by the rapid pace of technological development. The whole legislative process was rather like moving a mountain to bring forth a mouse, and it had brought into disrepute the Community's laudable efforts to create common industrial standards.

The most systematic expression of the new approach to the harmonization of technical standards was given by Lord Cockfield in the Internal Market White Paper. In this he called for a distinction in all internal market legislation to be made between 'what is essential to harmonize, and what may be left to mutual recognition of national standards'. In future, the traditional approach of legislative technical harmonization will be restricted to those areas where it is vital to create a uniform Continental market. Companies previously limited to national markets for products manufactured under national product standards will benefit from the economies of scale that the single internal market will create.

In 1985 the Commission acknowledged that exclusive reliance on Article 100 of the Treaty, which required a unanimous vote by the Council of Ministers to secure passage of all technical harmonization legislation, would be likely to present the same sort of difficulties experienced in the past. It therefore announced its intention to pursue legislative harmonization under Articles 30–36, which prohibited national governments from adopting policies which constituted an 'arbitrary discrimination or a disguised restriction on trade between member states'.

However, by the time the Single European Act had been ratified in 1987 the Commission's ability to secure legislative approval of technical harmonization measures by the Council of Ministers had been immeasurably strengthened. Article 100a of the amended Treaty introduced the principle of qualified majority voting for all measures 'which have as their object the establishment and functioning of the internal market'. The built-in institutional unanimity had been bypassed, allowing the Commission to press ahead with the task of laying the foundations of a single internal market. Henceforth, all legislative technical harmonization measures will be confined to establishing minimum health and safety requirements, conformity with which will guarantee manufacturers the right of access to the markets of other member states. In addition, legislative technical harmonization will be complemented by the systematic implementation of the principle of mutual recognition of non-essential national product standards. On the assumption that all such regulations are designed to lay down minimum health and safety standards, it follows that all governments have basically the same objectives in mind.

Following a series of seminal judgments by the European Court of Justice, notably the 1979 Cassis de Dijon ruling, which specified that Community law demands the mutual acceptance of goods from one member state by other member states, the Internal Market White Paper laid down that in future:

> The general principle should be approved that, if a product is lawfully manufactured and marketed in one member state, there is no reason why it should not move freely throughout the Community. The objectives of national legislation in this respect are essentially identical. Although they may take different forms, they amount to the same thing.

As a result, member states must now accept products from other member states which are manufactured to a different design but which nonetheless perform the same as those manufactured to national technical standards. This principle (which may in retrospect seem to be nothing more than common sense) is in fact little short of a revolution, given the historical context of Community attempts to harmonize technical standards. Moreover, working on the principle that it is better to privatize as much harmonization as possible, the task of establishing European-wide product standards has now been taken out of the hands of the bureaucrats and allocated to the new European standards institutes such as the European Committee for Standardization (CEN), the European Committee for Electrotechnical Standardization (CENELEC) and the European Telecommunications Standards Institute (ETSI).

Each organization, composed of industry experts and representatives of consumer bodies, has been authorized by the Commission to build on legislative technical harmonization by developing common industrial product standards applicable throughout the EC. So far, Britain's participation on the new standard-setting organizations has been extremely poor, and many of the key positions have already gone to West Germany and France. At a meeting of 300 senior business executives in Glasgow in October 1988, Lynda Chalker, Minister of State at the Foreign Office, expressed the Government's concern that Britain was being overshadowed by its Continental rivals, and warned that: 'The common standards which get adopted in Europe are bound to bear the character of the countries which put the most effort into their creation.' Similarly, product testing and certification procedures, which are used by national regulatory authorities to ensure that imported goods actually comply with national technical standards and regulations before being granted authorization for sale in the national market, are now also subject to the principle of mutual recognition.

The old system of national product testing and certification procedures (which meant, for example, that before a British-made vehicle could be sold on the Italian market its brakes would have to be sent to Italian inspectors for testing before going back to Britain for installation and eventual shipment back to Italy) is finally on its way out. Member states who continue to protect their national markets from Community competition by taking refuge in Article 36 of the Treaty, granting them the right to restrict imports because they do not conform to their 'essential requirements', will no longer have grounds for doing so. If the new approach is successful, the different essential requirements of member states will be replaced by harmonized Community essential requirements.

In order that member states do not sabotage this strategy by continuing to lay down national product standards independent of the work of the new European standards institutes they are now obliged to notify the Commission in advance of their intention to introduce any new regulations and technical standards that could have an impact on other member states. Under a Directive on Mutual Information Procedures, which came into effect in January 1985, the Commission also has the power to prevent member states from implementing any new technical regulations until it has established whether they create any new barriers to intra-Community trade. To date, over 30 such technical standards have been blocked by Brussels.

According to Commission statistics, about 60% of the total number of complaints received from member states concerning other member states who fail to honour the provisions of the Treaty relate to the Common Market provisions of Articles 30–36. Because of its limited resources, the Commission has only been able to resolve less than half of these infractions, which has acted as a significant brake on progress towards the creation of a genuine internal market. However, under the new multidimensional strategy for harmonizing technical standards, Commission officials are confident that the combined impact of legislative technical harmonization, the principle of mutual recognition of non-essential national technical standards, the work of the new standardization organizations and the recently implemented mutual information procedures will produce a considerable improvement in the record of member states adhering to Community regulations. A new directive tightening up existing legislation on cross-frontier public procurement procedures (and another extending these procedures to the hitherto-excluded sectors of telecommunications, water, transport and energy) will give the Commission's strategy an additional impetus. Once adopted, these directives will require all public works and supply contracts to incorporate Community technical standards.

The new approach should also be strengthened as a result of the establishment in September 1988 of Eurocert, a Brussels-based organization, composed of national inspection and certification bodies from Britain, Belgium, France, Luxembourg, Portugal, Spain, Sweden and Switzerland, which is designed to ensure that product certificates issued by one member state will be recognized and accepted without difficulty by all other member states. The success of this initiative will depend on mutual confidence between the various national inspection and certification bodies, each of which will be required to have a stringent internal quality-assurance system, subject to regular audits by other members of Eurocert.

Yet for all its improvements over the traditional approach to technical harmonization, the new strategy is not without its problems. Where differing technical standards are not essential to cross-frontier trade, few difficulties should present themselves. However, in those cases where technical differences are essential (and they are many) the picture is considerably less optimistic. No amount of mutual recognition will, for example, enable a three-pin electrical plug to fit into a two-pin socket. Mutual recognition will not by itself establish the kind of European-wide industrial standards needed to create the economies of scale that would be offered by Community-wide industrial standards. It will be many years, perhaps decades, before the new technical standards authorities have completed the task of harmonizing essential technical standards.

The cost of divergent technical standards

Less than a year after the Community's new harmonization procedures were fully in place the Commission published a report outlining its estimates of the total cost of all fiscal, physical and technical barriers to trade within the EC. The report, *The European Challenge 1992: The Benefits of a Single Market*, was the first to attempt to quantify how much European companies were losing as a result of border controls, protectionist public procurement policies and divergent national product standards.

The report was compiled under the chairmanship of Paolo Cecchini, a special adviser to the Commission, and was based on a survey of 11,000 business executives, conducted by 15 companies of consultants, academics, economists and Commission personnel. The central conclusion of this unprecedented two-year study was that effective implementation of the White Paper Internal Market programme would save European industry about £130 billion, the equivalent of some 5% of the Community's gross domestic product. The precision of the report's estimates has been the subject of a heated dispute, but few have denied that they are pointing in the right direction.

In addition to demonstrating the cost of maintaining twelve separate markets the report also highlighted the opportunities for economic growth, job creation, reduced costs, improved productivity, increased competition, greater professional and business mobility and enhanced consumer choice that were there for the taking. 'Now we have the hard evidence, the confirmation of what those who are engaged in the building of Europe have always known: that the failure to achieve a single market has been costing European industry millions in unnecessary costs and opportunities,' Lord Cockfield said in his foreword. However, even more revealing than the overall estimated costs of market fragmentation was the report's examination of the costs of market fragmentation in specific areas, such as border and administrative red tape, public procurement and divergent technical standards in particular.

According to the Cecchini survey, divergent national technical standards were the second most important obstacle to the creation of the internal market after administrative formalities and border controls. The operation of some 100,000 different technical specifications across European industry meant that European companies were compelled to operate in a technical Tower of Babel, which was losing them billions of pounds because of duplicated product development, lost economies of scale and an enforced competitive disadvantage in relation to their counterparts in Japan and the United States.

This situation was particularly acute in the high-technology sectors, where companies can no longer survive by selling solely in national markets. To have any prospect of competing with their Japanese and American rivals, European companies needed a domestic market of Continental proportions to achieve the volume of sales required to recoup the large expenditures entailed in research and development.

The automobile industry

Perhaps the most obvious beneficiary of the introduction of common technical standards across European industry is that of the automobile sector. In fact, the 1992 process should end the long-standing fragmentation of the European auto market and begin the age of the Euro-car. At present, the 12 million models sold annually in the European Community have to conform with a bewildering variety of national technical and safety standards, which deprive manufacturers of potentially substantial economies of scale.

Some countries (principally France and Italy) fear that the creation of a single market for the auto sector will enable external producers (such as Japan) to increase their penetration of the European market. However, the Commission appears set on introducing some 44 mandatory regulations —governing all aspects of auto production, from the depth of tyre tread and the brilliance of headlamps to the level of permissible toxic exhaust emissions—by the middle of 1992.

Anxieties over increased foreign competition may hold up the Commission's plans but they are unlikely to be prevented outright. Once installed, the new system will replace the existing patchwork of voluntary standards, enabling a vehicle made in one country to be sold freely in any other. Similar measures are also likely to follow for buses, trucks and motorcycles.

The telecommunications sector

In the telecommunications sector the costs of the divergent technical standards imposed on all three categories of telecommunications technology, customer premises equipment, such as telephones, facsimile and telex machines; transmission equipment, such as wire, cable and antennas; and the central office equipment needed to interface the growing variety of telecommunication services were estimated by the Cecchini report to be in excess of 25% of the £17.5 billion the European telecommunications market was worth in 1986. Moreover, these barriers were increasing at an alarming rate under the pressures of rapid technological innovation.

It is not necessary to look hard or far to locate the primary cause of this lamentable state of affairs. Hitherto, the various national telecommunications authorities, the government Post Telegraph and Telephone (PTT) organizations in Europe, such as the West German Bundespost and the French Direction Générale des Télécommunications, as well as the recently privatized British Telecom in Britain, were responsible for establishing technical standards for the European telecommunications industry, through an organization known as the European

Confederation of Postal and Telecommunications Administrations (CEPT).

Despite initially high aspirations, CEPT proved to be a failure. Production of telecommunications equipment continued to be carried out on a national basis, with the PTTs discriminating in favour of local manufacturers while relying on national technical standards to prevent European competition. Consequently, the harmonization of technical standards has been taken away from CEPT and allocated to the new Community standards organizations. Even more absurd has been the development of new telecommunications technologies on a national basis, notably packet-switching. This is a method of breaking down information into digital messages for transmission over telephone networks, used extensively by office workers in the form of electronic mail services and vital for office communications. However, because of the difficulties involved in tailoring each national system to another it is estimated that only three out of every four transmissions are successful.

However, the Internal Market White Paper, and the 1987 Green Paper on the liberalization of the telecommunications industry, is expected to bring about a considerable transformation in the Community's telecommunications sector. The deregulation programme calls for the introduction of cross-frontier competition in the supply of terminal equipment by 1990, the end of national monopolies in the provision of value-added services such as electronic mail boxes, remote databases and voice messaging by the end of 1991 and some degree of price harmonization in an effort to bring tariffs into line across the Community by 1992.

Perhaps the most important single measure of all is the creation of ETSI, which is empowered to accelerate agreement on harmonizing European technical specifications and certification procedures. ETSI was established in Nice in March 1987, and had its inaugural meeting three months later under the directorship of Professor Diodato Gagliardi. Unlike CEPT, ETSI has its own building, a permanent director and a staff of twelve, with provisions for more staff once its workload begins to increase.

Most observers were very surprised by the speed at which the new organization was created, raising expectations that ETSI would register equally rapid progress in the field of establishing common technical standards for the high-growth digital mobile telephone sector. Keeping to time-honoured tradition, Europe had built its first generation of cellular telephone systems on the basis of incompatible technical standards. Any European business executive travelling by car from London to Paris and on to Rome, and who needed to keep in constant touch with headquarters, would need three mobile telephones to do so.

During negotiations on technical standards for the second generation of mobile cellular telephones most European countries favoured the use of a narrow transmission band, while France and West Germany proposed the adoption of the wide band. After months of difficult negotiations,

France and West Germany finally capitulated. The breakthrough was widely acknowledged to be unprecedented. However, the difficulty in arriving at common technical standards for the next generation of mobile cellular telephones showed the enormity of the task facing ETSI. Despite this success, even the most optimistic observers expect the standardization process to be slow and patchy, effectively ruling out the prospect of large-scale standardization in the telecommunications sector by 1992.

Technical standards as barriers to foreign trade

Shortly after the new technical standards organizations were in place, they were subject to many criticisms from abroad. American politicians in particular were concerned that one of the consequences of the new organizations would be European technical standards which would exclude US products from the European domestic market. Richard Mosbacker, President Bush's outspoken Commerce Secretary, accused the Commission of engaging in an ingenious form of protectionism through the standards-setting organizations. These fears were also expressed in a constant stream of US newspaper reports, which were given added credence by the House of Representatives Foreign Affairs Committee in its report on standards published in June 1988.

However, in a letter published in the *Financial Times* the same month, Roy MacDowell, the former President of the International Electrotechnical Commission (IEC), a Geneva-based organization responsible for drawing up worldwide electrotechnical standards, challenged this 'pessimistic US view'. MacDowell pointed out that most electrotechnical standards in Community countries were 'already based on standards written by the International Electrotechnical Commission'.

Furthermore, he pointed out that the IEC was a world organization whose standards are formulated by experts from all member countries —including the United States. America was therefore 'already in a position to participate directly in European harmonization through the international forum provided by the IEC'. Moreover, the Commission has given an undertaking to the world trade body, the General Agreement on Tariffs and Trade, to adopt existing world standards as the new European ones.

MacDowell added that an agreement also exists between the IEC and its sister Community organization, CENELEC, 'under the terms of which information on European standardization and harmonization activities is transmitted to non-European countries via the IEC headquarters in Geneva'. As a result, the 'principles of openness and transparency' demanded by Secretary Mosbacker were already in operation.

The pharmaceuticals sector

As in the telecommunications sector, the creation of a single market for the European pharmaceuticals industry, worth some £20 billion a year, faces complex problems. So far, the Commission's attempts to reconcile the need for strict control on the quality, safety and efficacy of new drugs with industry's desire for more efficient drug-registration and sales-authorization procedures have not convinced industry officials or national authorities that the objective of creating an internal market for the pharmaceuticals sector will be realized by 1992. Under the present system a pharmaceuticals company wishing to introduce a new product into a particular market must submit it to the appropriate national registration authority, which is responsible for establishing whether the drug is safe and actually does what the manufacturers claim of it. However, because each member state has its own registration procedure, acquiring twelve separate approvals to market a new pharmaceutical product (each of which can take in excess of two years), this is a laborious and expensive process which takes up the time allowed for drug patent protection.

Furthermore, the major purchasers of pharmaceuticals in the EC are the state-owned health authorities, which exercise considerable influence on the price at which drugs are sold. The great variation in national public health authority pricing policies (which invariably discriminate in favour of domestic drug manufacturers) also have a direct influence on company profits. Removal of such barriers would save the European pharmaceuticals sector an estimated 1% of the industry's annual costs. The pharmaceuticals companies maintain that, on average, it takes ten years to develop a new drug at a cost of £50 million, and unless the Community is able to introduce uniform registration, market-authorization and pricing procedures they are sceptical of their ability to compete effectively with their foreign rivals in the race to produce the next generation of high-technology drugs which require increasingly heavy investment in research and development—the return on which is never guaranteed. However, in the wake of the Thalidomide tragedy in the 1960s most European governments introduced complex and time-consuming drug-testing procedures (for example, Britain's 1968 Medicines Act) to reassure public opinion about the safety of the drugs they were consuming. Such anxieties have since been heightened by the appalling side-effects of the anti-arthritic drug, Opren.

The Commission is currently in the process of examining two potential solutions to this dilemma. The first envisages the creation of a central drug-licensing organization (similar to the US Food and Drug Administration) which would be responsible for testing all new drugs. This would have the merit of streamlining national drug registration and authorization procedures, and permitting any new drug to go on sale throughout the Community once it had been given a European seal of approval. Some industry officials, however, have already expressed fears that a European drug-licensing authority would become too bureaucratic. The alternative is a more decentralized system based on a combination of the establishment of mandatory Community-wide testing procedures and the mutual recognition of member states' registration and marketing requirements. While this system may avoid the dangers of excessive bureaucracy, it almost seems calculated to arouse national anxieties over whether other member states' testing procedures would be as effective as their own.

As far as other aspects of the programme are concerned, the Commission has already produced a draft directive on price controls which would require the national public health authorities to make their pricing systems more open, thereby giving pharmaceuticals companies more certainty about the price at which their products will eventually be sold. A major breakthrough was achieved in December 1986 with the adoption of a package of directives setting out market-authorization procedures for high-technology medicines. The Commission has also been consulting the pharmaceuticals industry and the national regulatory bodies about their preference for a new EC drug regulatory system, and is expected to issue its proposals by the end of 1989. However, the issue remains so sensitive that few expect the new drug testing and certification arrangements to be in operation by the 1992 deadline.

The construction sector

Contrary to popular perceptions, the European construction products industry is a major influence in cross-frontier trade. In 1985 the Community market for construction products was valued at around £70 billion, but the prospects for substantial future growth are tarnished by the enormous variations in customer specifications for building materials such as bricks, glass, plaster, concrete, aggregates, timber and steel. The cost of market fragmentation has been put at some £55 million a year, while their removal could generate an additional £1 billion in extra business.

In Britain, the construction and construction products industry is already a highly competitive sector, where profit margins are tight. Consequently, British companies are more likely to find new business in Europe than Continental companies are likely to find in Britain. Leading British construction and construction product companies, notably Trafalgar House, Wimpey, Laing and Tarmac, have already established their presence in Continental Europe with a view to exploiting the potential offered by the creation of the internal market. Nonetheless, the British construction industry appears to be lagging behind some of its European rivals, particularly in France, where overall preparations for a European construction industry without frontiers appear to be considerably more advanced.

Unlike most industries, construction is both a service and a product. Prospective clients have an understandable preference for using construction companies with whom they are familiar and in whom they have confidence. This puts a high premium on having a physical presence in a given market and acquiring familiarity with the local environment. Such efforts would be to little avail if a construction company, having established itself in a particular market, was effectively prohibited from operating in it because the technical specifications of the construction products being used were unacceptable to the regulatory authority of the host country. However, the experience of one French company, which had to fight for five years to obtain the technical certification to sell its steel girders in West Germany, demonstrated that such obstacles are all too frequent.

As in other major industrial sectors, technical specifications and product certification procedures are used to keep competition in the construction sector from other member states to an absolute minimum. The Cecchini report even claimed that the 'so called inherent divergencies in customer requirements may be largely a case of national tastes determined by national regulations'.

The Internal Market White Paper, in accordance with the harmonization and mutual recognition procedures outlined above, proposes a basic framework of European technical standards for construction products, in accordance with mutually accepted criteria of stability, safety and health. The standards organization (CEN) is currently drawing up a European code of technical standards for the construction industry, and although it is clear that the new standards will not be ready by 1992, the Commission has agreed to accept and enforce the mutual recognition of current national standards in the interim.

The foodstuffs sector

A similar approach has been used in the foodstuffs sector. Here the Commission's strategy involves the adoption of a series of general framework directives, governing the areas of additives, flavouring, labelling, packaging, public inspection and irradiation. These directives will establish the broad principles to which national food laws must adhere, leaving the details to be worked out largely by the Commission and the European Food Industry Association (CIAA) in a series of more specific foodstuffs directives.

The strategy is designed to capitalize on a succession of rulings by the European Court of Justice, notably the 1987 one against Greece and West Germany for prohibiting imports of beer that did not conform to national 'beer purity' laws and the 1988 ruling against Italy for prohibiting imports of pasta made from soft rather than hard wheat. The judgments have established that if a food product is legally manufactured and sold in one member state it can be manufactured and sold in all.

The new approach, as in so many other areas, represents a significant departure from the past. The old system of food standards harmonization focused on the specific composition of foodstuffs (known as recipe law) on a case-by-case basis. In the field of additives alone there are an estimated 40,000 applications, making regulation of each a practical impossibility. On the principle that it is better to delegate as much harmonization to the private sector as possible, the CIAA, composed of the various trade bodies of the European foodstuffs industry, is now responsible for compiling compositional standards. As much research on foodstuff additives has already been carried out there is no need for the CIAA to start from the beginning, and the Commission has restricted its legislative activity to the protection of public health, consumer information, fair trading and public inspection. This change of direction represents a modest victory for Britain, which has persistently argued for the abolition of recipe law.

There is agreement on the immediate horizon on a host of quality and packaging regulations for the food and drink industry, including common procedures for verifying the quality of food imported from other member states (particularly important in the wake of growing public concern over salmonella and listeria poisoning), along with common rules on irradiated food and the labelling of health foods. The internal market for foodstuffs, excluding labelling, is therefore all but complete.

The implications of the successful creation of an internal market for the European foodstuffs industry (which now looks more optimistic than at any time since the White Paper was launched) are far-reaching. Small manufacturers, unless they are able to develop small national niche markets on a European scale, can expect much competition from their European counterparts. Many family food concerns, which owe their existence to the fragmentation of the European market and who are unable to form cross-border alliances, are likely to fail. Larger companies, who will benefit from the economies of scale that the abolition of trade barriers will produce, should find themselves facing the prospect of new markets emerging throughout the Community.

With a large European market now on the horizon it seems almost inevitable that foodstuffs manufacturers, processors and distributors will follow the trilingual labelling precedent set by the French manufacturer of Benedicta Mayonnaise, whose jars of salad dressing are already available in local supermarkets with a single French, British and Dutch label —assuming, of course, that the Commission keeps labelling requirements to a minimum. In the restructuring that is likely to follow the opening up of national markets some smaller companies may fall by the wayside, but consumers will benefit from lower prices brought about by increased competition and a significant expansion of the variety of food products available for consumption.

Other sectors

The White Paper envisages applying the same strategy to every sector fragmented by divergent national technical standards, whether in the car, civil engineering or chemical industries. The same approach has also been applied to sectors outside manufacturing, including public procurement, air, sea and road transport, veterinary and plant controls, the free movement of workers and professionals, capital movements and financial services.

The White Paper singles out the liberalization of financial services, such as insurance policies, mortgages, consumer credit and unit trusts, as a potentially major source of economic growth and job creation. The Commission's proposals for deregulation are based on the co-ordination of national rules governing the authorization of companies wishing to operate in the financial services sector. The proposed Community regulatory system is to be based on the principle of 'home country control'. Supervisory responsibilities will lie with the appropriate authorities in the member state in which the company is based, regardless of which member state the company is operating in. Ironically, in most countries it is the governments of the member states who are pressing hard for deregulation, often in the face of bitter resistance from financial service institutions, such as those in West Germany, who are very comfortable in their protected national markets and do not relish the prospect of competition from across the border.

Checklist of changes

- The traditional case-by-case approach to the harmonization of different product technical standards has been replaced by legislative harmonization where necessary and mutual recognition where possible.
- All essential technical harmonization measures will be brought into force by majority voting.
- These legislative measures will stipulate an obligtory minimum of health and safety standards, conformity with which will guarantee manufacturers the right of access to the markets of other member states.
- Legislative technical harmonization will be complemented by systematic implementation of the principle of mutual recognition for non-essential product standards, reinforced by the 1979 Cassis de Dijon ruling.
- The task of establishing European-wide technical standards has been allocated to the new European standards-setting organizations such as CEN, CENELEC and ETSI.
- The traditional system of national product testing and certification procedures will also be subject to mutual recognition.
- Under the directive governing mutual information procedures, the European Commission has the power to prevent member states from implementing any new technical standard likely to create additional barriers to trade.
- The White Paper programme calls for the introduction of cross-frontier competition in the supply of terminal equipment by 1990, the end of national monopolies in the provision of value-added services by the end of 1989 and some degree of tariff price harmonization by 1992.

- National drug registration and authorization procedures will be streamlined with the introduction of either a central drug-licensing authority or mandatory Community-wide testing procedures, along with mutual recognition of member states' registration and marketing requirements.
- National public health authorities will be required to introduce more open drug pricing policies.
- Essential technical standards will be laid down for all other sectors, including the construction, car, civil engineering, and chemical industries. The same approach has also been adopted for sectors outside manufacturing, notably financial services and foodstuffs.

5 DRUGS, CRIME AND TERRORISM
Policing a Europe without frontiers

One of the main benefits of 1992 is the promise it holds out of free movement—the fulfilment of the dream expressed in 1951 by Ernest Bevin, Foreign Secretary in the Attlee government after the war, that one day he would be 'able to take a ticket at Victoria Station and go anywhere I damn well please'. Conversely, one of the main fears about 1992—expressed most forcefully in Britain but not only in Britain—is that it will create 'an internal market' for terrorism and drug trafficking. In her forceful speech at the College of Europe in Bruges in September 1988 Mrs Thatcher supported 1992 in so far as it opened up markets, widened consumer choice and encouraged enterprise, but declared it to be a 'matter of plain common sense' that frontier controls could not be totally abolished if citizens were to be protected.

This demand for the retention of frontier controls contradicts the undertakings contained in Article 8a of the Single European Act, which defines the internal market specifically as an 'area without internal frontiers'. Andreas Papandreou, Greek Prime Minister and the then President of the Council of Ministers, accused Thatcher of 'putting in question, unilaterally, an Act which binds the Twelve by validated international treaty'. The Act does have a loophole, in the form of a General Declaration allowing states to 'take such steps as they consider necessary' to prevent drug smuggling, terrorism and illegal immigration. However, the Declaration is subordinate to the overall aim of abolition of frontiers, and EC leaders agreed to avoid national controls by laying down 'common measures' on visas, immigration and extradition while also intensifying police co-operation throughout the EC.

Under the 1992 process, in other words, as agreed in negotiations for the Single European Act, the apprehension of criminals and terrorists is provided for through the strengthening of external frontiers, European-wide police and intelligence co-operation, and common visa and immigration policies on the grounds that most arrests do not, in any case, take place at air- or seaports or border crossings. Where they do, the criminals have often in reality been tracked for miles through police co-operation (for example, from Spain or Italy to a Channel port) and the frontier is simply a convenient location for a police or customs operation.

As the impact of the Thatcher speech in Bruges demonstrated, the abolition of frontiers arouses fears of threats ranging from gunmen to rabies, and raises directly the issue of national sovereignty. It may be a mistake, however, to conclude that a majority of people therefore oppose the abolition of borders, provided that measures against crime are adequate. No aspect of the internal market programme has captured the imagination of European public opinion as much as the proposal to abolish the Community's internal frontiers and replace them with a single external one. In an age marked by ever-increasing amounts of intra-Community tourism and travel the prospect of being able to move from Britain to France, West Germany, Greece or Spain without obligatory travel documents, inspection at internal frontiers and time-consuming delays is perhaps the single most tangible benefit of the Community's economic integration process. In a survey published in July 1988 by Euro-Barometer, the Community's public opinion research organization, the elimination of frontier controls was identified by 64% of the sample as one of the ten most popular aspects of the entire internal market programme.

There can be little doubt that the Commission has been emboldened in its determination to press ahead with the abolition of internal frontiers by the decision of the so-called Schengen Group, made up of the Benelux countries, West Germany and France, to introduce their own border-free zone by 1990—regardless of progress among the Twelve. But the removal of the Berlin Wall, and the advent of free movement between East and West Germany, raised serious objections among other Schengen countries over the viability of the free borders plan. The Commission clearly regards the Schengen initiative as the laboratory for its own proposals for a frontier-free Europe, and is confident that its anticipated success will help to force the more reluctant member states into following the Schengen example.

In February 1989, for example, Martin Bangemann, the new Commissioner responsible for the internal market, announced the Commission's intention to press ahead with the introduction of common policies governing extradition, the right of asylum and the granting of visas. Bangemann's extraordinary claim that the entire edifice could be in place within six months seemed reckless in the extreme, but he also used the occasion to hint that the Commission might be prepared to accept the introduction of spot checks at frontier posts to replace systematic border controls, which observers in Brussels interpreted as an attempt to win Britain over to the controversial scheme.

Moving from one member state to another as one moves from Kent to Essex or Yorkshire to Lincolnshire is also a major attraction for European companies trading across national frontiers. Industry has been compelled to shoulder an immense burden as a consequence of the delays, red tape, form filling, and transport and handling charges associated with the maintenance of frontier formalities. The European Commission argues forcibly that the complete removal of these physical barriers to trade will not only reduce costs and stimulate competition but will also encourage many smaller firms (who have traditionally been inhibited from expanding beyond national borders because of the costs involved) to seek new markets throughout the Community.

The Commission's proposals have met much criticism. The fear that any attempt to abolish internal frontier controls to facilitate free movement for business executives, labour and tourists will have the potentially disastrous side-effect of laying the foundations of an internal market for terrorists, drug traffickers, criminals and dangerous diseases such as rabies has been most commonly expressed in Britain, Ireland, Denmark and Greece. During a debate in the European Parliament in December 1985, shortly after publication of the Internal Market White Paper, the basic arguments of the anti- and pro-abolitionists were stated in terms that have been repeated in much the same form ever since.

Bob Cryer, the Labour MEP for Sheffield, challenged Lord Cockfield by saying: 'Would the Commissioner accept, with his well-known enthusiasm for the removal of all frontiers, that neither he nor anybody else has produced any solution to the question which keeps being raised . . . how one can control increased drug smuggling, how one can control rabies and how one can control the spread of plant diseases if customs supervision and frontiers are entirely removed as he wishes?' In his customary sardonic manner, Lord Cockfield replied: 'It was made clear in the White Paper that there were a number of problems, particularly in the field of terrorism and drug trafficking, which would require careful consideration before the full White Paper proposals are implemented.' The Commissioner then went on to give Cryer a lesson in how to work from first principles.

> If, for example, you were considering how to deal with the drug problem and assumed that you had no frontiers to start with, would you end up by saying that the right solution to the drug problem was the creation of national frontiers? I very much doubt whether you would. In fact most of the drug seizures are not made at national frontiers at all, nor are they made as a result of routine checks on every single person who goes from one country to another. I agree that these are very important problems, they need to be studied, and they need to be studied with an open mind.

The Commission's proposals, in fact, offer the basis for a fundamental transformation in the way the Community organizes its defences against terrorists, drug traffickers, criminals and plant and animal diseases. However, Britain is still looking for a 'balance of advantage' between free movement and control of crime.

The case for the abolition of internal frontier controls

Despite the abolition of customs duties and quantitative restrictions imposed on intra-Community trade by individual member states that followed the completion of the single external tariff in 1968, customs posts have remained a feature of national frontiers, even though they have been largely deprived of the function that gave them their name. Because there are no longer intra-Community customs duties on goods and services at internal frontiers, customs posts no longer really exist within the EC, even if the signs suggest otherwise. What are still often referred to as customs posts are in fact frontier control posts; they are only customs posts for goods entering member states from outside the Community. Duty on alcohol and tobacco, for example, are excise, not custom duties.

The White Paper describes internal frontier controls as the most visible example of the continued division of the European Community into twelve national segments. Concomitantly, their removal would be the clearest sign of the integration of the member states into a genuine single market. The need to remove these internal frontier controls does not arise simply out of any idealistic or aesthetic sentiment. Rather, it stems from the practical necessity of stimulating economic growth by removing all physical barriers to trade as part of the Commission's overall strategy of making European industry more competitive in world markets.

According to Cecchini's report, the cost of these frontier controls is intolerably high, from both the perspective of the companies who have to go through them and the governments who have to administer them. The report estimates that some 25% of company profits are taken up by frontier control-related costs and delays, the equivalent of 2% of the value of each trans-frontier consignment of goods, which works out at roughly £6 billion every year. Frontier controls were identified by business executives as the single greatest obstacle to the expansion of intra-Community trade and a crippling burden on the smaller companies. Moreover, they cost Community governments an estimated £670 million a year in taxpayers' money to administer. The report also estimated that their removal could be worth around £10.5 billion in new trading opportunities, the equivalent of about 3% of the present value of intra-Community trade.

The Commission clearly shares the concerns of member states regarding the growth of terrorism, drug trafficking and major crime, and the role played by internal frontier controls in attempting to control these problems. However, the White Paper insists that:

> Frontier controls are by no means the only or most effective measures in this regard. If the objective of abolishing all internal frontier controls is to be met, alternative means of protection will need to be found or, where they exist, strengthened.

It accepts that many of the proposed changes will present difficulties for member states, and time will be needed for the necessary adjustments to be made. But it is quite adamant that such difficulties 'should not be allowed permanently to frustrate the achievement of the greater progress . . .'.

The White Paper then goes on to list all the internal areas in which common policies need to be developed, such as indirect taxation, plant and veterinary controls, the movement of individuals and the collection of trade statistics. Focusing on the movement of individuals, it points out that most of the Commission's initiatives (notably the introduction of the European passport) 'have been aimed at making checks at internal frontiers more flexible as they cannot be abolished altogether until, in line with the concerns expressed by the European Council, adequate safeguards are introduced against terrorism and drugs'. Meanwhile, the Commission envisages the gradual introduction of separate channels for Community citizens at sea- and airports, just as we already have for British nationals re-entering Britain at Gatwick or Heathrow, and the abolition of systematic controls over departures to other member states. Metal detectors at airports would remain in place, and member states would retain the right to re-introduce systematic frontier controls in the event of an emergency.

Crime and detection across frontiers

Turning to the external areas in which common policies need to be developed, the White Paper outlines a programme for the approximation of national legislation governing public security, illegal immigration, the possession of firearms, and visa and extradition policy, all of which will be enforced at the Community's external border. By 1992 the Commission hopes to arrive at the situation in which individuals can travel freely from one member state to another without having to undergo systematic checks on entry.

What lies behind the Commission's proposals, in addition to the attempt to reduce the costs borne by companies involved in intra-Community trade and the irritations endured by Community citizens travelling from one member state to another, is a recognition that terrorism, gun running, drug trafficking and major crime have long ceased to be national problems. As challenges to the fabric of both political and civil society everywhere in the Community, logic and reason would suggest that they are best dealt with on a Community-wide basis.

Furthermore, there is only a limited benefit to be obtained from effective frontier controls around Britain if British armed forces personnel on the Continent remain vulnerable to terrorist attacks. The continued fragmentation of member state policies in these areas works to the advantage of the terrorist, the drug trafficker and the major criminal. What the Community needs is a strict external frontier to act as the first line of defence against these organizations and individuals in the first place, backed up internally by increased co-operation between national law-enforcement and intelligence organizations. Such co-operation is already responsible for the great majority of terrorist apprehensions and confiscations of drug consignments, long before they get to internal frontier controls.

Addressing a London audience in November 1986, Lord Cockfield emphasized this point:

> The way to deal with these problems is not simply to retreat behind national frontiers, to man the barricades against our fellow European citizens . . . There is no *a priori* reason to suppose that reinforcing the internal frontiers of the Community as we know them today is likely to prove the most effective way of dealing with these problems. And in so far as—inevitably—it obstructs the objective of creating a Europe without frontiers, it carries a heavy cost to trade, to industry, and ultimately to all our citizens . . . There are no customs officers on Hadrian's Wall, or immigration officials manning Offa's Dyke. That is what our ambition is to create.

Police and intelligence co-operation: the Trevi Group

The attempt to improve co-ordination between national police forces pre-dates the White Paper by a decade. Although the Treaty of Rome does not provide for measures designed to combat terrorism, drug trafficking and major crime, the Council of Ministers, meeting in Trevi, Italy, in December 1975, recognized the growing necessity of improving co-operation between the interior and justice departments of member states. Ministers agreed to set up three groups to deal with terrorism, drug trafficking and crime, which were supplemented with a fourth in October 1986 dealing with illegal immigration. Strictly speaking, the initiative, known as the Trevi Group or Trevi Process, exists quite independently of Community institutions, although for convenience it is often referred to as if it were a normal function of the Council of Ministers.

Despite a promising start, Interior and Justice Ministers did not meet again for almost ten years. However, as soon as Middle East conflicts began to spill over into the streets of European capitals the Community was forced to react. Since 1986, Interior and Justice Ministers, senior police and intelligence officers, and forensic scientists have been meeting in secret with increasing frequency to exchange information and ideas on how to stem the rising tide of international crime. These exchanges have been instrumental in breaking down traditional professional and national rivalries and laying the basis of trust and mutual respect, without which any attempt to increase cross-frontier co-operation would simply founder.

Following a series of bombing outrages in Paris in 1986 by the so-called Solidarity Committee for Arab Prisoners, who were attempting to intimidate the French authorities into releasing three Arab terrorists, an emergency Trevi Group meeting was held in London at the request of Paris in September 1986, with Douglas Hurd, the Home Secretary, acting as President of the Council of Ministers. The meeting produced an agreement to improve the flow of intelligence and information, develop a co-ordinated response between member states, identify and close the loopholes through which terrorists gain entry into the Community and tackle the political problems which create terrorist violence in the first place.

At the end of the meeting Hurd described terrorists as being increasingly members of organizations which operate across national frontiers, who have access to substantial sums of money, arms, equipment, technical knowledge and training, which was forcing governments and their counter-terrorist agencies to organize themselves on a Community-wide basis. 'These new measures will help us to target terrorists' movements, supplies of money, arms and equipment, so that we can harry and disrupt them,' and would be followed up with further practical measures, the minister said.

In October 1986 Community Interior and Justice Ministers met to discuss the security implications of the Commission's proposals to abolish internal frontiers by 1992, in which the Commission was represented by Lord Cockfield. They agreed to launch a concerted assault against terrorists, drug traffickers, criminals and, for the first time, illegal immigrants, while simultaneously pledging themselves to the goal of free movement around the Community for all law-abiding citizens. The ministers agreed to consider the possibility of harmonizing member state visa and right of asylum policies, increase co-operation against the abuse of passports and exchange information gathered at spot checks on internal frontiers. Hurd publicly stated that the objectives of allowing free movement of Community nationals, while restricting criminals, were not irreconcilable. However, he then went on to insist that Britain would continue to conduct a full examination of every passport, reflecting Britain's actual but as yet unstated conviction that they were indeed irreconcilable.

Aspirations for closer and more effective action between member states appeared to receive a setback towards the end of the month, when Sir Geoffrey Howe, the then Foreign Secretary, demanded a united Community response against Syria, following evidence indicating Syrian complicity in the attempted bombing in April of an El Al airliner at Heathrow by Nezar Hindawi. The request was initially greeted with a mixture of caution, scepticism and outright hostility. After much agonizing, the Community, with the exception of Greece, agreed to a ban on all new arms sales and high-level visits to Syria, a review of Syrian embassy and consular staffs, and tighter security for the national carrier, Syrianair. Although Sir Geoffrey put a brave face on the agreement, he had clearly wanted much tougher action—much earlier.

The subject was also high on the agenda at the EC summit meeting in London that December. The meeting produced a communiqué committing member states to three principles: no concessions to terrorists or their sponsors, solidarity in preventing terrorism and bringing the perpetrators to justice and (in a veiled reference to the delay in reacting to the Hindawi affair) a concerted response to terrorist attacks. It was also revealed that the Trevi Group had produced a secret document listing those countries and organizations responsible for recent terrorist outrages and who continued to pose a serious threat to public security in the Community. Again, however, Greece refused to sign—a position that was modified substantially after the terrorist attack on the *City of Poros* cruiser in July 1988, which resulted in the death of 11 passengers.

Although the member states were moving in the direction of increased co-operation the increase in kidnappings in Beirut had placed an enormous strain on the Community's declared commitment to adopt a united front in the face of terrorist threats. During 1987, France and West Germany, both of whom held known terrorists believed to be responsible for a variety of hijackings and assassinations, were under pressure to release them in exchange for their own nationals held hostage in Beirut. Despite the temptation to waver from the principles outlined in the December communiqué it was becoming clearer that the only effective response to terrorism, whether internal or external, was a collective one.

At a meeting of Community Justice Ministers in Brussels in July 1987 member states took another step forward by agreeing to streamline extradition procedures, allowing nationals sentenced in one member state to opt to serve their sentence in their state of origin, and laying down that an individual could not be prosecuted more than once for the same offence anywhere in the Community. During the summit meeting between the leading industrialized countries in Venice in June 1987 an agreement to prohibit flights from any country failing to prosecute or extradite terrorists involved in offences involving aircraft was signed, adding considerably to the sanctions available against state-sponsored terrorism. During the EC summit meeting in Hanover in June 1988 Chancellor Helmut Kohl of West Germany even went so far as to suggest the creation of a European police agency modelled on the American Federal Bureau of Investigation. The idea was not warmly received, but while it may still be too premature to start thinking along these lines it is likely to attract more serious consideration in the years ahead.

The next major breakthrough was made following a series of IRA attacks on British armed forces personnel in West Germany and the Netherlands in 1988. Community Interior Ministers meeting in Munich in July 1988 agreed to further increases in exchanges of information and forensic evidence, a study on the security implications of 1992 and, perhaps most important of all, to launch an examination into possible

Community-wide legislation to examine the bank accounts of terrorist organizations and seize their financial assets.

During its periodic review of the Prevention of Terrorism Act Britain had decided to introduce a new provision granting the government the power to inspect bank accounts (and confiscate their contents) where there was a suspicion that the money could be used to finance terrorist activities. However, Hurd was fully aware that there was little point in Britain acting in isolation. The legislation would be useless if terrorist organizations could move their accounts around Community banks. It was clearly apparent (although no government minister has yet conceded the point) that Britain could no longer take refuge in its island status from terrorists, drug traffickers or criminals.

However, the days when criminals can hide their ill-gotten gains in Continental retreats such as the Costa Brava may now be numbered. The success of the 1986 Drug Trafficking Offences Act, and the 1988 Criminal Justice Act (both of which gave British courts powers to confiscate the proceeds from drug trafficking and other forms of major crime), has encouraged the Home Office to try to persuade its Community partners to adopt similar laws.

Admittedly, France and West Germany retain grave reservations over such a development, but progress has been particularly promising with Spain. Although still a long way off, the Home Office's ultimate objective is to facilitate the introduction of a fully harmonized system of judicial seizure for the proceeds of major crime—effectively preventing criminals from laundering money through Continental banks, and enabling the Community to establish a policy of 'no hiding place' for criminal fortunes.

The case against the abolition of frontiers

Nevertheless, the fact that terrorists such as West Germany's Red Army Faction, or RAF (heirs to the notorious Baader–Meinhof Gang), the IRA and the Italian Red Brigades remain active gives cause for concern. The terrorists, too, are preparing for 1992, as was shown by the attempted murder in September 1988 of Hans Tietmeyer, a senior Bonn official, by the RAF with the active help of the Red Brigades, as part of a co-ordinated terrorist effort to disrupt an IMF ministerial meeting in Berlin. Similarly, the murder of Herr Alfred Herrhausen, the chief executive of Deutsche Bank, who was blown up in his bullet-proof Mercedes in November 1989, was yet another reminder that the RAF was still active. Partly because of such incidents, Britain's police forces, backed up by many of their Continental colleagues, have grave reservations about the proposed abolition of frontier controls.

During the annual meeting of the International Union of Police Federations (IUPF) in August 1988, which represents over 500,000 officers, a resolution was passed against abolishing frontier controls by a majority of one. However, most of Europe's police forces appeared to think that abolition was inevitable. But what irritated them more than anything was the failure of EC governments to consult them over the implications of abolition. This is a shortcoming which member states ought to rectify as soon as possible. Peter Tanner, the Secretary of the British Police Federation and President of the IUPF, also warned that if internal borders were to be abolished there would need to be rapid progress on establishing common procedures for extradition, criminal justice and the right of hot pursuit across borders, all of which the Commission hopes to have in place before the 1992 deadline expires.

The surprise announcement in November 1988 by the Belgian Cabinet to overturn the recommendation by the Belgian judiciary to extradite Patrick Ryan, the former Roman Catholic priest wanted by Scotland Yard in connection with four offences of conspiracy to commit murder and illegal possession of explosives, caused exasperation in Downing Street and overshadowed the forthcoming EC summit meeting in Rhodes. The rejection of the extradition request, originally made on 9 September, almost three months after Ryan had been detained by the Belgian authorities for entering the country with a false passport, was prompted by the Government's fear of possible IRA retaliation if Ryan, then on hunger strike in St Gilles prison in Brussels, died on Belgian soil. This was the first time that Belgium had denied an extradition request from a NATO partner for over 20 years, and it took the issue of increased co-operation against terrorism to the top of the Community's agenda.

During an otherwise low-key summit meeting at Rhodes in December, Mrs Thatcher had some frank exchanges with her Belgian and Irish counterparts over the Ryan affair. However, the controversy at least resulted in a new initiative to tackle the problems of controlling terrorists, drug traffickers and criminals, in an internal market without frontiers. The twelve heads of government agreed to appoint a special official to take charge of intergovernmental negotiations on controlling terrorism, drug trafficking and illegal immigration, in advance of a Trevi Group meeting in December in Athens on the problems presented by international crime and the abolition of internal frontiers.

Although the Commission is engaged in an attempt to wipe out a whole range of plant and animal diseases across Europe, British public opinion has tended to focus on the danger of rabies. These anxieties are not difficult to understand. *La rage* is a killer, and Britain has been free of the disease for over 60 years. However, there is much truth in the observation that Britain's island status, far from easing popular anxieties over the spread of rabies, has actually heightened them. In reality, the threat posed by rabies is marginal. In over 40 years of quarantine controls Britain has never found one animal with rabies. According to statistics collected by the International Organization of Epizootics, there were 19,000 cases of rabies recorded in the whole of continental Europe for 1985. Of this total, 14,000 were foxes, 3000 were other wild animals and 200 were domestic animals.

There was one recorded case of rabies among the human population—and that was in Finland.

Rabies is overwhelmingly confined to wild animals, most of which are foxes. Even so, the Commission is taking no chances. Officials have been monitoring closely a series of field tests with an oral vaccine for wild animals. If the tests prove successful the Commission is expected to launch a Community-wide rabies-eradication programme, which holds out the promise of eliminating the disease completely. Moreover, the Home Office has made it clear that Britain will retain its quarantine controls at sea- and airports. The Home Office has also been closely involved with the Euro-tunnel contractors on devising ways to prevent animals from crawling along the floor of the tunnel. In short, Britain's defences against rabies will be as effective as ever. Equally as important, Europe's defences against rabies will be strengthened by the internal market programme.

Partly because there is still some time to elapse before the Community's external frontier is in place, Britain has shown a deep ambivalence towards the Commission's proposal to abolish all internal frontier controls by 1992, and is clearly leaning in the direction of keeping them intact. Reflecting on the Commission's proposals in October 1986, the Home Secretary said:

> A lot depends on the way we can strengthen our external frontiers. The more effective we are in keeping drugs, terrorists and major criminals out of the Community in the first place, the easier it will be to relax our internal controls.

Even so, the minister warned that 'it was not around the corner'.

Now 1992 is just around the corner, and the British position has hardened considerably. At the June 1988 meeting of the Trevi Group in Munich Hurd insisted that:

> Frontier controls do provide an effective means of dealing with these problems. They are not 100 per cent effective but they are more effective than internal arrangements.

Hurd seemed to be suggesting that Britain had its own ideas about European integration—a sort of internal market *avec frontières*. Addressing the annual conference of the Association of Chief Police Officers in Eastbourne a month before, the minister declared: 'We owe it to ourselves, and to our fellow citizens, to continue to do all we can to see that the terrorist, the drug trafficker or criminal, is not the unintended beneficiary of changes designed for the development of the Community, and the benefit of law-abiding Community citizens.' As a result of such anxieties, particularly after Britain's anger over the refusal of Belgium to extradite a suspected IRA terrorist, the Trevi Group, meeting in Athens in December

1988, agreed to examine the possibility of introducing a common extradition policy.

Controlling crime in the single market

These statements raise two fundamental questions about the proposed abolition of internal frontier controls. First, are these so-called internal arrangements—increased police co-operation, the creation of common policies on extradition, confiscation of terrorists' assets, immigration and the right of hot pursuit across national borders—more effective than internal frontier controls? British ministers think not, but at the same time acknowledge that without parallel legislation in other member states Britain's attempt to control terrorism and drug trafficking will be to little avail.

Moreover, while there are isolated examples of the efficacy of internal frontier controls, such as the chance apprehension of two IRA gunmen by a West German border guard in September 1988, the great majority of terrorists, drug traffickers and criminals are merely arrested at frontier control points, having been identified as a result of co-operation between Community intelligence agencies long before. Furthermore, the most difficult internal frontier to monitor in the entire Community is the border between Ulster and the Irish Republic—which has no frontier controls.

Second, a major fear is that if Britain decides to keep its internal frontier controls there will be no changes benefiting law-abiding Community citizens. Movement in and out of Britain will remain more or less as time consuming and costly as it is at present. The Commission insists that one either has internal frontier controls or one does not—there is no half-way house—and it is disingenuous to suggest that we can have both.

At the kernel of the dispute over the abolition of frontier controls lies one of the many historic differences between Britain and its European neighbours. Continental Europeans have tended to rely more on individual identity cards than frontier controls for the apprehension of criminals—an idea which has never been particularly popular in Britain. However, at an address given at the Crime in Europe Conference in York in September 1988 David Faulkner, a deputy Under-Secretary of State at the Home Office, suggested that Britain might be forced to re-evaluate its traditional hostility to the introduction of a national identity card as a result of growing pressures for greater freedom of movement around the Community. At the Rhodes summit in December 1988 Mrs Thatcher raised the idea of EC identity cards without either endorsing or rejecting it.

This, coupled with intensive police and intelligence co-operation under Trevi arrangements and common EC policies on immigration and extradition, may point the way forward and allow the Single European Act's commitment to 'an area without internal frontiers' to be fulfilled. The alternative—the retention of national controls by Britain in isolation from the other Eleven—could lead to action against Britain in the European

Court after 1992, which was not what the framers of the Act had in mind and is not what other members of the EC wish to see happen.

However, Britain is confident that the Single European Act does allow member states to retain internal frontiers. It has also challenged Lord Cockfield's claim that the great majority of drug seizures are made as a result of increased co-operation between national police forces.

A report released in Brussels in March 1989, based on statistics collected by the Home Office, showed that 36% of the volume of drugs seized in 1986 came from or via another EC country. That figure rose to 41% in 1987, and provisional data for 1988 shows an increase to 44%. While acknowledging that 'investigators depend on frontier staff to intercept intelligence targets', it nonetheless insisted that 'seizures made "cold" or according to "profiles" of likely smuggling types, depend on officers being at the frontier to observe, select, question and examine'.

Checklist of changes

- The European Commission hopes to oversee the complete abolition of all internal frontier controls (the so-called physical barriers to trade) by the end of 1992.
- The abolition of internal frontiers will result in significant cost reductions for companies involved in cross-frontier trade, and will also make travel and tourism for the ordinary citizen considerably easier.
- The manpower and resources freed from internal frontier controls can then be redirected towards defending the Community from terrorists, drug traffickers and other criminals at the Community's external frontiers.
- The approximation of member states' fiscal taxation arrangements will eliminate the need to collect value added tax at internal frontiers.
- There will be increased co-operation between national police and intelligence forces in the fight against terrorists and criminals.
- Common Community initiatives on immigration, visa, extradition and right of asylum policies, the possession of firearms, confiscation of terrorists' and criminal assets, and the right of hot pursuit across national borders may also be introduced.
- Common programmes for the elimination of animal and plant diseases, possibly including rabies, will also be implemented.

6 CONTRACTS AND TENDERS
Public purchasing policy in the single market

Although the principle of free trade is the cornerstone of the Treaty of Rome, the past 30 years have demonstrated that public procurement is the last area in which anyone would ever find it in operation. According to the provisions of Articles 30–36, member states are obliged to remove all quantitative restrictions (or any other measures having an equivalent effect) that obstruct the free movement of goods within the Community. Similarly, Articles 59–66 make it incumbent on member states to remove all obstacles in the way of the free flow of services across national frontiers. However, like so many other commitments entered into by national governments, these particular provisions were signed with the best intentions and promptly filed away.

The public purchasing programmes of central and local government (which includes their agencies and enterprises) have persistently reflected the defensive and parochial outlook displayed by the once-famous group of secretaries from Croydon who launched the 'I'm backing Britain' campaign in the 1960s. Both were motivated by the intensely patriotic (if somewhat economically misguided) conviction that buying national was the answer to Britain's economic difficulties.

During the past 30 years the growth of cross-border trade in goods and services in the private sector has been impressive. By comparison, the volume of such trade in the public sector has been comparatively static. There is a marked contrast between the demand by national governments for the private sector to adjust to the laws of supply and demand, on the one hand, and the way in which the public sector has been allowed to seek refuge behind national barriers, on the other. This raises charges of double standards.

The national bias of public purchasing bodies in favour of domestic manufacturers and suppliers covers three broad categories of goods and services:

1 All basic supply goods, ranging from office equipment to commercial vehicles and school and hospital supplies;
2 Public works such as roads, buildings, bridges and other civil engineering projects;
3 The so-called 'big-ticket items', which include sophisticated telecommunications and scientific facilities and power-generating and defence equipment.

The justifications used by member states to support biased national public procurement policies have depended on social considerations, economic necessity and outright national pride. At its most basic, governments have argued that domestic political exigencies have forced them to place public procurement contracts locally in order to reduce unemployment in declining industries or to support emerging industries in the early stages of development. More compelling, perhaps, has been the insistence that major industries such as telecommunications, aerospace and defence (which have massive research and development costs and where governments are frequently the only significant purchaser) would face collapse without government help. The implications of such a collapse, it is claimed, go far beyond considerations of social policy and regional development and into the realm of national security. All too often, however, economic necessity, social policy and strategic considerations have contained more than a hint of national pride. Governments have repeatedly asked themselves how an advanced industrialized country can be worthy of the name if it cannot support its own steel, car or defence industries.

However, it has become increasingly evident that the inescapable problem with a world view that stops at national boundaries will lead to long-term economic annihilation. Public procurement programmes that discriminate in favour of national champions reinforce the market fragmentation of the European economy, and cost the member states billions of pounds a year in unnecessary premiums to local firms. Market fragmentation denies companies the economies of scale they need to survive without government help, and leaves them vulnerable to competition from their larger external rivals. In the short term, discrimination in favour of local producers and suppliers may be a palliative for economically declining regions and companies unable or unwilling to survive without government assistance. However, in the long term it cannot generate the kind of competitive environment that companies need to survive in the increasingly competitive international economy.

The cost of national public procurement policies

According to the survey on the costs of European market fragmentation conducted on behalf of the European Commission by Cecchini in 1987, the value of all public purchasing contracts in 1986 was in excess of £355 billion, or £20 billion more than the value of all intra-Community trade during the same year. The sum of £355 billion is equivalent to 15% of the combined gross domestic product of all twelve member states, and therefore constitutes one of the most important single categories of European economic activity.

The Cecchini survey acknowledged that a sizeable portion of this sum was allocated to the purchase of goods and services that were inherently non-competitive, non-tradable or required in such small volumes that few manufacturers or suppliers outside the country in question would be prepared to compete against their domestic rivals. However, the survey insisted that, even making allowances for this factor, the estimated value of member states' annual public purchasing contracts were in the region of £230 billion. Of this total, less than 2% went to bidders outside national boundaries, which was costing the Community an estimated additional £14.5 billion a year. The assumptions and projections lying behind these figures have been the subject of a bitter dispute. The authors of the Cecchini study, in their enthusiasm to demonstrate the costs of discriminatory public purchasing policies, have been accused of considerably overstating their case.

It would be foolhardy, however, to accept the claim advanced by member states that the cost of national bias in public procurement programmes is negligible. No government likes to be accused, especially by bureaucrats in Brussels, of squandering public money. However, according to a report on the internal market published by Britain's independent Royal Institute of International Affairs in 1987, the costs of national discrimination in public purchasing was estimated at about £14 billion a year, thereby vindicating the Commission's estimates. It is therefore evident that national governments pay far more than they should for their purchases of works, goods and services, and in so doing finance inefficient and uncompetitive producers. An examination of some of the key sectors of the European economy would illustrate this point.

The European telecommunications market has become the classic example of the absurdity of protecting national markets from external competition by favouring national producers through biased public purchasing programmes. The Community market for telephone exchange systems is worth about £5 billion a year. However, the market is divided between eleven national producers, who are now installing no less than seven different exchange systems, five of which have been developed by European companies, most of whom are state owned.

If public procurement was opened to cross-border competition telephone exchange manufacturers would have a major incentive to link up, rationalize the number of exchange systems on offer and thereby reduce development costs, which would, in turn, be reflected in cheaper prices. In anticipation of 1992, a number of telecommunications companies have already begun to restructure their operations. The acquisition of AT&T's European interests by the French telecommunications company Alcatel, the purchase of the French company CGCT by the Swedish giant Ericsson and the link-up between the telecommunications divisions of GEC and Plessey represent the first wave of mergers in the European telecommunications industry.

Such distortions are also evident in other industrial sectors. The European locomotive industry, for example, is valued at about £70 million a year. There are no less than 16 locomotive manufacturers (compared to two in the United States) competing in an industry that has a 50%

overcapacity and is characterized by little intra-EC trade. Boilermaking presents a similar picture. The market is worth an estimated £1.5 billion a year. There are 12 EC manufacturers (compared to six in the United States), and it is characterized by a phenomenal 80% overcapacity with negligible intra-EC trade. The same is true of turbine generator manufacturers. There are ten European manufacturers (compared to two in the United States) chasing orders in a European market that is valued at about £1.5 billion a year, and which has 40% overcapacity. Indeed, it would be difficult to identify a handful of industries that do not rely on the industrial equivalent of social security for their survival.

However, there is more to the cost of discriminatory public purchasing than simple market fragmentation. According to the European Commission, 'protectionist support, often portrayed as a shot in the arm for industry, is in fact a striking example of governments' shooting themselves, and their competitive ideals, in the foot'. Even more alarming is the report's prediction that 'unless restrictions on public purchasing are swept away, far from strategic industries being protected, whole areas of industry which have high multiplier effects on other sectors of manufacturing could cease to be viable'.

Opening up public procurement: round one

Because the member states had failed to honour the free-trade provisions of Articles 30–36 and 59–66 of the Treaty (and had shown no indications of ever doing so of their own volition) the need for additional legislation was abundantly evident. During the 1970s two directives were issued in an effort to remedy this situation, the 1971 Directive on Public Works and the 1977 Directive on Public Supplies.

The directives replaced divergent national procedures for issuing public procurement contracts with a Community-wide procedure governing all public works contracts over £670,000 and all public supply contracts over £134,000. Consequently, all public authorities responsible for awarding contracts falling above these thresholds were required to ensure that their invitations to tender were brought to the attention of companies and suppliers anywhere in the Community. This could be achieved comparatively easily by publication of tendering opportunities in the supplement to the *Official Journal of the European Communities*. The directives also made it illegal to split up tenders so that individually they fell beneath the two thresholds.

Under the new directives the contract-awarding bodies were explicitly prohibited from discriminating against non-national contractors or suppliers under the provisions of Articles 30–36. These articles prohibit all quotas on imports and exports between member states or any measure, whether by law, regulation or administrative practice, which has an equivalent effect. There are two exceptions to this requirement. First, member states are permitted to restrict trade on grounds of public morality, public policy, public health or public security. Second, they are permitted to restrict trade where the product in question fails to meet the member state's essential technical standards. However, any member state attempting to abuse these two let-out clauses could find itself before the European Court of Justice.

In an attempt to encourage public bodies to think in commercial rather than patriotic terms the two directives set out a series of objective criteria for evaluating competing tenders, and made it incumbent on the public bodies to award contracts to those companies who had submitted the lowest-priced or most economically advantageous offers. Where a contractor or supplier had evidence or suspected that it had been discriminated against by the awarding body it was empowered to register a complaint with the Director General for the Internal Market. The Commission could then conduct an investigation into the award procedure. If the investigation confirmed that discrimination had taken place, a formal letter could be sent to the member state asking it to answer the infringement allegation. If the member state failed to answer by the specified date, or if the answer was unsatisfactory, the case could be passed on to the European Court of Justice.

Although regarded as a major step forward in the cause of intra-Community free trade, the significance of the two new directives was soon demonstrated to be rather more apparent than real. In order to secure acceptance by the Council of Ministers the teeth of the original intention to open up public procurement to cross-border competition had been drawn out—one by one.

Under the terms of the two directives, a contract-awarding body had the choice of two basic types of tendering procedure which effectively enabled the authority to preserve its traditional national biases intact. The first is the open procedure, which requires offers to tender to be made available to all potential bidders. The second is the restricted procedure, in which only the contractor or supplier invited to tender may do so. Moreover, all construction and supply contracts awarded by the public authorities responsible for air, land and sea transport; the production and distribution of drinking water; the exploration, development and distribution of coal, oil, electricity and gas; and the development and maintenance of the telecommunications industry were excluded from the scope of the two directives. By the time they came into force, less than 20% of Community public procurement contracts were affected by them.

If this minimalist attempt to promote competition in public procurement became too onerous, the contract-awarding bodies were soon to demonstrate their ingenuity in finding new ways of evading the new works and supply directives in the limited areas in which they applied. Member states' failure to respect their commitments has varied from mild abuse of tendering procedures to outright violation and evasion. The two directives have still not been properly incorporated into national law in a number of member states, and failure to publish advance notification of contracts in the *Official Journal* has been widespread.

Most awarding authorities have insisted that contractors and suppliers adhere to national technical specifications, even in those areas where Community technical standards have been established. Tenders have been systematically divided up into separate contracts in order to fall below the thresholds at which publication in the *Official Journal* is mandatory. Use of the open tenders procedure has been kept to a minimum, while the conditions under which restricted procedures are permitted have been interpreted broadly. Some member states have not even bothered with such subtleties, preferring instead to ignore the conditions under which restricted procedures can be used while systematically eliminating tenders from other member states.

The Commission's powers of enforcement were no match for the ability of member states to ignore the two directives. It proved to be extremely difficult for construction or supply companies to produce evidence demonstrating that they had been discriminated against illegally. On the rare occasions such evidence was found, a company faced up to a two-year wait before the European Court of Justice could hear the case, by which time a construction project was invariably completed and a supply contract long consumed. There was, however, one lesson to come out of the public works and supply directives that was to prove invaluable in the future: how not to make the same mistake twice.

The White Paper and public procurement

Recognizing the political sensitivity surrounding the issue of national bias in public purchasing, the Internal Market White Paper announced the Commission's intention to establish the Advisory Committee on the Opening Up of Public Procurement. This was to be staffed by representatives from the Commission, the member states and the public bodies with responsibilities for awarding contracts. By examining the reasons why the public works and public supply directives had failed to prove effective, and by developing a closer understanding of the needs of the public purchasing bodies, the Advisory Committee set about drafting a strategy for the Commission's second assault on a practice it had denounced as 'economic incest'.

The White Paper gave an outline of the kinds of areas the Commission had identified as those in need of urgent attention. These included closing the loopholes in the existing public works and supply directives, tightening procedures for advance publication of tendering opportunities, providing construction and supply companies with effective means of redress where public purchasing procedures have been breached and, most sensitive of all, extending the contract-awarding procedures to the four excluded sectors.

In the eighteen months that followed the publication of the White Paper the atmosphere of foreboding concerning the prospects for opening up public procurement gradually gave way to cautious grounds for optimism. In three consecutive summit meetings (in The Hague in June 1986, London in December 1986 and Brussels in February 1987) an unprecedented consensus had emerged singling out progress on public procurement as one of the priority areas of the internal market programme.

Member states had finally taken the first tentative steps towards overcoming their traditional reluctance to submit their cherished public sectors to the laws of supply and demand. It was a long-overdue acknowledgement that, in the context of continued government retrenchment and persistent restraint on public spending, the contract-awarding bodies had to abandon their misguided patriotism and pay more attention to commercial considerations when awarding public purchasing contracts.

Opening up public procurement: round two

Reflecting the priorities laid out in the White Paper, and acting on the recommendations formulated by the Advisory Committee on Opening Up Public Procurement, the Commission first concentrated on the existing public works and supply directives. A new Public Supplies Directive was proposed in March 1988, amending the 1977 Public Supplies Directive, and became effective in January 1989.

The type of supply contracts covered by the new directive, ranging from office equipment to employees' clothing, was clearly defined, and the rules for calculating their value for the purposes of applying the £134,000 threshold at which it had to be published in the *Official Journal* (or *Tenders Electronic Daily*, the Community's online database) were made more explicit. The open tenders procedure was made the rule, and any attempt by a contract-awarding body to use the restricted tenders procedure had to be justified to the Commission. Procurement authorities are now also required to give advance notice of their annual purchasing requirements in an attempt to enable supply companies to prepare for potential contracts in advance. All public bodies, from the House of Lords down to the local High Street library, are now required to open all supply contracts over the designated threshold to cross-border competition.

A proposal to amend the 1971 Public Works Directive has proved somewhat more difficult to draft, but the broad outline of the Commission's intentions has already been made known. The existing £670,000 threshold at which all public works contracts have to be published in the *Official Journal* has been made obsolete by the rising costs of construction work over the past 15 years, and is to be replaced by a new £3.35 million threshold. Contracts for public works whose value exceeds the new higher ceiling will have to be advertised in the *Official Journal*. Both categories of contract will, however, remain subject to all other Community rules governing tendering procedures.

The Commission also intends to extend the scope of the existing directive on public works by introducing a wider definition of contract-awarding bodies subject to its provisions, including the non-governmental agencies financed from public funds. As in the case of public supply contracts, the availability of restricted procedures is to be sharply curtailed and the open procedure is to become the norm. In order to ensure that the contract-awarding bodies have adhered to the new tendering procedures they will be required to explain on request why they have decided to reject a particular bid and submit a report to the Commission on each award decision. In future, recognition of Community technical standards will be mandatory. The Council of Ministers is expected to adopt the new Public Works Directive by the end of 1988 for implementation in 1989.

Following the emerging consensus on the need to ensure greater compliance with Community regulations governing public procurement, in July 1987 the Commission submitted to Council a draft directive on proposals to improve the means of redress available to companies who have been illegally discriminated against by public purchasing authorities. Because of the nature of public procurement (and the inordinate amount of time it takes the European Court of Justice to pass judgment on infractions of Community law) the Commission has focused its efforts on prevention rather than cure. Once a building has been completed it would be difficult, even for bureaucrats in Brussels, to demand that it be demolished because the awarding body had discriminated in favour of a national construction company.

The proposed prevention strategy contains three separate but inter-locking elements. First, the Commission would be empowered to suspend for three months any contract award if the awarding authority failed to make adequate provision for cross-border competition. The awarding authority would then be required to make good its breach of Community tendering procedures by issuing a new call to tender complying with the provisions of the public purchasing directives. If an awarding body persisted in its error it would be incumbent on the government of the member states to compel the awarding body to respect Community law. Second, should this prove unsuccessful, the company would then be able to challenge national tendering procedures through the national courts without having to register a complaint with the Commission first. Viol-ations of public purchasing directives are likely to be met with large fines. Finally, if all else fails, the Commission reserves the right to take the member state to the European Court of Justice under the provisions of Article 169 of the Treaty. The Commission has indicated that borderline cases will be overlooked, and that it will only act where there is evidence of a clear and blatant infringement of the rules. Council is expected to endorse the Commission's proposals for effective redress towards the end of 1988 for implementation early in 1989.

Acceptance of the proposed directive on compliance with Community tendering procedures has been described by the Commission as vital in order 'to increase the credibility of the Community's efforts to break down the psychological reluctance of traders, industrialists, and more particularly, small and medium-sized enterprises, to bid across frontiers for public works contracts'. In June 1988 the Commission unveiled its wide-ranging proposals to incorporate the four excluded sectors (telecommunications, energy, transport and water), which have so far remained immune from cross-border competition, into the Community's system for awarding construction and supply contracts, thereby fulfilling a priority commitment in its goal of completing the internal market by 1992.

Before making its proposals the Commission took into account the extensive analysis of the four excluded sectors conducted by the Advisory Committee on Opening Up Public Procurement. This examination demonstrated that biased patterns of public procurement could not simply be attributed to the public status of the organizations operating in the four sectors. Similar difficulties could be expected even if all four sectors were in private hands. Far more important was the actual structure of the sector itself, whether electricity, gas, coal or oil in the energy sector; the seaports, airports and rail networks and municipal mass transport systems in the transport sector; the purification and distribution functions of the water sector; and the development and supply of telecommunications equipment in the communications sector. The Advisory Committee found that all four sectors were inherently monopolistic, consequently insulated from competition and characterized by a highly developed propensity to 'buy national'.

The main reason for the excluded sectors being left out of the scope of the 1970s directives on public purchasing was that the pattern of ownership throughout the Community varied considerably from private to public or a mixture of the two, and the Commission faced great difficulty in trying to find some regulatory formula that adequately catered for the different forms of ownership. The new directive ignores this question, and focuses instead on the more important area of state influence. Any organization in the four excluded sectors (whether publicly or privately owned) that is subject to official or unofficial pressures to place public procurement contracts with local firms will be subject to the new directive. The intention is not to force these organizations to buy foreign, but to ensure that they are free to exercise their commercial judgement, independently of nationalistic public purchasing pressures.

Because the organizations operating in the excluded sectors are more sensitive to industrial and commercial considerations than the public and administrative bodies covered by the existing directives on public purchasing, the new directive provides a considerably more flexible tendering procedure. The organizations can choose between requesting tenders on a contract-by-contract basis or periodically calling for expressions of interest from would-be contractors or suppliers. They can also avail themselves of the option to maintain a pool of contractors and suppliers, on condition that the terms of entrance to the pool are made public and that foreign companies have the same rights of access as national companies. A new system (known as a negotiated procedure) has been introduced in which an awarding body can enter into talks with prospective contractors or suppliers, but only where the response from open or restricted procedures has been unsatisfactory, or where issues of national security or defence are at stake. As with previous directives, Community technical standards must be used wherever possible. The telecommunications sector was the subject of a separate directive in 1989, and electricity is to be in 1990.

The excluded sectors directive will cover all supply contracts valued at £134,000 and above, which the Commission estimates is enough to buy 4.5 miles of fibre-optic cable, two buses or a small crane, and all works contracts valued at £3.3 million and above, enough to pay for 6.5 miles of standard or 1.5 miles of high-speed railway line or the dredging of a major port. Access to the Community's public purchasing market by organizations from outside the EC can be excluded where more than 50% of the value of the contract is provided by companies outside the twelve member states.

Completing the Commission's internal market programme in the field of public purchasing is a new directive covering the flourishing market for telecommunications, known as Open Network Provision. In December 1988, the Commission announced its intention to launch an ambitious and highly controversial plan to compel member states to open up their national telecommunications services industries to free competition throughout the Community by 1991.

The plan, which will be implemented under the competition provisions of Article 90 of the Treaty of Rome, will make it incumbent on member states to relinquish their monopoly rights over the burgeoning telecommunications services sector. Only voice telephony and telex services will remain outside the scope of the directive. In a separate but related move, the Commission also submitted to the Council of Ministers a draft directive calling for the introduction of harmonized technical standards, in an effort to open up the telecommunications networks to all equipment manufacturers, and thus bring an end to the arbitrary power of the private and state-owned phone companies to decide who has access to the network.

But the telecommunications services plan, which would open up the vast majority of the Community's £44 billion telecommunications services industry to free competition, was confronted with bitter opposition from a variety of member states, principally West Germany, France and Italy, all of whom continue to exercise a virtually exclusive monopoly over their telecommunications services sector. The plan also faced opposition from Britain, on procedural grounds (despite the UK government's commitment to the objectives of the proposal), because it was convinced that the

Commission was overstepping the limit of its powers by refusing to adhere to the normal procedure of drawing up a draft directive for approval by the Council of Ministers.

The plan was originally scheduled for finalization in March 1989, and would have eliminated all telecommunications services monopolies by January 1991. However, it proved so controversial that the Commission was forced to consider a one-year extension of the liberalization timetable in order to defuse some of the angry reactions its ambitious proposals had generated.

The Commission is already being taken to the European Court of Justice by France, following its decision in June to issue its own directive forcing member states to open up the Community's terminal equipment market to cross-border competition. But the Commission, backed by the powerful commercial telecommunications companies, is confident that the Court of Justice will uphold its authority to liberalize the telecommunications sector under the powers granted to it by the EC's founding treaty—as it already has done in the field of competition policy and the liberalization of the air transport industry.

The Commission is also confident that it will emerge victorious in the impending battle over the proposed liberalization of telecommunications services. As one official said: 'Eventually, the member states will have to reconcile themselves to the fact that they are signatories to the Treaty of Rome.' Yet there is no disguising the growing anxiety among the governments of member states over the Commission's determination to ride roughshod over national sensibilities—using every power at its disposal, and forcing them to adhere to the Community's timetable for the completion of the internal market by 1992. The Commission hopes to implement a new directive by 1992 covering the liberalization of telecommunications services, which will include everything from electronic mail to data processing and teleshopping.

Checklist of changes

- The loopholes in the 1971 directive on public works and the 1977 directive on public supplies will be closed and procedures for advance publication of tendering opportunities will be tightened up.
- Public bodies will be required to open all supply contracts worth more than £134,000 and all public works contracts worth more than £3.3 million to cross-border competition.
- In order to make sure that the contract-awarding bodies adhere to the new procedures they will be required to explain why they have rejected particular bids.
- There will be a wider definition of contract-awarding bodies, recognition of Community technical standards will become

mandatory, and all works contracts above £3.3 million will have to be advertised in the *Official Journal*.

- The means of redress for companies who have been illegally discriminated against by the public purchasing authorities will also be improved, and substantial fines are likely to be imposed on anyone violating the Community's public purchasing directives.
- The four excluded sectors (telecommunications, energy, transport and water) will also be incorporated into the Community's systems of awarding construction and supply contracts.

7 THE PROFESSIONS
Freedom of establishment and mutual recognition of professional qualifications

The attempt to create a single European market would be fatally flawed without a single market for labour. Along with capital, goods and services, the free movement of labour, whether unskilled, skilled or professional, is one of the vital factors of production necessary for the efficient functioning of the Community's economy. Indeed, in many respects the internal market programme would simply not work without the abolition of national labour markets and the freedom for labour to move around the Community in search of more attractive conditions of employment and new opportunities to exploit.

The need to eliminate the barriers preventing the free movement of labour is particularly acute in the case of the service sector, which has recorded impressive rates of growth in recent years and will continue to do so only in an atmosphere of free competition. However, the benefits to be obtained from increased competition between goods, capital and services apply with equal force to every aspect of the labour market. The free movement of labour also constitutes one of the central elements of the European Commission's determination to create a 'Citizens' Europe', in which such freedoms are enshrined in Community law.

The Treaty of Rome already provides the legal basis for Community citizens to establish themselves in any member state and to be treated equally with the citizens of the host state. Article 52 lays down that 'restrictions on the freedom of establishment of nationals of a member state in the territory of another member state shall be abolished by progressive stages . . . such progressive abolition shall also apply to restrictions on the setting up of agencies, branches or subsidiaries by nationals of any member state established in the territory of any member state'. It also specifies that 'freedom of establishment shall include the right to take up and pursue activities as self-employed persons, and to set up and manage undertakings', while Article 57, as amended by the Single European Act, made it incumbent on the Council of Ministers to issue directives facilitating the mutual recognition of 'diplomas, certificates and other evidence of formal qualifications', enabling individuals who qualify in one member state to practise without hindrance in any other.

In an effort to allay the anxieties of member states about the employment of other Community nationals in certain sensitive sectors, principally those of national defence and security, the objective of creating the conditions for the free movement of labour cannot be allowed to prejudice the right of member states to regulate those sectors vital to 'public policy, public security and public health'. However, member states are explicitly prohibited under Article 53 from introducing any new restrictions on the right of Community nationals to establish themselves and take up their professions in any member state of their choosing.

As a result of two landmark rulings by the European Court of Justice in 1974, the right of Community citizens to work in any member state, without discrimination, was further reinforced. However, despite the theoretical right of establishment, a complex web of national regulations governing skills and professions in most member states has proved to be virtually impenetrable for non-nationals, unless they have been prepared to take their professional or vocational examinations all over again. Free movement has effectively been circumscribed by the various national regulations governing access to everything, from plumbing and carpentry to medicine and corporate law. Having qualified in a given field in one member state, the ability to work or practise elsewhere in the Community was frequently barred because of national differences in training periods and qualifications, or because member states simply refused to recognize equivalent qualifications obtained in other member states in order to protect their professional and labour markets from intra-Community competition.

Previous attempts to create a free market for labour

Because most of the barriers to the free circulation of labour arise out of different national educational traditions, reinforced by the fact that professions and skills are essentially nationally based, the European Commission had previously tried to eliminate the differences in member states' level and length of training requirements on a case-by-case basis. The negotiations co-ordinating professional qualifications were both difficult and protracted, but, by 1985, significant progress had been made. Some eight directives had been issued by the Council of Ministers, harmonizing national requirements to take up and practise a variety of professions in any member state. These included directives for doctors (1975), nurses (1977), dentists (1978), veterinary surgeons (1978), midwives (1980), architects (1985), pharmacists (1985) and general practitioners (1986), which was to become the last of the sectoral directives designed to facilitate increased professional mobility.

At the time, the directive governing training for GPs was seen as the dawning of the age of the Euro-doctor. The measure was basically a consolidation and updating of the 1975 directive on essential medical qualifications for GPs, based largely on the British model. British GPs are already required to undergo six years' basic training, followed by three years' practical experience in the National Health Service before becoming fully qualified. By 1990, all other member states will also require two years' practical experience in addition to the basic training requirements. Yet while the measure established uniform Community training requirements for GPs, very few have so far availed themselves of their freedom to work in any member state. According to Commission estimates, there are some 600,000 doctors practising in the Community, only 2000 of whom work in member states other than the one in which they qualified. Language, as in so many other areas, remains the single greatest obstacle to professional mobility in the internal market.

Although the negotiations which led to the implementation of the eight professional mobility directives have helped to build links between related professions in the twelve member states, they were nonetheless a laborious and time-consuming process. The negotiations for the directive governing architects took 17 years to complete, thus acquiring the dubious distinction of becoming one of the longest discussions over a single piece of legislation in the Community's history. Nor was this an isolated phenomenon. The negotiations for the directive for pharmacists came a close second, having taken 16 years to complete, while the proposal for the free movement of lawyers had been on the negotiating table for over a decade with no sign of a breakthrough. With some 80 or so professions still to go, the Commission will be fortunate to have completed the task of creating an internal market for professionals this side of 2092.

Along with many other of the Commission's 1992 initiatives in the internal market programme, the prospects for rapid progress were enhanced immeasurably by abandoning the traditional approach of case-by-case harmonization in favour of a mutual recognition. During the EC summit meeting at Fontainebleau in June 1984 member states gave their approval to a scheme designed to build on the existing legal foundations for the freedom of establishment by introducing the principle of a general system of mutual recognition for all higher education qualifications. With its mandate in hand, the Commission promptly set about drawing up radical new proposals for creation of an internal market for labour and the professions.

The Internal Market White Paper made a sweeping assault on the remaining barriers to the free movement of labour. It declared that:

> The Commission considers it crucial that the obstacles which still exist within the Community to free movement for the self-employed and employees be removed by 1992. It considers that Community citizens should be free to engage in their professions throughout the Community, if they so wish, without the obligation to adhere to formalities which, in the final analysis, could serve to discourage such movement.

It also pointed out that, as far as employees were concerned, free movement was now virtually complete, and a succession of rulings by the European Court of Justice had already severely curtailed the right of the public authorities in the various member states to reserve positions for their own nationals. However, certain problems still remained to be solved—for example, obstacles preventing the free movement and residence of Community migrant workers, particularly those living on the frontier of one member state and employed in another. Proposals to remove both the cumbersome administrative procedures governing the acquisition of residence permits in different member states and the taxation of frontier-migrant workers were put forward as potential solutions, and are still awaiting approval by the Council of Ministers.

In addition, the White Paper announced a two-stage programme designed to bring about the essential comparability of different member state vocational training qualifications. The first part of the programme calls for the prompt approximation of vocational proficiency certificates among member states, while the second stage involves the introduction of a European vocational training card by 1990, serving as proof in all member states that the holder has been awarded with a universally recognized vocational training qualification.

In May 1987, and after much acrimonious debate between the Twelve, the Council of Ministers endorsed a multimillion pound Commission proposal to increase student exchanges between Community universities. Known as ERASMUS, the programme (originally budgeted at £125 million and subsequently trimmed to £60 million) will enable an estimated 5% of students in higher education to spend part of their courses in another Community country. Britain is expected to receive about £12 million, much of which will be spent in the form of a travel allowance of about £1500 for some 25,000 British students. The programme will run for three years, and is expected to be implemented by 1990.

The Commission also declared its intention to propose legislation facilitating the mutual recognition of apprenticeship courses, as well as measures to ensure that freedom of movement is not restricted to only those gainfully employed. One of the most important initiatives in this respect is the 1987 programme to increase co-operation between further educational establishments, designed to promote increased mobility of students around the Community and act as an encouragement for the acquisition of language skills. However, while much of this work remains to be completed, member states have been able to agree on a general system for the mutual recognition of higher education degrees, which has been described as the single most important step towards the creation of a free market for people and services.

Mutual recognition of professional diplomas

In July 1985 the Commission put forward its proposal to create the basic conditions for the free movement of citizens who wish to take up a profession subject to regulation in another member state, and in which access is conditional on holding a specific degree of higher education. It was the first example of the Commission's attempts to create a 'Citizens' Europe', and is based on the principle that what was good for one member state was also good for all others. The proposal does not cover those professions already subject to sectoral directives, such as doctors, dentists and architects, but applies to everyone else, including surveyors, accountants, lawyers, physiotherapists, opticians and psychologists.

Initially, the Commission's proposals were greeted with some reservation by member states, notably Britain and France. Commission officials argued that the general recognition directive would only work on the basis of mutual trust and co-operation between member states. However, it was one thing to say that professionals from one member state would practise according to the requirements of other member states, and quite another to suggest that differences between member states in training and professional practice could be easily overcome on the basis of mutual trust and co-operation, combined with a probationary period of practical experience.

The legal profession, as represented by the Consultative Committee of European Bars, insisted that some mechanism (for example, an aptitude test to determine whether a lawyer from one member state was competent to practise in another) had to be incorporated into the proposal. The Commission objected to such modifications on the grounds that the professions were merely trying to preserve their closed-shop privileges, and that if it granted special concessions for lawyers, every other profession would soon be seeking preferential treatment, thereby undermining the whole purpose of the directive. Besides, one Commission official said indignantly: 'When it comes to the point, is a German lawyer really likely to seek to defend a client in a British court without knowing British law and being able to speak the language?'

At a meeting of the Council of Ministers in Luxembourg in June 1988 ministers agreed a compromise, allowing member states the freedom to decide whether to require non-national professionals to undergo a period of probation or sit an aptitude test before practising in their respective territories. Much to the irritation of the Commission, particularly Lord Cockfield, the compromise also made aptitude tests obligatory for all professions involved in legal work, provided that they were not another examination of 'the entire corpus of knowledge'. After a reading by the European Parliament, the directive was formally approved by the Council of Ministers at the end of 1988 and will come into force in 1990.

The directive is predicated on four guiding principles. First, it is general in character, and will be applied to all regulated professions for which a three-year university degree is required. Second, mutual recognition is based on confidence and trust between member states, thereby avoiding the need to harmonize the different education and training schemes for the different professions among all member states. Third, the directive states that recognition is given to the 'finished product', defined as a fully qualified professional who has completed any training required in addition to obtaining a university degree. Foreign nationals can also use the same professional titles as domestic nationals. Finally, where important differences exist between the same profession among different member states, national authorities have the right to examine the competence of individual professionals by means of an aptitude test or a period of probation at their discretion.

The directive also makes special provision for the chartered bodies of Great Britain and the Republic of Ireland. These bodies, which regulate professional standards, are unique to Britain and Ireland. However, while membership of a chartered body is not based on the same level of higher education required in other EC member states in order to practise a particular profession, for the purposes of the directive there is no difference between them. Members of chartered bodies now have access to their sister professions in the Community, and, by the same token, their sister professions also have access to membership of the chartered bodies.

The agreement was described by Francis Maude, the junior trade minister, as 'an essential element in a genuine single market, leading to lower prices for services, and increased opportunities abroad'. It also gives European professionals greater freedom to move around the Community's internal market than is enjoyed by their American counterparts in their domestic market. However, proposals to extend similar rights of mobility to students, pensioners and the unemployed found considerably less sympathy from Britain, supported by Denmark, and remain effectively deadlocked. The Commission has, however, made clear its determination to prevent the new mobility freedoms from being restricted only to those gainfully employed, and will no doubt try again later.

In theory, the agreement on a 'general system for the recognition of higher education diplomas awarded on completion of professional education and training of at least three years' duration' provides an estimated 10 million Community professionals with the freedom to live and work in any member state of their choosing. As an instrument for the promotion of professional mobility, the initiative has been described by the Commission as being 'better than a passport'. However, the Commission is clearly unhappy about the incorporation of aptitude tests into the directive, and has declared its determination to monitor the situation closely in order to prevent the professions from erecting new barriers. Any attempt by member states to preserve their national markets for professional services for their own professionals (such as the attempt in 1988 by French lawyers to keep their British rivals out of France's expanding market for financial services) is likely to meet retaliation from Brussels.

UK professions affected by the Mutual Recognition Directive

1 Institute of Chartered Accountants in England and Wales
2 Institute of Chartered Accountants of Scotland
3 Institute of Chartered Accountants in Ireland
4 Chartered Association of Certified Accountants
5 Chartered Institute of Loss Adjusters
6 Chartered Institute of Management Accountants
7 Institute of Chartered Secretaries and Administrators
8 Chartered Insurance Institute
9 Institute of Actuaries
10 Faculty of Actuaries
11 Chartered Institute of Bankers
12 Institute of Bankers in Scotland
13 Royal Institution of Chartered Surveyors
14 Royal Town Planning Institute
15 Chartered Society of Physiotherapists
16 Royal Society of Chemistry
17 British Psychological Society
18 Library Association
19 Institute of Chartered Foresters
20 Chartered Institute of Building
21 Engineering Council
22 Institute of Energy
23 Institution of Structural Engineers
24 Institution of Civil Engineers
25 Institution of Mining Engineers
26 Institution of Mining and Metallurgy
27 Institution of Electrical Engineers
28 Institution of Gas Engineers
29 Institution of Mechanical Engineers
30 Institution of Chemical Engineers
31 Institution of Production Engineers
32 Institution of Marine Engineers
33 Royal Institution of Naval Architects
34 Royal Aeronautical Society
35 Institute of Metals
36 Chartered Institution of Building Services Engineers
37 Institute of Measurement and Control
38 British Computer Society

The language barrier

Although welcoming the internal market programme as a much-needed stimulus for European industry, many critics have argued that, no matter how many technical, physical and fiscal barriers to trade are dismantled between now and 1992, the linguistic one will remain intact, effectively condemning the Community to permanent fragmentation. Even if all the directives are implemented by the deadline, language will remain the greatest single barrier preventing the creation of a genuine internal market. Linguistic differences are an unfortunate but brutal fact of life, and they will always be with us. They may be of minimal significance where member states have a long tradition of close economic ties, such as the historic relationship between Britain and Holland, but where no such relationship exists, any attempt to break new ground will be difficult—if not impossible—without the requisite linguistic skills.

At the institutional level the Community functions effectively only because it spends large sums of money on interpreters and translators, who account for about one in three of all Community employees. There are nine official languages in the Community: English, French, German, Italian, Spanish, Greek, Danish, Dutch and Portuguese, with Irish as an unofficial working language. Without the services of legions of interpreters and translators, the Community's modest bureaucratic machine, under strain at the best of times, would come to a precipitate halt. Few companies can afford to spend similar sums on interpreters and translators, so what hope is there for the internal market—especially for countries like Britain and France, which have a poor reputation for acquiring foreign-language skills?

According to a survey of 1500 British companies conducted by Newcastle-upon-Tyne Polytechnic in 1988, the language barrier is far more significant than most British companies appreciate. This showed that a severe shortage of staff speaking European languages was costing British industry millions of pounds every year in lost contracts. Moreover, it found that while English has become the leading language in diplomacy, science and technology, it has been steadily losing ground to European languages in the fields of commerce and industry.

Perhaps even more alarming was the fact that this trend had been observed since Britain joined the Community in 1973, but a disturbing proportion of British companies had failed to take appropriate action, preferring instead to 'muddle through' by inundating foreign consulates with untranslated and (for the most part) 'unintelligible' trade literature. The survey discovered a direct correlation between export performance and linguistic competence, and found that Britain's trade deficit in manufactured goods, particularly in the car, textile, iron, steel, resins and plastics sectors, could be reversed if a more balanced trade relationship could be established with just three countries, West Germany, Italy and Japan. Emphasizing the importance of language skills, the report noted that: 'It is not fortuitous that West Germany, Italy and Japan came respectively second, fourth and sixth in the rank order of foreign languages most lacking in British companies.'

Warning British firms that there was little doubt that the survival of manufacturing industry in Britain will come to depend on exports to non-English speaking countries, the authors stressed that: 'The key European languages—German, French, Spanish and Italian—are likely to play an increasingly important role in UK–EC trade if Britain is not only to maintain its market share, but also to increase it.' However, the omens are not favourable. In the decade between 1973 and 1983 the volume of manufactured goods imported into Britain from the Community rose by 300%, while Britain could manage only a modest 66% in the other direction. 'Other countries,' the report said, 'have mastered our language and market, but we have not reciprocated to the same extent. This deficiency, moreover, seems to apply to firms all over Britain.'

The survey also found that, in spite of a marginal increase in company awareness of the importance of language competence since the 1980s, there remained a marked reluctance for companies to employ individuals as much for their linguistic as for their technical skills. Many companies had been deterred from recruiting linguists because of the poor cost-effectiveness of employing a specialist if the frequency of foreign-language use was low. However, the consequences of underestimating the utility of linguists were inescapable. 'British companies are losing valuable trading opportunities for the lack of the right skills in the right languages, and many without realizing it,' the report concluded.

It is clear that it will be the linguists who will manage European industry and commerce in the 1990s. There is already a considerable premium in Europe for people with linguistic skills, and as the competition between European companies (as well as US and Japanese ones located inside the Community) intensifies, they are likely to become a scarce and extremely valuable resource—commanding ever-increasing financial rewards.

However, British students appear to be on course for allowing their Continental counterparts to take the largest share of the anticipated growth in the language market. David Smith, chairman of the 1988 Headmasters' Conference, a forum representing Britain's leading independent schools, warned his colleagues that many of Britain's schools and colleges were simply not prepared to cope with the challenge presented by 1992—particularly as far as foreign languages were concerned. Such predictions appear to be borne out by the statistical evidence. Despite the growing involvement of Japanese companies throughout the European (and especially the British) economy, British universities produce barely 50 Japanese-language graduates a year, while the number of university applications to study other foreign languages is declining steadily.

Although there is good cause to be concerned about the number of linguists produced by the education system, the problem is by no means confined to Britain. However, an attempt by the Commission to promote language teaching through the Lingua programme rapidly turned into an example of how Brussels, in its enthusiasm to promote the European ideal, has a marked tendency to overreach itself. The programme was an attempt to enforce the teaching of two languages at schools throughout Europe, as well as establish a new pupil exchange scheme.

In May 1989, Britain bitterly opposed the project, primarily on the grounds that the Commission had no powers under the Treaty of Rome to legislate in the field of secondary education. Downing Street also felt that the £160 million programme was 'poor value for money'. Domestic commentators felt that to have allowed the plan to be implemented, even for such laudable reasons, would have been to set a precedent that could have had serious repercussions for secondary education in the future.

Eventually, a compromise was reached in which the revised £130 million Lingua programme excluded all reference to secondary schools, and concentrated instead on promoting language teaching in post-secondary fields such as teacher exchanges, vocational training and language instruction for trainees in management, tourism and business studies.

Checklist of changes

- Introduction of the general system of mutual recognition for all higher education qualifications will enable professionals to practise anywhere in the Community.
- Member states will be entitled to require an aptitude test or a period of probation for all professionals involved in legal work before allowing professionals from other Community countries to practise on their own territory.
- The eight sectoral directives governing professional mobility, passed prior to the White Paper programme, are not affected by the general directive on the mutual recognition of professional qualifications.
- The European Commission intends to introduce a two-stage programme designed to make member states' vocational training qualifications comparable, along with a European vocational training card serving as proof that the holder has been awarded a universally recognizable vocational training qualification.
- Student exchanges between Community universities and higher education colleges will be increased.
- Proposals for a directive governing the mutual recognition of apprenticeships will also be implemented.
- Legislation designed to remove the cumbersome administrative procedures governing the acquisition of residence permits in different member states and the taxation of frontier migrant workers will also be forthcoming.

8 A FISTFUL OF ECUs
Financial services, the EMS and monetary union

Three fast-moving developments are transforming fiscal and monetary affairs in Britain and Europe: the new directive on banking across frontiers on the basis of a single licence; the agreement fully to liberalize capital movements within the EC by 1 July 1990; and the commitment by Mrs Thatcher (reluctantly) and other summit leaders (enthusiastically) at Madrid in June 1989 to the first phase of a three-stage programme for achieving economic and monetary union (EMU), combined with the decision reached at Strasbourg in December 1989 to convene an inter-governmental conference in December 1990 to revise the Treaty of Rome, thus paving the way for full economic and monetary union. The last has caused much controversy both in the EC and in Britain, where the unity of the ruling Conservative Party is increasingly under strain over Europe and EMU has become the touchstone of Britain's European commitment.

This emerged at the Strasbourg summit in December 1989, when Mrs Thatcher repeated what she had said in her Mansion House speech in November: that EMU was not a British priority, least of all at a time when rapid developments in Eastern Europe called—in her view—for cautious rather than headlong progress toward monetary union enshrined in a new treaty. This would 'take the heart of democratic control out of parliamentary accountability.' But not all ministers share this view. Tensions within the British government over the issue surfaced dramatically on October 27, 1989, when Nigel Lawson resigned as Chancellor of the Exchequer because of Mrs Thatcher's refusal to sack her economic adviser, Sir Alan Walters, a noted opponent of British entry to the Exchange Rate Mechanism (ERM) of the European Monetary System (EMS).

Lawson later spelled out his differences with Thatcher over Europe, declaring that British membership of the ERM was in his view central to the government's resolve to beat inflation: 'Indeed, given the existence of the EMS, our continuing non-participation in the ERM cannot fail to cast practical doubt on that resolve.' Britain could not have influence in Europe unless it joined the EMS fully, Lawson said, adding that Thatcher was 'incapable of appointing ministers she trusts and then having them carry out policy.' The effect of the row was damaging, and led to a fall in Tory popularity, coming as it did after an earlier Cabinet re-shuffle in August, described by *Time* magazine as a 'Shuffle Shambles.' In the wake of Lawson's departure in October, John Major, appointed Foreign Secretary only three months before in place of Sir Geoffrey Howe, was suddenly made Chancellor, Douglas Hurd was moved from the Home Office to the

Foreign Office, David Waddington was appointed Home Secretary, and Nicholas Ridley moved to the Department of Trade and Industry.

As Mrs Thatcher herself observed at Madrid, the phased plan for EMU has implications far beyond the purely financial and monetary. Britain welcomes the prospect of financial liberalization; but monetary union is another matter. Like all EC economic blueprints, it has powerful political overtones, with consequences for national sovereignty. At the heart of the matter is the question of whether we are heading—despite British reservations—for a unified monetary area with a common banking system and a single currency, an aim furthered by President Mitterrand and the French EC Presidency in the second half of 1989 after the Madrid summit.

The three-stage plan: the Delors report and the Madrid summit

Plans for EMU stem from a report on monetary union ordered by the EC summit at Hanover in 1988 and prepared by Delors as Commission President, with heads of central banks and other experts serving on his committee. It was published in April 1989. At Madrid, British objections to the visionary thrust of the Delors report prevented its full adoption as official policy. However, the Madrid leaders did agree that the first phase of EMU would amount to 'increased economic and monetary co-ordination' among the Twelve, beginning at the same time as capital movements liberalization in mid-1990. They also agreed, again in the face of British opposition, to prepare 'completely and adequately' an Inter-Governmental Conference (IGC) on stages two and three, understood (not least by France and West Germany) to include the evolution of a federal banking structure, as recommended by the Delors report, and possibly a single currency, both of which would require treaty amendments. Moreover, President Mitterrand, who took over the EC Presidency from Felipe Gonzalez of Spain after Madrid, argues that acceptance of stage one also necessarily entails eventual acceptance of the other stages, an idea contained in the now-celebrated Paragraph 39 of the Delors report ('a decision to enter upon the first stage should be a decision to embark on the entire process') but vigorously contested by Mrs Thatcher. Some believe Mrs Thatcher is assuming that stage one of EMU will take until 1992 and beyond, so that stages two and three will never be reached. This may be a miscalculation. As the *Financial Times* observed in an editorial on 23 June 1989: 'After 40 years of experience, it should be burnt into the consciousness of a British Prime Minister that she may slow down an evolution on which all other members of the EC are resolved; she may influence its form; but she will not stop it.'

The three proposed stages are:

1 Greater economic convergence from 1 July 1990, with all currencies

inside the EMS; central bank governors able to make proposals to the Council of Ministers; possible creation of a European Reserve Fund.

2 More collective decision making, though with national governments retaining ultimate control of fiscal and monetary policy; non-binding rules for national budget deficits; establishment of a European System of Central Banks (ESCB); fewer exchange rate realignments.

3 Fixed exchange rates; single currency introduced; binding deficit constraints; ESCB acquires far-reaching powers over national reserves and EC fiscal policy.

Under stage one of the Delors plan, therefore—the only stage for which a starting date has been set—all EC currencies would be committed to joining the European Monetary System (EMS), a move which puts immediate pressure on sterling to join. The Spanish peseta duly joined the EMS on 19 June 1989 (Greece and Portugal remained outside for the time being). Mrs Thatcher, who until Madrid had always insisted that the pound would join the EMS only 'when the time is ripe' (taken by many to mean 'never'), for the first time gave a list of specific conditions: the pound would join when UK inflation was down to the EC average; when France and Italy had emulated Britain in scrapping exchange controls; when the internal market had been completed; when a free market in financial services had been achieved; and when competition policy had been strengthened.

Sceptics saw this as simply a more subtle delaying tactic. Certainly, there is little doubt that Britain, which at Madrid yet again found itself in a minority of one, agreed to 'phase one' in the hope of resisting full monetary union in the long term. Mrs Thatcher, in this view, joined the bandwagon to slow it down. Yet France, West Germany, Italy and Spain clearly believe—and said at Madrid—that monetary union will require the setting up of new institutions and possibly further Treaty of Rome amendments, which in turn will entail further devolution of powers from national parliaments to Brussels. This, Mrs Thatcher objected, would amount to 'the biggest transfer of national authority we have ever had', and would be rejected by Parliament. Equally, Mrs Thatcher strongly opposed the proposal for an Inter-Governmental Conference on the precise timetable for EMU, but was outvoted—a repeat performance of the Milan summit of 1985, when she failed to prevent the setting up of an IGC to formulate what then became the Single European Act (see Chapter 3).

At Madrid, Mrs Thatcher accepted that she was outnumbered. 'I have not the slightest shadow of doubt we shall vote against it,' she said of the IGC proposal, 'and I have not the slightest doubt we shall be in a minority.' Britain would not boycott the conference, since 'it is never right to leave an empty chair'. But Mrs Thatcher reminded her partners that IGC outcomes must be unanimous. She served warning that she saw 'nothing automatic' about going beyond phase one, and that she saw absolutely no need for a single European currency. The Delors plan was not the only option, Mrs Thatcher declared, and the EC would not 'go pell mell' into monetary union. Lord Young, as the then Trade and Industry Secretary, warned in an address to the Bruges Group that EMU as conceived by Delors would lead to a single European government, 'with national parliaments turned into local councils or museums'. Nigel Lawson, the Chancellor of the Exchequer, attacked the Delors report in April 1989 as a recipe for a United States of Europe, 'a concept of the European Community which we do not share'. On the other hand, it was Lawson who—to the apparent dismay of Mrs Thatcher—paved the way for the Madrid compromise on 'phase one' by agreeing at a meeting of Finance Ministers at S'Agaró on the Costa Brava at the end of May 1989 that currency union and Euro bank proposals were worth considering, if only because debate would make the problems involved all the more apparent.

During a Finance Ministers meeting at the French Mediterranean resort of Antibes in September, Lawson tried to deflect criticism that Britain was dragging its feet on monetary union by putting forward his alternative to the Delors Plan. In essence, the idea involved making EC currencies legal tender in each member state. But critics argued that while the scheme could possibly work for business, enabling companies to buy and sell in the currency of their choice, it was unlikely to be popular with the average citizen who would find himself having to act as a one man *bureau de change*.

The debate on financial liberalization and monetary union is thus another—and crucial—aspect of the tug of war between 1992 'pragmatists' and 'visionaries'. Mrs Thatcher, as the arch-pragmatist, seems to be being pulled further towards the visionary version that she would wish. The senior British Commissioner in Brussels, Sir Leon Brittan, aligned himself with the Eleven in June 1989 when he told the Association of District Councils in Torquay there was 'no economic justification' for further 'unwise delay' in bringing sterling into the EMS.

Some of the more radical ideas on monetary union—for example, the setting up of a fully fledged, all-powerful European Bank—have been modified, with the Delors report leaning towards co-ordination rather than centralization. As John Williamson of the Washington Institute for International Economics wrote to *The Economist* after Madrid, the Twelve 'do not need to have a fiscal policy that is identical either among themselves or over time, but only that there should be a mechanism to ensure that the aggregate outcome will be consistent with macroeconomic stability'. However, the Delors plan still envisages an ESCB to manage exchange rates and regulate money supply, and the replacement of national currencies by the European Currency Unit (ECU). Robin Leigh-Pemberton, Governor of the Bank of England, who served on the Delors committee and endorsed its findings, noted that the three phases of EMU implied 'fundamental and far-reaching changes to national sovereignty', but opposed any 'forcing of the pace' towards—for example—a single currency. At Madrid, Mitterrand described Mrs Thatcher as a 'brake on European union' because of her stern defence of sovereignty in monetary affairs, leading her to retort that this was 'a bit rich' coming from the leader of a country which had yet to abolish exchange controls.

Freedom of capital movements from mid-1990

The official EC Cecchini report on the anticipated benefits of 1992 suggests that deregulation and the absence of artificial barriers will have a major impact on financial services—banks, insurance and securities. To reverse the formula, freedom in financial services could provide the motor for much of the 1992 programme, as capital moves about the integrated market and banks compete across borders to offer services. EC officials put the 1992 saving to the financial services sector at between £14 and £15 billion. The four areas targeted for immediate 1992 integration are capital movements, insurance, banking and securities.

All 25 financial service proposals in the 1985 White Paper have been tabled. Some directives have been in force for some time, such as the 1985 law liberalizing the marketing of mutual funds and unit trusts—although British unit trust companies complain that they are still excluded from mutual trust markets in Europe, where distribution networks have been largely built up by banks and advertising is restricted. Other areas are even more complex, from motor insurance to 'own initiative' life insurance and group pension schemes. However, the governing principle of 'home country control' is firmly established, meaning that 'the home country supervising financial institutions should be responsible for the authorization of financial operators and the application of key prudential rules to those operators throughout the Community' (Geoffrey Fitchew, Director General of DG XV).

The liberalization of capital movements is already bringing an unrestricted market in financial services closer. The basis for this lies in Article 67 of the Treaty of Rome, which provides for all member states to 'abolish all restrictions on the movement of capital belonging to persons resident in the Community'. Some loosening up of capital flows did take place after EC directives were passed in the 1960s, but it has taken the 1992 impetus to provide the final push. Britain, with its traditional strengths in the field, is likely to benefit more than most other EC countries from free capital flows, a prospect welcomed in the City and Whitehall. Britain abolished exchange controls as early as 1979, though not entirely for reasons to do with the EC.

The Cecchini report anticipates 'substantial economic gains' from the integration of financial markets, because of the pivotal role such services play in acting as the catalyst for European economies in general. The report calculates that the integration in 1992 of banking and credit insurance, brokerage and securities will save the Community 'in the order of 22 billion ECU'—about £15 billion. In the eight countries where financial integration is to take place—Britain, France, West Germany, the Benelux nations, Denmark and Italy (Spain, Ireland, Greece and Portugal are excluded until after 1992, the latter two until 1995), the report found 'notably wide margins' in prices charged at present for mortgages, motor insurance and consumer credit. The 'competitive pressures of integration' will level these differentials out, to the benefit of the consumer, Cecchini suggests.

The first part of the Commission's two-stage plan for free capital flows across frontiers began in February 1987, with the liberalization of cross-border transactions in unit trusts, unlisted securities and long-term trade credits: the second phase, agreed in June 1988, completes the process by providing for full liberalization beginning in July 1990. In banking, there is already a degree of free competition: but in practice, as Cecchini noted: 'It appears difficult for many banks to compete successfully in other Community countries because new establishment involves considerable costs not borne by existing domestic banking networks.' The Second Banking Directive, tabled in January 1988 and adopted by the Council on 19 June 1989, deals with these hidden barriers—including restrictions on foreign involvement in local banks, prevalent in Southern Europe—and lays the basis for a single licensing system, while seeking to allay US fears and tighten up on possible abuses (see below).

Insurance and securities

Similar restrictions are to be swept away in insurance and securities trading. There has been widespread irritation over barriers put up by insurance firms in West Germany, where non-German insurance companies must have a permanent local establishment, and have to pay penalizing tax rates which the Commission regards as discriminatory. The principle was tested in the European Court in 1986, when West German insurers complained that they had been fined for obtaining for clients low-cost industrial and marine insurance in Britain. Due to these test cases, and qualified majority voting, a directive on cross-border competition in non-life insurance for commercial customers is already on the statute books.

In their study on *Europe's Domestic Market*, Jacques Pelkmans and Alan Winters write that 'insurance probably offers more scope for British gains from the European Domestic Market than does banking'. The 1986 ruling by the European Court freed co-insurance from restrictions, and set out once and for all the right of establishment for insurance companies in other EC states. As in other areas, barriers to cross-border trade in insurance were supposed to disappear in accordance with earlier directives, notably the 1978 directive on co-insurance. In practice it has taken the 1992 process to crack—or start to crack—a particularly tough nut.

The non-life directive, passed in June 1988 and due to come into force in 1990, permits cross-frontier trade by larger companies, defined as those with a minimum turnover of 24 million ECUs (£16 million) or over 500 employees. It covers transport risks—marine and aviation, general liability, property and fire. Because national governments derive substantial income from life insurance tax, and because tax on insurance still differs from country to country, the directive concedes that tax can still be collected by the state within which the risk is insured.

Agreement on common insurance policies throughout Europe is still a long way off, but there are likely to be a growing number of cross-border mergers in insurance, as the recent acquisition of Equity and Life by the French Compagnie du Midi illustrates. The business could just as well flow the other way: British companies such as Royal Insurance are actively expanding their Continental operations.

Securities dealers, on the other hand, are less pleased with EC plans. The Securities and Investments Board and the Securities Association have lobbied hard in Brussels against directives which they believe will place tightly regulated British firms at a disadvantage to less-regulated Continental competitors. They also dislike the idea of an EC trading mentality under which non-EC firms will be excluded where possible. The Commission issued proposals in this field at the end of 1988. The hope in Brussels is that by 1993, if not 1992, the differing EC country regulations governing securities trading will be brought into line. (See also the section on the Second Banking Directive, below.) A harmonization directive on brokerage and investment houses is also under consideration in Brussels, on the assumption that cross-border speculation will increase.

Mortgages across frontiers

In theory, banks and finance houses across the EC will compete with each other after 1992 in offering home loans. The extent which this happens will depend on how far home loan practices are harmonized. At present they differ widely, as does home ownership, which is high in Britain and Spain (64% owner occupation), and in Ireland (74%) but low in West Germany (37%) and the Netherlands (44%), where rented accommodation is the norm. The Commission has therefore not sought to table a mortgage finance directive, but instead is incorporating the mutual recognition of home loan standards into the Second Banking Directive. French, Danish and Dutch finance houses have already set up subsidiaries in the UK to offer mortgages to home buyers. However, this is not seen as a real threat by any of the major building societies. They, in turn, are making modest forays into the Continental housing market: Abbey National has a Spanish subsidiary, Abbeycorp (with Swiss involvement) and the Midland Bank's French subsidiary is making inroads into the French mortgage business. Building society managers expect to see more cross-border activity of this kind in 1992. However, an EC-wide regulated home loan market is some way off, especially since countries like West Germany operate strict rules for home loans through tightly regulated finance institutions, with home buyers obliged to prove that they have saved a high proportion of the value of the house. Some UK finance houses already offer ECU mortgages, based on the ECU basket of European currencies.

Export Credit Guarantees

Another intriguing question is whether the practice of using national state agencies such as the Export Credits Guarantee Department (ECGD) to support trading ventures will continue to make sense either for intra-European trade or for EC-based trade with the rest of the world. It is possible that, as the financial barriers come down, credit insurance will increasingly pass to private rather than government institutions, or a combination of the two, along the lines of existing West German private insurance companies, which reinsure with the government.

Export finance not only underwrites the export risk, it also insures the exporter against bankruptcy by foreign customers. However, in theory, a Dutch or French insurer could undercut the ECGD by offering British exporters the same service for exports to Holland or France, on the same terms as the ECGD but with the advantage of local knowledge. Moreover, the concept of 'national exports' will become increasingly outdated in the single market, and the concept of 'European' exports to non-EC countries will come to the fore. This could lead in the long run to the development of a pan-European export credit agency.

Capital transfers and insider trading: avoiding a 'spiv's charter'

The June 1988 directive on completing capital movements liberalization by July 1990 is a textbook example of the passage of a 1992 directive from draft proposal to law in the face of Twelve differing national standpoints. Britain's initial objection was that the free flow of capital across frontiers should not be regarded as a step towards the harmonization of indirect taxes, over which the UK retains its veto. But others also had reservations.

France in particular, under the socialist government of Michel Rocard, expressed strong doubts, arguing that if EC citizens were able freely to move capital around the Community this could only encourage fraud and tax evasion. This objection was met by an undertaking from the Commission that it would report back on ways of strengthening cross-border tax inspection to prevent abuses. France, unlike Britain, has no pay-as-you-earn (PAYE) tax system, and French tax officials rely on their right to obtain information from banks—a further reason for French objections to the directive. The City of London is bound to benefit from liberalization as EC capital flows to a proven financial centre, with market capitalization totalling $500 billion. Only West Germany comes close, with $160 billion, while financial markets in France and Italy have $100 billion or less. However, anxieties about fraud persist in London as well as in Paris. A further misgiving in London is that EC investors may regard the City as over-regulated under the 1986 Financial Services Act—drawn up by the government without any recognition of the implications of 1992—and that the City may lose out by standing aloof from moves towards a European Bank.

Fears that the removal of restrictions on bank account movements within the EC could benefit tax dodgers and other villains rather than *bona fide* business executives and bank customers have been partly met by the new directive on insider dealing agreed by Finance Ministers in Luxembourg in June 1989, at the same time as the Second Banking Directive. The Commission's original proposals were adapted to meet the demands of the British Bankers Association and City institutions, to the point where they closely resemble UK legislation by laying down a narrow definition of insider trading, embracing both 'primary' and 'secondary' insiders who misuse information about a company they work for or are 'closely associated with', while allowing normal stock market activities to go ahead unhindered. The directive requires EC countries to co-operate across frontiers in tracking down illegal stock exchange activity. All states are obliged to bring their national laws into line with the directive by 1 June 1992, causing problems for Belgium, Italy, Ireland and West Germany, which have little or no insider trading legislation.

Another proposal, for taxing bank interest and investment income at source, has had a less favourable reception. Such a withholding tax, proposed variously at 10% or 15%, would apply to National Savings and building society accounts, and would help—for example—to allay French fears of a diversion of savings to tax-free Luxembourg. However, when in July 1989 Pierre Beregevoy, the French Finance Minister, chaired a discussion on reducing tax evasion in an era of free capital flows, Mme Christiane Scrivener, the Commissioner for Fiscal Affairs, stressed co-operation against fraud rather than a withholding tax, a clear admission that the tax was unpopular. Lawson declared flatly that he took this omission to mean that the withholding tax idea was 'dead'. John Banham, the CBI director general, urged Lawson to oppose the tax as 'misguided', since it would add to business costs and raise interest rates. West Germany announced in July 1989 it was scrapping its own unpopular 10% withholding tax and said it would seek 'a more viable tax on investment earnings' together with its EC partners.

The Second Banking Directive, solvency ratios and reciprocity

The Second Banking Directive, adopted in June 1989 (subject to a second reading by the European Parliament), is a powerful force propelling the European banking world towards a financial revolution. Under the directive, due to come into force on 1 January 1993, any High Street bank in an EC member country will be able to operate throughout the Community on the basis of a single licence issued in its country of origin—not in the 'host' country. In other words, the directive accepts the principle that it is enough for banks to be properly authorized and supervised in their home country for them to be able to deal in deposits and loans of both cash and securities in any of the other states. The directive alters a situation in which banks can only open subsidiaries in another country, subject to local controls. Host countries retain the right to control bank liquidity for reasons of monetary policy.

Under the directive, Lloyds or National Westminster will be able to operate on the Continent without local authorization—and equally, Crédit Lyonnais or the Dresdner Bank can operate in Britain, competing with British banks in offering a range of services. British banks claim to be ready for the fray: Barclays, for example, says it has 3200 offices 'from Munich to Murcia, Paris to Piraeus', with Barclays de Zoete Wedd particularly strong in France, Spain and the Netherlands (*1992: What Does the Future Hold for Your Business?*, Barclays Corporate Marketing Department). The Bank of England suggested in a survey in June 1989 (*The Single European Market: Survey of the UK Financial Services Industry*) that France, Italy and Spain offer the best markets for UK bank expansion.

Only post-1992 practice will show how far this can develop: for example, national home loan regulations will still differ widely. West German home buyers have to prove they have saved one third of the proposed mortgage. Banks licensed to operate throughout the EC must have a minimum working capital of £3.5 million and provide Brussels with information on their larger shareholders. Solvency ratios have proved a sticking point: under the Basle agreement of July 1988, reflected in an EC draft directive, the Group of Ten agreed that a bank's funds must constitute at least 8% of its risk-weighted assets. Both West Germany and Denmark object that mortgage lending, which plays a large role in their banking activities, is given too high a risk weighting both in the Basle agreement on solvency ratios and in the subsequent EC directive. (UK discount houses are exempted because of their 'special nature'.)

Ordinary bank customers will be more concerned with the standardization of cashpoint bank cards, beginning in Belgium, West Germany, Denmark and—surprisingly—Portugal and Spain, with banks in those countries negotiating joint agreements on customer access to computerized networks. Such Euro-networks or even bank mergers will become a common feature as 1992 approaches.

Non-EC banks will have access to the EC, but the EC will retaliate by withholding approval for non-EC banking operations if EC banks are not given comparable treatment in third countries. This softens earlier proposals under which automatic penalties would have been imposed on non-EC banks from countries which created difficulties for European banks. According to Willy de Clercq, the then External Affairs Commissioner, speaking in Austria in August 1988: 'Our view is that Community credit institutions should have equal access to the financial markets of non-European countries. The Commission will check on a case-by-case basis whether similar institutions from all member states are given the same treatment in the non-Community country concerned.' However, in September 1988, Lord Young, the then Trade and Industry Secretary, told a meeting of the Italian Chamber of Commerce in London that the reciprocity proposal would erect a wall of protectionism round Europe and threaten London's position as a key financial centre open to allcomers. His view is supported by the Bank of England, which opposes interference by Brussels which might, for example, prevent a US bank from opening in London because an undercapitalized Portuguese bank had been barred from the United States.

This had given rise to anxiety in the United States, where the federal banking authorities maintain that reciprocity would require radical changes in US interstate banking law. To meet this, the directive was reformulated to provide for 'case-by-case' negotiations with countries where commercial and investment banking are legally separate. It remains unclear, however, just how the EC's 1992 banking plans will overlap with the international supervisory regulations being drafted by the Bank for International Settlements in Basle, although the BIS is involved in EC deliberations.

Remaining details to be cleared up involve how national laws requiring banks to disclose information for tax purposes will be retained. Governments retain their powers to control national instruments of fiscal policy such as interest rates—but in time, this may also be eroded if the co-ordination of interest rates becomes a consequence of economic integration and EMS management in 1992 conditions. For Britain, a further problem arises in the field of securities, listed by the directive as one of the 'core activities' of banking, along with deposits, loans, credit, portfolio management and leasing. The Securities and Investment Board (SIB), which controls security dealings in Britain, has shown little enthusiasm for the single licensing system, and neither has the British Bankers' Association. A key clause limits the right of banks to own stakes in industrial and other non-banking companies, with holdings limited to 50% of the banks' capital and to 10% of capital for each holding.

The City is in a strong position, however, with a daily foreign exchange turnover of $90 billion, compared to $50 billion in New York and Tokyo. It attracts business because of its skills and its liberal regulatory system, both assets for 1992. This could put British banks in a strong position as cross-border banking strategies emerge: the cross-shareholding link-up between the Royal Bank of Scotland and Banco Santander of Spain—plus its West German and Belgian subsidiaries, announced in October 1988—is just one example, though the first to involve a UK bank. Other link-ups aimed at 1992 include a deal between Amro Bank in the Netherlands and the Société Génerale of Belgium; the purchase by the Deutsche Bank of Banca d'America e d'Italia; a joint venture between Belgium's Générale de Banque and the Amsterdam–Rotterdam Bank; and the acquisition by

Crédit Lyonnais of a controlling interest in Credito Bergamasco of Italy. In July 1989 Hypotheken und Wechsel Bank of Bavaria took a 50% stake in Foreign and Colonial Management, the British fund management group, which said it was 'positioning itself firmly on the 1992 express'. In November 1989 Morgan Grenfell announced it had agreed to a 1.5 billion dollar takeover bid by Deutsche Bank, a move said by the German bank to reflect 'the pre-eminence of London in Europe in corporate finance and asset management.'

The attraction of such deals lies in increased capital assets and market access, but they also usually involve the harmonization of computerized cash-card services and point-of-sale systems, the most obvious benefit to customers. Consumer credit is a likely growth area in 1992, with further expansion by systems such as Eurocard and Visa. The European Council for Payment Systems, which groups forty banks, is working on compatibility for all electronic card systems.

The European Monetary System: will the pound ever join?

After Madrid and Strasbourg, Britain is more than ever confronted with the question of whether the pound can remain free-floating outside the European Monetary System in an EC which has free capital flows, a single licencing system for banking, and free competition in insurance. Pierre Beregevoy, the French Finance Minister, puts it bluntly: 'A common monetary policy cannot work effectively as long as Great Britain remains outside the EMS exchange mechanism.' After the summer and autumn Cabinet reshuffles both Nigel Lawson, the former Chancellor of the Exchequer, and Sir Geoffrey Howe, the former Foreign Secretary—both victims of a head-on clash with Mrs Thatcher over Europe and the EMS—continued to argue strongly that Mrs Thatcher's view was mistaken and EMS membership was essential to the struggle against inflation and the stability of sterling. In December 1989 Howe, as Deputy Prime Minister, predicted that the pound would join the ERM by the time of the next UK general election—in 1992.

Much political, media and academic opinion also favours committing the pound to the EMS at a point favourable to sterling. As indicated earlier, Mrs Thatcher herself has apparently swung round to the view that the pound could join under certain conditions, and some believe the move may be made during Britain's EC Presidency in 1992. Sir Leon Brittan has persistently reminded Mrs Thatcher that 'joining the EMS mechanism would help to make sure inflation carries on moving firmly down toward the levels enjoyed by Britain's partners already inside the system', adding that 'a 15% movement in exchange rates over a year can mean the difference between a useful profit and an unsustainable loss'. On the other hand, Tim Congdon, economic adviser to Gerrard & National and an opponent of EMS membership, declared in *The Times* on the eve of Madrid (26 June 1989) that the year when sterling was informally tied to the West German mark (March 1987–8) had proved a 'disaster', with credit growth out of control and inflationary pressure on the rise: 'The requirements of domestic credit constraint and exchange rate stability are in conflict, and the various countries [Britain and the rest of Europe], far from associating in a stable and integrated monetary union, suffer from a deep-seated financial incompatibility.'

Part of the resistance to committing sterling to the EMS stems from the perception of sterling as a symbol of national independence. From this perspective, keeping the pound out of the EMS amounts to another aspect of British resistance to full European integration. However, those who favour an independent pound also do so because they believe that the merits of the EMS have been exaggerated; because sterling has a global as well as European role; or because of a fear that, once inside the European Monetary System, sterling would be dominated by the deutschmark, the most powerful European currency.

Although it deals with financial services and capital movements, the White Paper of 1985 does not directly tackle the question of the EMS. The issue of sterling's membership or non-membership is therefore not, strictly speaking, part of 1992. The EMS, after all, dates from 1979, when the 1992 programme was but a glint in the Commission's collective eye. The EMS was designed as a way of stabilizing currency fluctuations after the collapse of the post-war Bretton Woods fixed exchange-rate system, and the partial failure of the subsequent European Snake, which allowed fluctuations within agreed limits. Unlike the Snake, the EMS is a system for full currency management, under which currencies participating in the Exchange Rate Mechanism, or ERM, have fixed rates against the European Currency Unit. The ECU, in turn, is based on a 'basket' of currencies participating in the EMS. Sterling, paradoxically, is part of the ECU 'basket' but not of the ERM itself. Greece and Portugal remain outside the EMS—but because their economies are too weak, rather than for doctrinal reasons. The peseta joined in June 1989, and is allowed (like the Italian lira) to fluctuate by up to 6% from its central rate.

The nine currencies which belong to the ERM have their ECU rate realigned at sessions of EEC Finance Ministers called for the purpose. Between realignment meetings, the central banks intervene in foreign exchange markets to support a member currency when it reaches its 'floor', drawing on a reserve called the European Monetary Co-operation Fund, based on member states' gold and currency reserves. Supporters of the EMS point to its stability since 1979, and to the steady reduction in inflation differentials. Many British business executives argue that planning would be much simpler if the pound were part of a stable currency system. Delors marked the tenth anniversary of the EMS in March 1989 by saying it had 'given the rest of the world a concrete example of the

Community's capacity to act together and create an island of stability in an ocean of monetary turbulence'.

Non-believers can point to the fact that France and West Germany are often in conflict over monetary policy, despite their membership of the EMS and the existence of a Franco-German Finance Council, set up in March 1988, as part of a joint effort to consolidate the Franco-German axis in the EC. French officials express open anger when the Bundesbank, the West German Central Bank, raises its interest rates and sets off a European chain reaction without consulting its French counterpart. This arouses French anxieties that the power of the deutschmark reflects the overall success of the West German economy, also demonstrated in a high West German standard of living. Part of the French drive for 1992, observers in Paris say, stems from a French belief that pooling sovereignty—for example, by agreeing to a European Central Bank or a federal banking system—will have the effect of curbing the rampant West German currency and economy.

Lloyds Bank's *International Financial Outlook for 1988* warned that the City could be 'isolated' if Britain remained 'on the sidelines' of monetary integration, and Sir Nicholas Goodison, chairman of the Stock Exchange, told a Commons committee that European monetary union—including a European Bank—was no longer a utopian dream. London financial markets stood to lose unless Britain took the first step of joining the EMS exchange rate mechanism before 1992, he said. Sir Leon Brittan told the International Stock Exchange in May 1989 that he was 'confident the City can maintain and develop its pre-eminent position as the financial centre of the European time zone'—provided Britain took a full part in EC plans. In July 1989 a report by the Commons select committee on trade and industry chaired by Kenneth Warren MP (*Financial Services and the Single European Market*) said Britain should join the EMS 'as soon as possible' to enable the City to be 'the financial gateway to Europe' in 1992. It said tax was a matter for governments, however, and in insurance brokers should be able to advertise life insurance abroad.

The ECU in your pocket: a future single currency?

The momentum towards monetary integration, including wider use of the ECU, is thus considerable. The ECU is still largely a notional currency, used as a unit of account for EMS realignments and EC internal calculations. But it is also increasingly in use as a unit of payment and reserve currency, and both travellers' cheques and Eurobonds can be ECU-denominated. One EC country—Belgium—has even issued ECU coins bearing a portrait of the sixteenth-century Emperor Charles V. The coins —5- and 50-ECU pieces, minted in silver and gold, respectively—are intended primarily as collectors' items, and sell for prices far above their face value. Yet they are legal tender in Belgium, in theory at least. In practice, few shops or restaurants actually take them, as we discovered when trying to pay with ECUs, and the issue is intended by the Belgian Government as a gesture in the direction of a future common currency.

A clearing house for ECU transactions was set up in October 1986 by a consortium of seven European banks, including Lloyds and the Crédit Lyonnais. One Luxembourg bank has even issued Visa credit cards in ECUs, and is planning a new 'smart' electronic version. At present, less than 1% of business transactions in the EC are invoiced in ECUs. But this is changing as 1992 approaches. The European Parliament's Economic and Monetary Affairs Committee argues that the prevalence of 'plastic money' offers greater scope for use of the ECU in 1992. In a report issued in 1987, the Committee urged use of the ECU for paying workers in EC border areas, with, for example, a Dutchman working over the border in West Germany holding a bank account in ECUs and converting them to marks or guilders as required. Some officials favour developing the ECU in this way as a 'parallel' currency, thus acquainting EC citizens with the ECU and enabling it to supplant national currencies in due course.

The ECU, meanwhile, remains little known in Britain, except to the money markets. When we offered Belgian-issued ECUs to London shop-keepers and bus drivers as an experiment while preparing this book, comments varied from 'What bright spark thought that one up?' (a bus driver) and 'We'd have to change all the tills and retrain the staff. Try Harrods—they might take them' (a DIY store supervisor) to 'It might be useful if you did a lot of travelling, but people are already getting angry about Brussels having a say in what goes on over here' (a policeman in Trafalgar Square). 'I'm very British—it just wouldn't seem like England if we had a European currency. Why can't they all change over to our money?' was a typical reaction (in this case a newspaper seller outside a London Underground station). Others object that ECU happens to be the name of a medieval French coin.

Nonetheless, Lord Cockfield, the architect of the 1992 White Paper, argued strongly before leaving office at the end of 1988 that a common currency was the inevitable and desirable consequence of the 1992 process. The Delors report of 1989 takes the same view. Non-EC countries which keep a close watch on 1992 appear equally convinced. One leading Soviet banking expert—Dr Thomas Alibegov, of the Moscow External Economic Bank—told Euro MPs in Strasbourg in July 1988 that the ECU was becoming the 'regional collective currency' of the EC, and as a consequence of the EMS there would need to be a European Bank to control the money supply by 1992. 'One must admit that the EMS has proved its viability in the difficult conditions of the strong rise and abrupt fall of the US dollar, together with a decrease in business activity and changes in prices for raw materials and energy products,' Dr Alibegov said.

The Government takes the view that the development of the ECU is a more acceptable path to monetary union than 'visionary' steps such as the creation of a European Bank. In August 1988 the Treasury took the unusual step of issuing bills denominated in ECUs, the first ECU-denominated bills to be internationally tradeable. The aim is to diversify Britain's reserves while at the same time encouraging the development of an ECU market in London, with the Bank of England hoping to build up holdings of 2 billion ECUs in investments. Commission officials were quick to warn, however, that the issuing of ECU-denominated bills could not be a substitute for other moves towards monetary union, and it remains an open question whether encouraging ECU development can be kept separate from other aspects of monetary integration such as the proposed European System of Central Banks.

Frankfurt versus London: the European Central Bank

Britain is not alone in expressing doubts about the European Bank proposal, even in the form of a federal structure co-ordinating the existing central banks. West Germany is divided, with Hans Dietrich Genscher, the Foreign Minister, wanting to move farther and faster than Helmut Kohl, the Chancellor. Karl Otto Pohl, chairman of the Bundesbank, is sceptical about a European Bank, arguing that it can only be considered after 1992, not before.

The communiqué issued at the Hanover summit of 1988 did not include the words 'European Central Bank', on Mrs Thatcher's insistence. The Prime Minister noted, with evident satisfaction, that pressure (largely from Genscher) for the summit itself to issue draft guidelines for a European Bank had successfully been resisted. Mrs Thatcher said she did not expect to see a European Central Bank in her lifetime, and added flatly: 'I do not share the vision of a United States of Europe and a single currency.' This reinforced her remark to the Commons on the eve of the summit that a Euro Bank could only come about when Parliament was dissolved and there was a European Government. Mrs Thatcher also made clear her opposition to the taxation of savings.

On the other hand, a number of EC leaders made it clear at Hanover that they regarded a European Bank as the object of monetary union. The communiqué recalled the objective of the 'progressive realization of economic and monetary union' as affirmed in the Single European Act, and established the Delors Committee to 'study and propose concrete stages leading toward this Union' by the time of the Madrid summit. The committee contained eleven EC Central Bank governors, including Robin Leigh-Pemberton, Governor of the Bank of England (eleven and not twelve governors, because Belgium and Luxembourg have a common franc); Delors; and four experts—Alexandre Lamfalussy, general manager of the Bank for International Settlements, Niels Thygesen, a Danish economics professor, Miguel Boyer, a former Spanish finance minister, and Frans Andriessen, former Dutch finance minister and EC Agriculture Commissioner in the first Delors Commission (now External Relations Commissioner). 'We have a structure and a date' declared President

Mitterrand of France after Hanover. 'We are on the right track. If there is to be monetary union there must be a central body to manage it. What remains to be settled is its relationship to the existing central banks.'

The options considered by Delors included:

1 The replacement of national central banks by a Bank of Europe;
2 Less radically, a European Bank, or Federal Reserve, controlled by the existing central banks;
3 Least radical of all, increased co-ordination among central banks.

Any of these options could be accompanied by the issuing of ECUs as a European currency to be used in parallel with national currencies—for example, for commercial transactions or to pay travel bills.

In the event, the Delors concept of an ESCB resembles option 2. However, even a central bank 'system' would entail new central banking institutions, and there are fears in the City that, whatever form it takes, a future Euro Bank will be located in Frankfurt—unless Britain reverses its stand to ensure that new central institutions come to London or are shared with Frankfurt. Writing in *The Times* in July 1988, John Young, economic adviser to Lloyds Bank, argued that: 'The longer Britain stays out of the EMS, the greater the likelihood that a federal Reserve bank located in Frankfurt might ultimately become the operational centre of official foreign exchange and money market intervention in the Community, posing a further threat to the pre-eminence of London among Europe's financial centres.'

The European Bank and the national veto
The debate in the near future will focus on whether new EC institutions —and therefore Treaty amendments—are a necessary part of the process of monetary integration set in train by the Delors report and the Madrid summit. In the last resort, could Britain veto the creation of a European Bank if it was supported by the other eleven states? After the Hanover summit, Dr David Owen, leader of the Social Democrat Party and former Labour Foreign Secretary, put it to Mrs Thatcher in the Commons that the special committee might conclude that the creation of a Euro Bank was necessary for the functioning of the internal market and the free flow of capital movements across frontiers. It could then be established, under Single Act procedures (Article 100a), by qualified majority voting, leaving Britain powerless to use its veto. The Prime Minister replied: 'He may be correct in theory, I do not think he is correct in any way in practice.'

In fact, Article 100a refers to the 300-odd internal market directives. It would require a very liberal interpretation of the majority voting rule to extend it to so fundamental a measure as the setting up of a European Bank. Monetary union, moreover, is covered by Article 102a of the Treaty of Rome, which states: 'Insofar as further development in the field of economic and monetary policy necessitates institutional changes, the provisions of Article 236 shall be applicable.' There can be little doubt that setting up a Euro Bank—or a federal institution of some kind—is just such an 'institutional change'. Article 236 states that institutional changes can only be made by a 'conference of representatives of the governments of member states' (in practice, a summit), and that such a conference can only amend the Treaty 'by common accord'—generally construed to mean by unanimity.

The national veto, in other words, is retained in monetary matters. Some Euro MPs, such as Peter Price, MEP for London South-East, and a member of the European Parliament's legal affairs committee, have argued that greater use of the ECU and other moves towards integration do not need a 'fully blown' Euro Bank but can be regulated through increased co-ordination among the central banks. Mrs Thatcher put it bluntly in her speech to the College of Europe at Bruges in September 1988: 'The key issue is not whether there should be a European Central Bank.' The immediate requirements were the free movement of capital ('We have it'), the abolition of exchange controls ('We abolished them in Britain in 1979') so that people can invest wherever they wish, a genuinely free market in financial services, and greater use of the ECU.

Nonetheless, if the pattern set by the Single European Act negotiations is followed, the proposed IGC on the second and third stages of monetary union is likely to end with a compromise which, through the sheer weight of Eleven against One, reflects the views of the majority. In reality, using Britain's veto would be a serious step indeed. Dr Owen argued in *The Times* in July 1988 that a Euro Bank would be set up

> whether Britain likes it or not. If Britain obstructs, as over the EMS, the others will simply move on, no doubt allowing us a similar semi-detached position, but dangerously marginalized. . . . Britain's lack of involvement would ensure that the central bank is set up in Frankfurt, Paris, or just possibly Brussels, when all logic dictates that it should be located in London.

Cash and credit across frontiers

Where does this leave Britain's financial services? The aftermath of the Big Bang of October 1986 and the development of electronic trading have certainly strengthened the City's claim to be the premier stock exchange and money market in Europe, and enable it to face 1992 with some confidence. Whether Britain joins in the move towards monetary union, however, will depend as much on political as on economic factors. What is certain is that we—as customers—stand to benefit from the 1992 process if it puts an end to a situation in which changing money around the EC means sizeable financial losses, while transferring money from bank to bank within the Community is a haphazard and costly business.

The European Consumers Bureau (BEUC), in a 1988 report, concluded that at present banks do not listen to clients' instructions when making money transfers: fail to make clear the cost of a transaction in advance: and charge both sender and payee even where the remitter had agreed to bear the costs. As for *bureaux de change*, BEUC also concluded, in a separate report, that travellers making a round trip of EC capitals would lose almost half their spending money just by paying handling charges—and by losing on official exchange rates. The Commission's plans for a directive to protect the rights of credit card holders around the Community have been diluted—to the relief of the credit card companies—but a code of conduct on liability in the event of loss or theft has been issued and will be followed by a directive if the code (which puts the burden on the company rather than the card holder) is not observed.

Whatever the theoretical advantages and disadvantages of monetary union and capital flows, and whatever doubts about a common European currency, the reaction of many business executives and travellers, tired of carrying envelopes of kroners, marks, francs and escudos in their pockets, could well be a heartfelt 'roll on the ECU' as the single market develops. Business and consumer pressures, as much as new directives, will dictate how far and how fast the liberalization of financial services goes.

Checklist of changes

- All restrictions on the movement of capital belonging to EC residents will be abolished by July 1990.
- There will be full liberalization of cross-border transactions in unit trusts, unlisted securities and long-term trade credits.
- There will be cross-border competition in non-life insurance for commercial clients.
- Restrictions preventing other EC nationals from holding securities or acting as brokers will be lifted.
- There could be mutual recognition of standards for mortgages.
- Any High Street bank will be able to operate throughout the Community on the basis of a single licence under the Second Banking Directive.
- A single licensing system for securities has been proposed.
- Existing credit card facilities will be increased.
- Use of the ECU (European Currency Unit) is to be expanded.
- A European Central Bank is under consideration.

9 MERGERS ACROSS FRONTIERS
Competition policy in the single market

The overriding objective of the internal market programme is to break down the fragmentation of the European economy into twelve separate and often conflicting components and create a single, unified market of 320 million producers and consumers. In essence, it is a strategy designed to benefit European business. The European Commission believes that companies, traditionally boxed into national markets, should be free to break out of their national confinement and link up with other European firms, whether through joint ventures or acquisitions.

Paradoxically, the Commission has two ostensibly irreconcilable goals:

1 To promote the restructuring of the European economy by allowing the various industrial sectors to consolidate their operations across national frontiers, shut down excess productive capacity, enhance economies of scale and reduce costs, thereby acquiring the kind of industrial strength needed to compete with American and Japanese companies on a more equal footing;

2 To prevent these newly restructured industries from engaging in the kind of practices that have earned big business a bad name the world over, such as illegal market-sharing arrangements, the abuse of dominant market positions to extract monopoly profits and attempts to prevent new competitors entering given markets.

The internal market programme would be an exercise in futility if, at the very moment national barriers to trade were levelled, European companies immediately set about raising them by introducing a new set of commercial barriers to trade and engaging in ingenious forms of anticompetitive behaviour. The Commission is fully aware that there is a contradiction between allowing companies to co-operate with each other across national borders when the temptation to abuse such freedom is likely to prove irresistible. However, it proposes to reconcile the irreconcilable by introducing a comprehensive competition policy, granting it the power to appraise all large-scale mergers which have a Community dimension and decide whether the proposed merger should be allowed to go ahead, whether the terms of the merger should be altered in the interests of free competition or whether it should be prohibited outright.

Under the provisions of the Treaty of Rome, the European Commission already possesses considerable powers to monitor certain categories of business activity. Article 85 prohibits as incompatible with the common market 'all agreements between undertakings, decisions by associations of undertakings and concerted practices which may affect trade between member states which have as their objective or effect the prevention or distortion of competition within the common market'. In short, any agreement or conspiracy by companies, individually or collectively, to fix prices, limit production or divide up the market is illegal, and it can be broken up before or after the event has taken place, and the offending companies subject to heavy fines. However, the Commission also has the power to give its approval to any restrictive practice where such an agreement 'contributes to improving the production or distribution of goods or to promoting technical or economic progress', an increasingly controversial area known as industrial policy.

Similarly, Article 86 states that 'Any abuse by one or more undertakings of a dominant position within the common market or in a substantial part of it shall be prohibited as incompatible with the common market in so far as it may affect trade between member states'. Consequently, any business abusing its dominant position can find itself the subject of a Commission investigation, and, if found guilty, be compelled to stop and made to pay a substantial fine. Article 86 also applies to mergers that would create a dominant position likely to be abused, but here the Commission can only act after the event has taken place, a limitation regarded by successive Competition Commissioners as the Achilles' heel of the Community's competition policy.

In the separate but related field of government subsidies to industry, known as state aids, Article 92 grants the Commission the power to make a prior decision whether (and at what level) aid can be given. It can also compel companies who have received state aid without the Commission's approval to pay it back. The Commission can, however, give approval to government subsidies where they are designed to promote economic development in areas of economic decline, but only the Commission is empowered to decide what government subsidies fall within this criterion.

Collectively, the ability to police restrictive market agreements, dominant market positions, mergers that are likely to lead to dominant market positions and state aids is an impressive range of powers at the disposal of the Commission to regulate competition within the Community. However, the Commission feels that its inability to scrutinize mergers before they have taken place is an obvious deficiency in its powers of competition enforcement. This deficiency has now become extremely acute as companies, in anticipation of the creation of the single internal market in 1992, have developed an appetite for US-style merger mania which has already led to a large increase in cross-frontier mergers and takeovers in an effort to strengthen their competitive positions. The Commission has been engaged since 1973 in a frequently acrimonious struggle with the Council of Ministers to fill this gap.

A comprehensive merger control policy

Few would dispute that until Peter Sutherland, the former Irish Commissioner for Competition Policy, joined the Commission in 1984 the attempt to obtain approval from the Council of Ministers for a directive on merger control had been given a low priority. No-one knew how the 38-year-old softly spoken Irishman would shape up to his new job. But for anyone prepared to look into his background, there was more than enough to indicate that here was a man who was going to upset the system.

Born the son of an insurance broker, he was educated at University College, Dublin, and the National University of Ireland, before becoming a barrister at the Irish, English and New York Bars. As the youngest-ever Attorney General in the government of Garret FitzGerald, he is credited with almost single-handedly persuading the Irish courts that IRA terrorists should no longer be able to evade extradition on the specious grounds that their actions were political and not criminal. Mr Sutherland was Ireland's fourth Commissioner since it joined the Community in 1973, and was to become universally acknowledged as the most rigorous Competition Commissioner Europe has ever had.

His success could be said to stem from a lifelong predilection for a good fight. During his university days he had a passion for rugby, and it is said that he fractured his nose no less than nine times, but refused to stop playing the game. He was to carry this enthusiasm for the scrum into adult life, and, in the course of his four-year term as Commissioner, forced many powerful corporate leaders and national politicians to leave the industrial playing field nursing their own bloody noses.

Presenting the Commission's sixteenth annual report on competition policy in July 1987, Sutherland gave notice to member states that he was determined to revive the stalled 1973 draft directive on mergers and takeovers. If they could not agree by the end of the year, at least in principle, to the necessity of augmenting the Commission's powers, he would use the full force of Articles 85 and 86 to try to fill the gap. Sutherland insisted that the new powers were needed to protect consumer interests, prevent mergers which distorted competition and provide companies with a predictable and effective Community-wide legal framework within which mergers and takeovers could be conducted.

Only Britain and France expressed reservations about the Commissioner's aspirations for new powers, and were confident that his threat to exploit existing legislation was little more than bluff. Then in November a decision by the European Court of Justice added considerable weight to Sutherland's warning. The Court approved an earlier decision by the Commission to allow the US company Philip Morris to take over a large minority stake in the UK-based company, Rothmans International, in the face of a legal challenge by British American Tobacco and R. J. Reynolds, on the grounds that the deal was against the interests of free competition.

However, in granting its seal of approval for the deal the Court also said that the Commission had a legal obligation to investigate any merger or acquisition that could lead to the creation or consolidation of a market dominance, and thereby violate the Community's competition code. It was a watershed decision. Hitherto, the Commission was under the impression that its powers under Article 85 were limited to investigations of price-fixing or market-sharing arrangements. However, the Court said that Article 85 could also be applied to mergers and acquisitions which might restrict competition (before the merger or acquisition went ahead), a decision which partially made up for the limitations of Article 86 governing mergers, which specifies that the Commission can act only after the deal has gone through. Now the Commission had the power to approve all mergers or acquisitions, except those between companies who do not have a dominant market position and whose combination would not lead to the creation of a dominant market position.

At an Internal Market Council the following month all member states except Britain and France (both of whom already have highly sophisticated merger control arrangements) granted their approval in principle to a comprehensive Community merger control policy. The Commission was then instructed to explore ways of overcoming the reservations expressed by London and Paris. A new, revised draft directive on mergers and acquisitions was tabled in March 1988, proposing that the Commission should have the power to regulate all mergers where the combined turnover of the companies involved exceeded £690 million, except where the company being taken over had an annual turnover of less than £33 million, or where 75% or more of the merged companies were in a single member state.

The proposal also called for a system of prior notification, powers to make dawn raids on company premises in search of incriminating evidence, fines of up to 10% of the combined company profits if the directive was violated and a commitment to speed up the bureaucratic process so that companies would be given a decision on whether the merger or acquisition could go ahead within a six-month period. 'Is it really acceptable,' asked Sutherland at a conference on 1992 in Paris the same month,

> that the same mergers between different companies in different member states should be subject to differing national laws, with the distinct possibility that conflicting decisions will be reached resulting from the fact that member states could apply different criteria? At least for important concentrations, which can have an impact on the internal market, the Community should be allowed to intervene.

Sutherland went on to warn that:

> Without a Community system of merger control, the door will
> remain open to the possibility that economic concentrations will be
> created in Europe which escape the existing rules. Clearly, such an
> outcome would contradict the very objectives that underpin the
> single market strategy—namely the creation of an environment for
> maximizing economic efficiency, competitiveness and technological
> progress.

Replying to Sutherland at the annual dinner of the Confederation of
British Industry in May, Lord Young, the then Secretary of State for Trade
and Industry, insisted that '1992 will not call for a sea change in mergers
policy—just a further evolution of the approach we have taken for many
years', effectively ruling out any British concessions on the Commission's
demand for a comprehensive merger control policy. In Luxembourg the
next month France decided to join its European neighbours and accept, in
principle, the need for such a policy, leaving Britain the only member state
to refuse to do so.

The junior trade minister, Francis Maude, denied that Britain was
isolated on the issue of merger control. Did this mean that the rest of the
Community was isolated from Britain? The minister could not be drawn
into a reply, and took refuge in the statement: 'We are not prepared to say
yes to the principle before we know the final form of the proposal.' In all
fairness to the embattled minister, Britain may have been isolated on the
question of the principle, but a number of member states had previously
expressed grave reservations about the details. France had indicated that
the £690 million threshold was too low, and Britain was not alone in its
anxiety that the six-month period for decisions could jeopardize prospective mergers, even if the Commission could adhere to it.

However, no-one was prepared for the bombshell dropped by John
Banham, the Director General of the Confederation of British Industry
(CBI). In a June statement that brought him into direct conflict with
government policy, Banham warned that:

> If counter-productive xenophobic arguments about hostile takeovers
> are to be avoided, it is essential that clear ground rules are set out
> and observed. The only pan-European agency able to ensure fair
> play in a free market is the European Commission.

Not content with pre-empting Lord Young, Banham then went on to claim
that one of the major reasons that British companies had not been able to
link up sufficiently in preparation for 1992 was a fear of violating Britain's
highly discretionary merger laws. According to Banham, not only were
new EC controls necessary but the government's failure to accept the

principle and get down to negotiating over the details was crippling the Department of Trade and Industry's campaign to prepare British business executives for the arrival of the internal market. Europe may have been open for business, Banham suggested, but Britain was not open for Europe.

Sutherland failed to get a merger control directive passed during his term of office, but he had managed to push the issue to the top of the European agenda. Moreover, he had won over eleven of the twelve member states to his point of view, leaving the British government isolated in Europe and cut off from its own business community. Despite this failure, he was nonetheless extremely effective in deploying the full weight of the Treaty of Rome against both companies and governments seeking an unfair competitive advantage over their rivals in the Community.

The enforcement of Articles 85 and 86

One of the most effective powers available to the Commission (powers denied to the Office of Fair Trading under British competition law) is the ability to make dawn raids on companies suspected of abusing a dominant position or engaging in a conspiracy to restrict free trade. In December 1985 the European Court of Justice found that Akzo, the Dutch chemicals multinational, had been abusing its dominant position by undercutting its prices in an attempt to force Engineering and Chemical Supplies Ltd, a small Gloucestershire-based firm, to withdraw from the organic peroxides market. The managing director of the company could obtain little protection under British law from the predatory pricing activities of a foreign rival. However, after receiving a complaint from the ECS, the Commission made a dawn raid on the Dutch company's premises and obtained all the incriminating evidence needed to secure a conviction. Akzo was fined £6.4 million, the ECS was still in business and the whole episode demonstrated how the Commission was able to come to the rescue of a small British firm (or indeed a small company anywhere in the Community) in the name of free competition.

In April 1986 15 international chemical companies (including the British firms ICI and Shell) were fined £38.75 million between them for engaging in an illegal price-fixing and market-sharing arrangement in polypropylene between 1977 and 1983, in violation of Article 85 governing conspiracies. However, in August the following year the Commission gave its approval for ICI and the Italian company Enichem to form the European Vinyls Corporation, a joint venture that planned to shut down 300,000 tonnes of excess capacity. Together, the two cases highlighted the Commission's dual approach towards business combinations. Agreements designed simply to fix prices will not be tolerated by Brussels, but agreements seeking to promote industrial restructuring are likely to get the Commission's blessing.

Although in December 1987 the Commission had given provisional approval of the conditions laid down by the Monopolies and Mergers Commission for British Airways' £250 million takeover of British Caledonian, it still had an obligation to make sure that the merger did not restrict the access of other carriers to routes shared by the two merged airlines as soon as the deal had gone ahead, under the authority granted it by Article 86. Once the Airlines of Britain Group (made up of British Midland Airways, Manx Airlines, Loganair and Eurocity Express) complained that the merger would lead to a restriction of trade the Commission launched its official investigation. The Community's powers to regulate the air transport industry had been severely circumscribed until the approval of a package of measures the same month, granting the Commission tough powers to monitor competition between the European airlines. The BA–BCal merger thus became a test case of the Commission's new authority to regulate the air transport industry.

By March 1988, when the Commission had announced its conditions on which the takeover would be authorized, it was abundantly clear that Sutherland was determined to carry out his threat to use the Treaty's competition powers to the full. British Airways was forced to surrender most of British Caledonian's European network to its smaller competitors, accept limitations on its use of landing and take-off slots at Gatwick Airport and comply with restrictions on extending its monopoly at Heathrow. Although these conditions were to remain in force for only four years, they were significantly more stringent than those demanded by the Monopolies and Mergers Commission. The deal was a major concession by Lord King, the company chairman, and another success for Commissioner Sutherland.

However, the significance of the affair went beyond the problems for the personalities involved. It emphasized the shortcomings of national merger regulation and highlighted yet again the case for impartial and effective merger control arrangements at Community level.

The attempt in 1988 by Nestlé, the Swiss foods group, to take over Rowntree, the British confectionery manufacturer, produced a nationalistic reaction almost identical to that which followed the attempt by the Italian entrepreneur, Carlo de Benedetti, to take over the Belgian conglomerate, Société Générale de Belgique. Both sides were motivated by the 'buy now or get bought later' ethic that has dominated Europe in the past few years. According to Gary Hamel of the London Business School, the large increase in cross-border mergers and acquisitions was the result of a realization by European companies that 'By 1992, all the good looking girls on the dance floor will have partners'.

At the same time, the two bids were a reminder that—at least psychologically—many businesses (and most member states) had yet to understand the implications of the European single market. Both bids were characterized as an assault on the very fabric of the nation by some outside predator intent on stealing a national asset. In an article in *The Times* in May 1988 Kenneth Dixon, the chairman of Rowntree, portrayed Kit Kat, Polo, Smarties and After Eight as an integral part of Britain's heritage, similar in stature only to the Crown Jewels, the Union Jack and the Houses of Parliament. The distinction between the company's interest and the national interest was lost completely, and the two concepts were projected as being identical and inseparable. By arguing (mistakenly, as it transpired) that the bid should be stopped because Swiss law prevented Swiss companies from being taken over by foreign companies, Dixon had inadvertently implied that if British companies enjoyed the same rights in Switzerland that Swiss companies enjoyed in Britain, he would have no ground to stand on. Likewise, de Benedetti (known in the Italian press as 'Carlo-Grab-It-All') was presented in Belgium as a swashbuckling marauder in search of foreign plunder. Observers felt that unless Société Générale was able to fend off the attack, Belgium would find itself under Italian domination.

In both cases the acquiring companies were not as predatory as the victims made out. Nestlé had been in Britain for 120 years, and as the manufacturer of Branston Pickle, Findus Frozen Foods and Nescafé coffee, was as much a part of the English cultural heritage as any box of Quality Street. Furthermore, it is simply not true that Swiss law prohibits foreign firms from taking over domestic ones. As Helmut Maucher, Nestlé's managing director, pointed out in his reply to Dixon's article in *The Times* the following week, Swiss companies can provide in their articles of association a provision granting them the right to refuse to register a shareholder, thereby making it extremely difficult for them to be taken over. However, companies who do this pay a heavy price, as unregistered shares trade at a much lower price than freely transferable ones. Besides, similar mechanisms are available to British companies seeking to protect themselves from unwelcome takeover bids.

Despite the rather colourful language of the Italian press, neither could de Benedetti be described as an avaricious raider. His companies, which include a variety of computer, publishing, car component, food and financial service concerns, employ over 100,000 people in Europe. Like Nestlé, his bid for a foreign company was motivated by a determination to be prepared for 1992. In the end, de Benedetti lost, and Nestlé was cleared by the Monopolies and Mergers Commission to go ahead with its bid for Rowntree. The experience of the two besieged companies was a salutary lesson for every other sleepy European firm that thought 1992 would not affect them. Sutherland could not intervene in either case, as there was no prima facie evidence for an investigation under the conspiracy or market dominance provisions of the Treaty. However, the bids demonstrated beyond doubt that, despite the promise of a European single market by 1992, economic nationalism remains a powerful force to be reckoned with by any company seeking to acquire firms in other member states.

While the Commission was unable to act in the Nestlé or de Benedetti bids, a bizarre combination of circumstances enabled it to intervene in the attempt by GC&C Brands to take over the Irish Distillers Group (IDG) with a £169 million bid before the deal went ahead—an event unprecedented in the history of Community competition policy. GC&C Brands, the consortium created in May 1988 by Grand Metropolitan, Allied Lyons and Guinness for the specific purpose of acquiring and then dismembering IDG, could barely disguise its surprise when it learnt on 29 July that the Commission was investigating it for conspiracy under Article 85. IDG, the makers of Jameson, Powers, Paddy and Bushmills whiskies, had complained to the Commission that GC&C was attempting to deprive its shareholders of the possibility of more competitive individual bids by creating the consortium.

In these circumstances the Commission's ability to approve mergers was not restricted to Article 86. Article 85 also applied, reinforced by the decision of the European Court of Justice over the Philip Morris case in November 1987. Commission officials could not recall another example of a joint venture takeover, but were delighted at the opportunity to show their strength in a takeover bid before it took place. The Commission's performance was widely seen as a test case, demonstrating how quickly and effectively it would be able to deal with mergers should the proposed directive on merger control ever get approval by the Council of Ministers.

The Commission issued its decision on 17 August—a record 20 days after the complaint was made—forcing the break-up of the consortium but allowing its individual members to go ahead with new individual bids. To emphasize the point, Sutherland issued a statement saying that: 'The Commission's intervention in the IDG case shows that it can and will act quickly and effectively to ensure that collusive practices restricting competition do not take place.'

The enforcement of Article 92

The Internal Market White Paper provides member states with a reminder of the Commission's declared intention to restrict illegal state aids with a rigorous application of Article 92. 'As the Commission moves to complete the internal market it will be necessary to ensure that anti-competitive practices do not engender new forms of local protectionism which would only lead to a re-partitioning of the market.' It goes on to point out that there is a tendency among some member states

> to spend large amounts of public funds on state aids to
> uncompetitive industries and enterprises. Often, they not only
> distort competition but also in the long run undermine efforts to
> increase European competitiveness.

Any government thinking that they were somehow exceptional was soon to receive a rude awakening. Initially, Delors had wanted Sutherland to adopt a soft line on government subsidies, but the Competition Commissioner insisted on a strict interpretation of the Treaty, and eventually got his way.

The Commission had already cut back large amounts of state assistance from the Community's ailing steel and ship building sectors before it turned its attention to the car industry. In March 1986 Sutherland launched an inquiry into plans by the West German motor group, Daimler-Benz, to build a £577 million car plant in Baden Württemberg. The local authorities had offered to pay for the preparation of the greenfield site and connect the plant to essential services. The Commission insisted that the offer constituted an illegal subsidy, and the offer was eventually withdrawn.

In December 1987 the British government was forced to trim £70 million from its £750 million aid package for the Rover Group as a condition of the sale of Leyland Trucks to DAF of the Netherlands. Three months later it was the turn of the French government to come under the Commission's scrutiny. It was given permission to give the state-owned company, Renault, a £1.9 billion subsidy, somewhat smaller than the government had initially sought, but only on the condition that its status was changed from a public to a private company subject to commercial law. It was also made clear that failure to carry out this commitment would be met by a demand that the subsidy be repaid. When Roger Fauroux, the French Industry Minister, announced in September 1988 that he had decided to keep Renault's public status intact, Sutherland made it abundantly clear that such action would give the Commission no option but to withdraw its consent for the proposed debt write-off. If France decided to go ahead with this write-off it would be summoned to the European Court of Justice.

The Commission is also currently investigating a £9.7 million subsidy from the Italian government to Alfa Romeo in 1985 and the sale of Alfa Romeo to Fiat in 1986. It considers that the price paid by Fiat was much lower than the value of Alfa Romeo, and thus involved an undisclosed illegal subsidy. Despite the evident reluctance of the Italian government to have its state aids subject to external scrutiny, the Commission has refused to back down.

By the time the British government had completed its plans for the privatization and sale of the Rover Group to British Aerospace in March 1988 for £150 million there should have been no doubt in anyone's mind that the deal could only go ahead after receiving the seal of approval from Brussels under Article 92—but there was. Professor Roland Smith, the chairman of British Aerospace, told MPs in parliament that if the Commission stepped in and demanded changes in Rover's proposed £800 million debt write-off he would pull out. Such talk may have been designed to intimidate the Commission, but it was to little avail. When the deal finally went through in July, Smith was forced to accept a £253 million reduction in the government's proposed cash injection into Rover.

The Commission had saved the British taxpayer millions of pounds in excess subsidy—although the National Audit Office later accused the Government of under-valuing Rover's assets—prompting the European Commission to demand an explanation. It had also fulfilled its obligations to make sure that the disposal of public companies did not confer an unfair advantage on the new owner in relation to other European enterprises operating in the same sector. However, no-one could say that British Aerospace had not come out with a bargain. The Commission will have just as much a say in the forthcoming privatizations of the remaining British state-owned companies and enterprises if any state aid is involved. Contrary to popular misapprehensions, any intervention will be based on the determination of the Commission to apply the competition rules fairly and effectively to all member states, and not out of any desire to make life difficult for Britain.

In July 1989, for example, the Commission approved a £731 million aid package for Short Brothers, the ailing Ulster-based aerospace company. The greater part of the package was for writing off accumulated debts and anticipated future losses, in an effort to make the company more attractive for sale to a foreign buyer—a practice traditionally disapproved by Brussels. However, because of the vital role the company plays in the economy of Northern Ireland, accounting for 10% of manufacturing employment in the region, the Commission was moved to make an exception to the rules against subsidies. Justifying its action, the Commission insisted that 'the social and economic consequences of a closure would be far reaching, and would inevitably result in a loss of confidence amongst potential outside investors who are crucial to Northern Ireland's economic development'.

The European Company Statute

Since June 1988, when Jacques Delors announced his intention to revive a long-standing Commission proposal to table plans for a European Company Statute as part of his personal commitment to add a 'social dimension' to the internal market programme, EC governments, companies and trades unions have been preparing for what promises to be a major showdown over the controversial issue of workers' rights.

In essence, the proposed European Company Statute would act as an alternative for companies currently required to register their existence and activities under national law. By incorporating under the European Company Statute, companies involved in cross-frontier mergers would be freed of the present requirement to adopt the company law of either member state. In addition to simplifying the legal situation, the Commission declared that the European Company Statute will also allow companies with operating losses in one member state to offset them against profits in another.

However, the proposal has a sting in its tail. In exchange for the benefits offered by the European Company Statute, companies would be required to accept certain minimum standards of worker participation in the running of the industries in which they are employed. Incorporation under the proposed legislation would be optional, not mandatory. The proposal has already received much criticism from Britain, which regards it as 'irrelevant', bitter opposition from UNICE, the European Employers' Federation, which fears it could become a millstone around the neck of European companies, and considerable scepticism from the European Trade Union Confederation, which insists that the proposals do not go far enough.

The idea of a European Company Statute is by no means new. The original proposal was made in 1970, following an initiative by France, but it proved so controversial that it was eventually shelved in 1982—a fate which befell all other attempts to revive the idea thereafter. It has, however, been brought back to life by Delors, in the conviction that the internal market programme could be placed in jeopardy unless the Community's workers believe that there is something in it for them too.

In a consultative document on the company statute circulated in the summer of 1988 the Commission outlined three models for worker involvement in company decision-making structures, each with varying degrees of worker participation. Officials have insisted that the proposal represents 'a modern approach for employer–worker relations throughout the EC', and that if consultations between governments, industry and trades unions showed enough support for the move, the Commission will go ahead and draft the legislation.

During preliminary discussions in Luxembourg in October 1988 the Commission expressed fears that, once the internal barriers to trade had been demolished, companies located in the more affluent Northern regions of the Community might be tempted to move some of their operations South, to avail themselves of cheaper labour costs and less stringent worker-protection legislation.

However, the Commission's argument received a hostile reception from member states anxious about the consequences of imposing new burdens on recently deregulated business, and from those who feared that the European Company Statute could provide a loophole enabling companies to bypass their own more restrictive worker-protection legislation. Francis Maude, the junior trade minister, told his European colleagues that the government had already consulted British companies about the proposal, and most saw little or no need for company law to be harmonized throughout the EC.

In her forthright speech in Bruges the previous month, Mrs Thatcher warned that the Community 'certainly does not need new regulations which raise the cost of employment, and make Europe's labour market less flexible and less competitive with overseas supplies'. The Prime Minister went on to state that if Europe was to have a company statute it must contain the least possible regulation, and warned that Britain would fight any attempt to introduce 'collectivism and corporatism' at the European level.

In the run-up to the Madrid summit in June 1989, Mrs Thatcher stepped up her assault against the social dimension or social charter (and, by implication, the European Company Statute). 'From all the accounts that I have received about the social charter,' she declared, 'it's more like a socialist charter.'

However, Delors remained determined to press ahead with the controversial project, and the following month managed to get the support of his fellow Commissioners to enact the proposals on the basis of majority voting instead of unanimity—thus removing the British veto. But just how much a threat the European Company Statute represents to British business interests remains a moot point. The choice of worker participation schemes available under the proposal range from full co-determination on the West German model to what has been described as 'a bland form of information and consultation'.

Nevertheless, the Commission's decision to push the measure through on the basis of majority voting is likely to provide an opportunity for those opposing the scheme, principally Britain, Ireland and the Netherlands, to mount a constitutional challenge in the European Court of Justice once it comes into operation.

The European business environment

The Commission plans to introduce a whole series of complementary measures in order to provide European companies with a common framework for conducting their operations. The Cecchini report speaks of the need to provide: 'a real home market . . . where companies trade without hindrance, but also one where they can operate in a cohesive regulatory environment . . . one where the rules of the game, if not the same, are not so different as to add major costs to doing business on a European-wide basis'.

In addition to the directive on the European Company Statute, such measures will include the creation of a Community trade mark, once the decision where to locate its headquarters has been made, and a European patent law to protect industrial and intellectual property rights, thereby avoiding the need to register patents in every member state. Measures designed to harmonize varying national audit and fiscal procedures are also expected.

Britain accepts need for EC merger control

With the UK's senior Commissioner (now Sir Leon Brittan) in charge of the sensitive Competition Policy dossier, and determined to continue the campaign launched by his illustrious predecessor, the government began to show signs of flexibility over the Community's demand for a comprehensive merger control policy. In January 1989, Lord Young, the then

Secretary of State for Trade and Industry, indicated for the first time that Britain would conform on the issue of new EC powers to approve all large-scale mergers.

After his first meeting with the 17-member Commission, Lord Young said that while Britain retained reservations about the proposed merger control regulation, it accepted the necessity of avoiding the problem of 'double jeopardy', where mergers had to be approved by both national and Community authorities. He suggested that it might be possible to reach an agreement whereby large mergers were approved by the Commission while smaller ones would be left to national bodies such as the Monopolies and Mergers Commission. Although he gave no indication of the turnover threshold that might initiate a Commission investigation (which is to be the subject of negotiations during the year), it was clear that the end of the Commission's 16-year campaign for new powers to regulate mergers was now in sight.

By April, Sir Leon had unveiled a new draft merger regulation which would grant the Commission powers to approve in advance all mergers where the combined turnover of the merged companies exceeded 5 billion ECUs. However, the revised turnover threshold is only a transitionary phase, and would remain in force until 1992, when it would fall to 2 billion ECUs.

After further talks in Brussels the following October, Britain, France and West Germany, agreed on the 5 billion ECU turnover threshold tabled earlier by Sir Leon. But final agreement on the measure proved elusive following the decision by Italy and a number of the smaller member states to hold out for a one billion ECU threshold, largely because they have little or no merger control apparatus of their own, rendering them dependent on Brussels for the monitoring of merger control. Nevertheless, all agreed at a further meeting in December, to sink their differences, granting the Commission sole power to bless or block large mergers.

Finally, the Commission's demand for what is known as an 'industrial policy override'—the power to waive the competition regulations in mergers which promote the economic interests of the Community against external competitors—has prompted a new argument over national sovereignty and the long-term cost of approving anti-competitive practices. West Germany, for example, does not want to see the Federal cartel office lose additional powers to Brussels, while the Department of Trade and Industry, now under Nicholas Ridley, has expressed fears that an industrial policy would grant a seal of approval to economic inefficiency by shielding national or Community companies from the forces of external competition. However, during the October meeting, ministers agreed that the inclusion of an industrial policy override should be abandoned, and that mergers should only be 'blessed or blocked' solely on competition grounds.

Checklist of changes

- The European Commission hopes to secure approval for a comprehensive merger control directive that will give Brussels the power to approve all large-scale mergers which have a Community dimension.
- The Commission will continue to exercise all its powers to appraise state aids to companies in both the private and public sectors in order to prevent governments engaging in anti-competitive practices.
- An optional European company statute, enabling companies involved in cross-frontier mergers to incorporate under European rather than national law, will also be introduced, along with measures designed to facilitate some degree of worker participation in company decision making.
- A series of measures aimed at providing European companies with a common framework for conducting their operations will be implemented, including a Community trade mark, a European patent law and legislation harmonizing variations in national audit and fiscal procedures.

10 VOICES AGAINST
Criticisms of 1992 from Left and Right

The programme for the completion of the single market by 1992 is designed to benefit businesses, consumers and travellers, but it does not arouse universal enthusiasm. There are fears that free movement will help criminals and terrorists in Europe and (mostly on the centre and right of the political spectrum) that 1992 will entail a serious loss of national sovereignty and enmesh Britain in European-style socialism. As Mrs Thatcher put it at Bruges:

> It is ironic that just when those countries such as the Soviet Union which have tried to run everything from the centre are learning that success depends on dispersing power and decisions away from the centre, some in the Community seem to want to move in the opposite direction. We have not successfully rolled back the frontiers of the state in Britain only to see them re-imposed at a European level.

The Left, while on the whole approving of 1992 after initial hostility, fears that cross-border activity by multinationals will benefit big business rather than ordinary employees, and lead to the erosion of workers' rights and health and safety standards—the 'social dimension'. Many business executives, for their part, fear that their companies will suffer commercial losses, or even fail.

Most of the critics of 1992 accept that, in Mrs Thatcher's words, 'by getting rid of barriers, by making it possible for companies to operate on a Europe-wide scale, we can best compete with the United States, Japan and the other new economic powers emerging in Asia and elsewhere'. This is the Government's view of a Europe 'open for enterprise'. However, not all sectors of industry share this view. DRI Europe, an international forecasting group, claimed in a report issued in July 1988 that the advent of the single market would not bring benefits on the scale envisaged by the Commission, least of all in sectors struggling for survival, such as the car industry. Harmonization of technical standards for and taxes on cars would be slow and incomplete, the report said. The 1992 programme did not envisage a policy for dealing with import threats from outside the Community. There would be cross-border trade distortions if VAT rates on cars were not brought into line, and companies such as Fiat and Renault could suffer sales losses so heavy that the French and Italian governments might try to maintain special restrictions on imports to protect them. Some fear that cross-border mergers in fields from banking to manufacturing will create Euro-conglomerates which will overpower small and medium-sized enterprises (SMEs) unable to compete in terms of resources and capital, even though the Single European Act specifically acknowledged the need to help SMEs in 1992.

The loss of national sovereignty

Even if such gloom is exaggerated, the 1992 process has aroused a widespread feeling (often nurtured by the tabloid press in Britain but also expressed by politicians and commentators) that power is ineluctably slipping out of the hands of national authorities and into those of faceless Eurocrats in Brussels. The case was perhaps best put by Brian Walden, the columnist, in the *Sunday Times* in July 1988, under the headline 'The line must be drawn at rule by Brussels'. After establishing his European credentials ('I admire Dutch tolerance, German cleanliness and efficiency, Italian family life and love of children, French worldliness and realism') Walden continued:

> But a nation is not a mere social arrangement that can be submerged into something better at the whim of planners and bureaucrats. The UK has not managed to solve its own nationality problems . . . Creating a single government for Western Europe is an infinitely more difficult operation than holding the UK together.

Comment of this kind has been encouraged by Delors' observation in June 1988 that an 'embryo' European government would emerge in the 1990s, and that 80% of economic and social legislation would be decided at the European level within ten years. The 1992 programme itself envisages no such development, since it is confined to the creation of the internal market. However, the critics have noticed that the process will not necessarily stop there. As Walden remarked:

> There is no point in subjecting Delors to an abusive tirade, because much of what he says is true. The creation of a single market is bound to mean that many decisions affecting our economic and social life will be taken in Brussels and Strasbourg. British politicians have been very slow to visualize what the new Europe will mean for national parliaments and national sovereignty . . . But I draw the line at a single European government.

The British people, Walden said, had not agreed to such a move when they voted in the 1975 EC referendum:

> and were specifically assured by several pro-Europeans, including me, that no such political arrangement was intended. We must dig

in our heels, before the EC is ruined by the haste and intemperance of political dreamers.

On a different level, the popular press has presented a picture of Britain surrendering sovereignty to Brussels. In August 1988 the *Star* newspaper carried a front-page headline reading '1992 Euro shocker', listing three points: 'Dearer clothes, food and power; our athletes to join Euro-team; Our troops to take orders in German.' 'Mrs Thatcher does not run Britain any more,' the report began:

> Nor does the Government. The Civil Service is powerless, and the highest courts in the land can be overruled. This is not the nightmare scenario of George Orwell's *1984*, it is the amazing reality of what life will be like in 1992. For that is the year when Britain will virtually disappear into a United States of Europe.

A favourite tabloid tactic is to add to such predictions some of the more eccentric proposals advanced by fringe elements in the EC, such as a small group of Euro MPs (who have little real power) for obliging British motorists to drive on the right or to cut their lawns between midday and 2 p.m. on Sundays.

While such reporting has little serious aim (apart from the arousal of indignation) there is genuine political concern among some commentators that by signing the Single European Act EC leaders have gone too far, and have created a monster which may get out of control. The tone was set by the debates in the Commons and Lords in 1986 as the Single European Act passed through both Houses of Parliament. Writing in *The Times* in May 1986, Sir Edward du Cann, MP for Taunton and president of the Conservative European Reform Group, summed up the Act as follows:

> The directive powers of the Commission are to be massively enhanced, the national veto is to be reduced in scope, progress toward European political union is to be accelerated. Thus, whether British people approve or disapprove, the establishment of a European super-state is under way.

Sir Edward added: 'Almost overnight and largely unnoticed by our fellow citizens, Britain's right to decide many practical matters, even her own destiny, is being surrendered to the majority vote and the interests of other nations not all of whom share our parliamentary traditions.'

The House of Lords Select Committee appointed to scrutinize the Act concluded that 'in the long term the position of the UK Parliament will become weaker'. Two eminent QCs, Peter Horsfield and Leolin Price, in *The Times* the same month said that the Act involved profound constitutional changes and was a step towards European political union. In the

House of Commons this view was most forcefully expressed by Teddy Taylor, Conservative MP for Southend, and a noted anti-Common Market campaigner. 'It would surely be in our national interests if the EC were to resolve its existing problems and implement its existing agreements before seeking further powers,' Taylor wrote to *The Times*:

> Is it wise to give even more power to the EC, which has so abysmally failed to resolve the crisis in its agricultural policy . . . More majority voting will simply mean more Euro laws being applied to the UK, which could well be wholly against our wishes or our interests. If this is not a major step towards federation, I wonder what is.

Paul Johnson, the columnist and historian, complained in *The Times* in June of public apathy as 'fundamental and irreversible changes' were pushed through, partly because of 'the sheer soporific effect of the leaden jargon with which the EC conceals its doings'. The Act was:

> a completely new treaty, which ought properly to have been placed on a level of significance equivalent to that of the original Treaty of Rome . . . When Britain joined the EC we had to accept that membership would involve some limitations to our national sovereignty. But the understanding was that these limitations were finite . . . and that any further limitations would be carefully negotiated by us from a position of strength within the EC.

As the Act passed over the final hurdle at Westminster, approval by the Lords, Lord Denning, former Master of the Rolls, warned that the aim of the Act was 'to transform Europe into a single nation with its own Parliament and its own legislation'. Westminster would become a 'subordinate body'.

For many, the EC is a 'fact of life', but one reluctantly accepted. British assertions of national sovereignty are greeted hypocritically on the Continent, right-wing critics say, since the French and other Europeans are adept at advancing their own national interests while claiming to be *communautaire*. According to Oliver Letwin, formerly a member of the Prime Minister's Policy Unit, fair competition and free movement of capital and labour within the EC under the 1992 programme are welcome, but have to be balanced against the fact that—as Enoch Powell once warned—Britain is losing its national autonomy:

> The idea that a majority group of French, West German, Italian, Belgian, Spanish, Portuguese and Irish ministers sitting behind closed doors in Brussels could pass what is effectively binding legislation on Britain, with our own parliament powerless to

intervene, would have struck anyone as a crazy proposition until recently. But this crazy proposition is now a fact.

In September 1988, *The Spectator* declared, after the row over the sacking of Lord Cockfield, that 'there is nothing to be gained from isolation from the Continent, and much to be said for institutionalized co-operation between powers which are geographically and politically close and on the whole friendly'. But it added that it was lukewarm about the European idea:

> Will people really accept that their lives can be ordered by Brussels? Will they only be prepared to accept this if Brussels is controlled by a powerful European Parliament? If so, what will be left of our own Parliament?

The *Sunday Telegraph* editor, Peregrine Worsthorne, argued that much right-wing opinion on the Continent is all too ready to accept 'collectivist' views of 1992, because:

> Quite simply they are not conservative in the way Mrs Thatcher is conservative. They are for the most part Christian Democrat, with deep roots in Catholic social and economic doctrine, which is light years away from Mrs Thatcher's brand of free enterprise economic and social doctrine.

Strong centralizing traditions are common to Left and Right on the Continent, 'making Leon Blum, the great French socialist, at one with Bismarck, the great German reactionary'.

Professor Elie Kedourie of London University, a noted authority on nationalism, agreed that the problem goes wider than arguments over harmonization:

> Whether through good luck or the wisdom of its political leaders, Britain has enjoyed for generations now a stable, constitutional mode of government in which the citizen has not had to fear for his freedom and where legality is the accepted norm and test for all official action. This is far from having been the case on the Continent where, since the French Revolution, a disagreeable, visionary and destructive style of politics has been in the habit of now and again erupting,

he said in *The Times* in September 1988. Spain, Greece, Italy and Germany all offer examples of instability and extremism. 'What is to hold such a disparate union together?' Kedourie asked. Writing in *The Independent*, Sir William Rees-Mogg, a former editor of *The Times*, suggested that Delors was trying to impose a socialist view of 1992, yet 'the European Commission has no remit to re-impose by subterfuge what Britain has thrown off after disastrous experience'.

Anti-Brussels feeling emerged during the European election in 1989, following the Government's warning to Brussels not to 'interfere' beyond its powers. *The Economist* commented that Mrs Thatcher's 'blind spot' about Europe was lethal, and she was 'ignoring the fact that much of what is happening in Western Europe is excellently Thatcherite and will continue to be if only she has the sense to embrace it with a bit of Continental warmth instead of treating it to unending English *froideur'*. James Elles MEP wrote in *The Times* on 26 June 1989 that 'The objective of the EC is not just simply to create an internal market. It is a means by which its member states can move, step by step, towards closer European integration, without actually specifying the destination.' But precisely because of this, thirteen academics, led by Lord Harris of Highcross, chairman of the Institute of Economic Affairs, in 1989 formed 'The Bruges Group'—more properly, The Campaign for a Europe of Sovereign States—to oppose European union in the spirit of Mrs Thatcher's Bruges speech. (The group had been initiated earlier by an Oxford undergraduate.) Edward Heath declared that 'any intelligent Conservative' could support a sharing of sovereignty, adding: 'Of course, if you go to a member of the British public and say, do you want your British pound and British pint of beer taken away by a lot of nasty foreign Marxists he will indignantly reply that no, he does not. But I believe the British public reject such false popularism, such distortions of the truth for the patronizing, self-serving hypocrisy that they are.' Jonathan Aitken MP replied that Britain was in danger of surrendering its sovereignty 'almost through sleepwalking'. Aitken said he was 'madly in favour of Europe', with a European wife, children born in Europe and 'lots of European friends'. But 'I am amazed at the willingness of some politicians to apparently throw out 900 years of constitutional history, headed by a sovereign parliament, in favour of what is still a European Blancmange . . . The Single European Act has been used by Delors and many others as a new Meccano set for constitutional, financial and legal experiments, a good many of which will turn out to be very damaging to this country' (*London International*, Summer 1989).

Democratic accountability

Criticisms of this kind carry a great deal of force and express widespread concern about integration. On the other hand, the Act was extensively discussed in Britain and other EC countries (as the comments themselves show) and it was ratified democratically. There was no secret about what it contained. According to an opinion poll published in *The Mail on Sunday* in September 1988, after Mrs Thatcher's speech in Bruges, two years later many Britons now accept a degree of integration with Europe and an erosion of sovereignty. The key question is how the resulting European institutions can be subjected to popular control. The Single European Act does provide for qualified majority voting in the Council of Ministers, and to this extent involves a loss of national sovereignty. On the other hand, joining the EC in the first place entailed some loss of sovereignty, and most supporters of European integration argue that by pooling sovereignty the EC becomes stronger and so more able to promote the interests of all its members. National governments, moreover, retain the right of veto in many vital areas, since the majority voting system applies to internal market matters only. However, there is a widespread perception that EC institutions must be more tightly controlled as European influence in our lives and work increases.

Some anti-EC feeling and comment reflects an unexpressed regret that Britain took the decision to join the Community in 1973. Others accept that EC accession was the right step, but regret that Mrs Thatcher subsequently put her name to the Single European Act, thus allowing the EC to take the process of integration a stage further. However, while such regrets are perfectly legitimate they can have no practical impact, since both the Accession Treaty and the Single European Act are accomplished facts, legally drawn up and ratified after long debate and negotiation. Britain, in the words of one senior EC diplomat, has 'passed the point of no return'.

The answer to fears of loss of control over our daily lives must therefore lie in increasing democratic control over the institutions of the EC, to ensure that EC developments meet British interests and concerns. This is the solution proposed, among others, by Bill Newton Dunn, Conservative MEP for Lincolnshire. The major omission in the 1992 programme, in Newton Dunn's view (which is widely shared by all parties in the European Parliament) is the lack of any provision for ensuring that, as integration proceeds, so democratic control over EC decision making is increased. Proposals are scrutinized at every stage as they pass through the decision-making procedures, particularly when they are approved by European Parliament committees. Nonetheless, in the final analysis decisions are made and proposals passed into law during deliberations of the Council of Ministers, which are confidential.

The argument for retaining confidentiality is that the Council of Ministers is not only a legislature but also a negotiating body, in which ministers win and concede points in a way likely to be impaired if the proceedings were made public. British Cabinet proceedings are not open to the press, the argument runs, so neither should those of the EC Council of Ministers be exposed to the public gaze. In any case, EC ministers all come from national parliaments and are therefore democratically accountable in their own countries.

However, the development of the 1992 process seems bound to lead to further demands for 'accountability', with at least partial media accession to Council meetings, instead of the present system under which Brussels-based correspondents are briefed by national spokesmen and have to find the whole picture (in so far as it can be found) by cultivating official contacts.

On 25 July 1989, as the newly elected European Parliament assembled for the session leading up to 1992, *The Times* noted that Conservative Euro MPs had for the first time been invited to hear the Prime Minister report to the 1922 Committee to increase MEP–MP liaison, but added:

> In practice, Westminster's machinery has been overwhelmed by the quantity and detail of European regulation. The European Parliament has remained weak. In the gap between lies the 'democratic deficit' . . . The approach to monitoring EC regulations taken so far by most Westminster MPs must rapidly change. The work of the select committee on European legislation and debates in the House are adequate only for considering general principles. EC matters need to cease being an alien subject and to be dispersed where they belong—an integral part of almost every aspect of national life considered by the House of Commons.

Attitudes on the Left

The demand for democratic accountability has also been taken up by the political left, and above all by the Labour Party, which, after a long period of hostility towards the EC, has given its support to the 1992 programme while at the same time seeking to ensure that the internal market not only benefits big business but also protects the rights of employees. Most of the Labour Party Group in the European Parliament, paradoxically, remains virulently anti-EC, but national Labour policy has altered.

The key event in the emergence of Labour's new policy was the decision at the beginning of 1988 by Neil Kinnock, the Party leader, to abandon Labour's previous commitment to withdrawing Britain from the EC if it won power. The intellectual ground for the change was prepared in a Fabian pamphlet written by David Martin, MEP, then leader of the Labour Group at Strasbourg, and published in February 1988, which argued that Labour should work with other socialist parties in Europe to 'bring common sense to the Common Market'. The aim, the pamphlet said, should be to increase social spending, redistribute resources as 1992 brought greater prosperity and protect the EC environment. In a preface Kinnock wrote: 'It is surely realistic to acknowledge that Britain's integration with the other European economies by 1990 will have proceeded so far that talk of economic withdrawal is both politically romantic and economically self-defeating.' The aim of socialism, Kinnock declared, was to 'prevent the hardship, exploitation and waste which can result from the operation of unregulated markets'. Labour's view of 1992, in other words, is diametrically opposed to that of the Right, which—in Kinnock's eyes—'puts profit before people'. He concluded that if the Left did not take part in 1992 there would be unimpeded movement to the complete economic and political domination of Western Europe by market power, with all of the effects on civil rights, environmental conditions, individual opportunities and collective provision which that implies. Leaving the European field to that is no more acceptable than leaving Britain to permanent Thatcherism.

On a visit to Brussels in February 1988 Kinnock followed this up by declaring flatly: 'The prospects for withdrawal in my view are nil.' In September 1988, in a speech to Labour Euro MPs in Glasgow, Kinnock urged all socialists to take part in 1992, remarking: 'If the single market was to mean nothing other than a big finance free-for-all, it would be a social, industrial and environmental catastrophe.' At the Labour Party Conference in Blackpool in October 1988 Kinnock took much the same line, accusing the Government of 'pathetically inadequate' preparations for 1992, and declaring that social justice had to be a central component of the single market if it was not to benefit rich regions and become 'expensive, ugly, a constant source of waste, and a constant source of tension between peoples'.

This appears to be accepted by a broad spectrum of left-wing opinion. In an article in the July–September 1988 issue of *The Political Quarterly* entitled 'Beyond One Nation Socialism: An Agenda for the European Left' Frances Morrell, former leader of the ILEA and a noted left-winger, argued that it was a mistake to examine the reasons for Labour's electoral decline, such as the loss of traditional working class support, in national rather than European terms:

> The shaping of Europe should not be abandoned to the Right. Labour, and indeed all Social Democratic Parties out of office, have a duty to oppose and to lead.

In July 1989 Glyn Ford, new leader of the Labour MEPs at Strasbourg, moved still further from Labour's anti-EC line, saying the Conservatives were 'hardly European' whereas 'we represent the party that is determined to work within the EC'. Kinnock supported this when visiting Strasbourg the same month, but, like Thatcher, was cautious on the pace of economic and monetary union.

The social dimension: a 1992 Workers' Charter?

Kinnock's lead has been followed by the trades union movement, whose espousal of 1992 was given great encouragement in September 1988, when Delors travelled to Bournemouth to appeal to the TUC to back the internal market. In doing so Delors—a French socialist—indirectly criticized the interpretation of 1992 advanced by Mrs Thatcher, and lent support to the Left's campaign for a 'social dimension'. 'It is impossible to build Europe only on deregulation,' he declared, to an ovation from the trades union delegates:

> 1992 is much more than the creation of an internal market abolishing barriers to the free movement of goods, services and investment. The internal market should be designed to benefit each and every citizen of the Community. It is therefore necessary to improve workers' living and working conditions, and to provide better protection for their health and safety at work.

He assured the TUC that he believed in 'social dialogue and collective bargaining' as pillars of a democratic society. These assertions won Delors TUC backing and the affectionate sobriquet 'Frère Jacques' (Brother Jacques). He had ceased to be, in the eyes of the Left, a soulless and overpaid international bureaucrat and had become the champion of the workers as the single market approached.

The significance of the change of heart in the Labour Party and the TUC lies partly in its impact on British politics. However, given the Conservative Party's current dominance of British politics, in the long run the most important impact of left-wing thinking on 1992 will be in the European context, where socialist parties are stronger and where some are in power. At the TUC in September 1988, Ron Todd, of the Transport and General Workers Union, speaking for the TUC General Council, called on British trades unionists to link up with their European counterparts to ensure that 1992 was moulded in the right direction. Todd admitted that the TUC had once been 'sceptical about there being any benefits in the European dimension'. But he added:

> The only card game in town at the moment is in a town called Brussels, and it's the game of poker . . . We've got to learn the rules, and pretty fast.

The TUC agreed to set up links with Continental unions to explore the possibilities of Europe-wide collective bargaining with employers, and called on the European Commission to produce a 'European Workers' Charter' to protect employees in cross-border mergers and takeovers.

Such a charter has been considered by the European Commission, and is favoured, in one form or another, by several of the EC countries which at present have socialist administrations. As it happens, three of them —Greece, Spain and France—hold the Presidency of the EC Council of Ministers consecutively. Felipe Gonzalez, the Spanish Prime Minister, who held the Presidency in the first half of 1989, is an enthusiastic proponent of the 'social dimension'. When Mrs Thatcher visited Madrid in September 1988 she expressed her opposition to new Europe-wide regulations on company law and worker participation in industry, remarking that the EC term 'social space' was imprecise:

It is a new piece of jargon. I am never quite sure what it is. But if it means having a regulation on Community company law, then I would oppose that particular thing. I am a democrat and I am a meritocrat and I believe you get on by merit, not by giving particular privileges to one particular group.

Gonzalez, however, insisted that a social dimension to 1992 was indispensable, with employees' rights protected and with help for the socially and economically disadvantaged.

The social dimension figured prominently in the European election campaign, when Michael Meacher, the Labour employment spokesman, leaked details of a report by a group of EC lawyers showing that Britain lagged behind other EC countries in rights of workers to annual leave, minimum wages and working hours. Norman Fowler, the Secretary of State for Employment, retorted that economic growth and job creation had brought down unemployment in Britain without the need for regulation or charters. At a meeting in Luxembourg of EC Labour and Employment Ministers in June 1989 he opposed the social charter, which, however, was backed by ten other states (Denmark abstained, saying it had to consult employers and trades unions at home). 'We are being asked to sign a blank cheque before anyone has defined what these rights would be and how much they would cost' Fowler declared. Britain also opposed the related proposal for a European Company Statute (see Chapter 9).

Proposals for a charter tabled in September 1988 by Manuel Marin of Spain, then Commissioner for Social Policy, were restricted to voluntary common measures for training schemes, common standards for social security benefits and common health and safety provisions, to which Britain has no objection. However, France and West Germany have since appealed to Mrs Vasso Papandreou of Greece, the present Commissioner, to follow the proposed charter—to be adopted at the Strasbourg summit at the end of 1989—with binding legislation on social issues and workers' rights by the mid-1990s. Mrs Papandreou issued a revised version of the charter in September 1989. In a letter to *The Times* on 29 June 1989 Norman Willis, TUC General Secretary, said the social charter 'would not seek to impose one particular model of worker participation on all member states'. But Mrs Thatcher dismissed the charter as 'backdoor socialism'. Michel Rocard, the French Prime Minister, memorably mixing his metaphors, accused her of having a view of Europe as 'a jungle, a house with its windows wide open to the winds, a plane without a pilot'. At the Madrid summit in June 1989 the issue was avoided but resurfaced under the French EC Presidency in the second half of 1989, when Mitterrand and Rocard actively pursued it in the run-up to the Strasbourg summit in December 1989.

The politicization of 1992

These developments show that the single market programme, initially seen as a technical one for harmonization and freer trade across frontiers, has rapidly acquired a party-political dimension as the reality of 1992 approaches. Anxieties on the Right about 'corporate socialism' and interference from Brussels at the expense of British cultural traditions and national sovereignty are matched by concern on the Left that the 1992 agenda has been set by conservative parties in power in Britain and Europe and by big business, which is able to influence both national governments and the European Commission.

The outcome of this debate is not clear, nor can we see how far the debate will shape 1992 and how much it will merely be a domestic political football to be kicked around for domestic political reasons. Speaking to West German trades unionists and business executives in Cologne in September 1988, Delors responded to criticisms from the Right by attacking the 'verbal excesses of the advocates of deregulation', and called for a 'new Keynes or Beveridge' to lay down a comprehensive EC social and employment programme for 1992, together with a plan for the redistribution of wealth. 'We thought we had this debate behind us,' Delors said, 'There can be no Europe without a social dimension . . . Europe must never become an instrument to weaken the trades unions.' The debate is far from over, however, and seems likely to intensify as 1992 approaches.

An indication of how strong the 1992 backlash might become was given in a speech by Sir John Hoskyns, the outgoing Director-General of the Institute of Directors, to an audience of 3,000 business executives in February 1989. Describing the internal market programme as a 'complete fiasco', Sir John attacked the Community and its institutions for 'shifting objectives, bad organization, wrong people, poor motivation, inadequate methods, weak management, personal politics and pilfering on a heroic scale'.

In addition to alleging that 'there are signs that the Brussels machine is becoming corrupted both intellectually and financially', Sir John astonished his audience by calling on the Community to scrap its 1992 achievements and start all over again! No less striking was the co-ordinated and instantaneous government assault on Sir John's provocative views.

Sir Geoffrey Howe, the then Foreign Secretary, later told a Birmingham press conference that: 'It is, quite frankly, perverse and faint-hearted to claim that the single market has been blown off course, or risks being submerged in collectivism or bureaucracy.' These sentiments were also echoed by Lord Young, who accused Sir John of ignoring 'many of the facts', and expressed fears that 'Sir John has been reading too many scare stories in the press and not attending closely enough to what was really happening'.

11 HARMONIZING TAXES
The VAT controversy

The harmonization of indirect taxation or, more accurately, the approximation of VAT (value added tax) and the harmonization of excise duties is regarded by the European Commission as central to the 1992 process. However, it arouses fundamental passions and fierce opposition—not least in Britain—for two main reasons. Taxation is traditionally the preserve of national governments, and not subject to supranational control; and the Commission's plans for VAT approximation, at least as originally tabled, would mean the ending of VAT zero-rating in Britain of basic goods such as food, fuel and children's clothing, a move any government would regard as politically sensitive—not to say explosive. Simultaneously, the harmonization of excise duties will have the effect of bringing down the cost to the consumer of cigarettes and alcohol. This gives rise to the charge that 'Brussels' is planning as part of 1992 to put up the price of food and children's shoes (socially useful products) while reducing the price of tobacco and spirits (socially harmful ones).

The measures put forward by the Commission have to be passed by the Council of Ministers to become law. As it happens, indirect taxation is one area in which the right of national veto has been retained. In any case, new proposals advanced by Mme Christiane Scrivener, the Commissioner for Fiscal Affairs, in May 1989, have made significant concessions allowing Britain to keep VAT zero rating on food, children's clothing and some other basic items, and giving all states greater flexibility in imposing tax rates on cigarettes, alcohol and tobacco.

Confusion between new proposals and court rulings
The debate over VAT and 1992 in Britain has been marked by the confusion of two separate points: the 1985 White Paper's plans for the removal of fiscal barriers; and rulings by the European Court on exemptions granted to Britain in 1977, when the Sixth VAT Directive was passed. The first refers to future proposals arising from the Single European Act; the second to a directive which is already in existence. Both tend to be regarded as interference by Brussels in British tax affairs, although this overlooks the fact that Britain has already agreed to the principle of VAT harmonization by putting its name to the 1977 directive (during the last Labour Government).

The 1977 concession does not mean that Britain or any other state is obliged to comply with the White Paper's vision of the removal of all fiscal barriers. Indeed, the Commission's proposals are currently going through a process of modification to meet the objections not only of Britain but also of other countries where VAT rates are either higher or lower than the proposed VAT bands contained in the draft 1992 directive. The Commission can (and does) argue that VAT approximation has long been on the agenda in one form or another. On the other hand, its approach to the problem illustrates the delicacy of the issue, especially the approach adopted in the 1992 White Paper itself.

The White Paper section on fiscal barriers (Section Three) was one of the most controversial aspects of the original 1992 programme. The Commission was well aware of this, as the careful if sometimes argumentative language of the White Paper shows. Section Three was the only one to depart from the overall principle of 1992—that member states should accept common goals and work their way towards them through mutual recognition, with adjustments made afterwards as the realities of the single market developed. Instead, the White Paper made a direct attempt to force EC governments to approximate their indirect tax rates.

It begins by noting that the removal of frontier controls 'is bound to have inescapable implications for the member states as far as indirect taxes are concerned'. In 1968, at the time of the customs union, it was already apparent that 'the mere removal of tariffs' would not create a true common market, and that differences in turnover taxes 'were the source of serious distortion'. The Treaty of Rome itself, the White Paper said, had provided for Commission proposals on the approximation of indirect taxation 'when this was needed for the completion of the internal market' (Articles 99 and 100). This remains the basis of the Commission's drive for VAT approximation: that VAT differentials distort trade in a frontier-free Europe; and that harmonization—or approximation—is necessary for the completion of the single market. Both are distrusted by anti-Marketeers and by a number of EC governments.

VAT has always appealed to EC policymakers as an instrument of fiscal policy because of its relative simplicity—as a principle, that is, not in terms of its complex paperwork for both business executives and VAT inspectors. Now used in all twelve EC states, with Portugal the last to come into line in 1989, VAT is a tax levied at each stage of the process of production and marketing but collected by the government of the country at the point of sale. In practice, however, VAT rates vary considerably from one country to another. A system of limited allowances has been developed for the carrying of tax-free goods across EC borders, but this causes problems for countries like Denmark and Ireland, which have tried (illegally, according to the Commission, which is threatening to take them to the European Court) to restrict such allowances to *bona fide* travellers by imposing arbitrary definitions of what constitutes a traveller.

Steps towards harmonization of indirect taxes

The first major step towards harmonization came in 1967, at the time of the

Six, when turnover taxes were replaced by VAT levied on a common basis through a series of VAT directives (the First VAT Directive, the Second VAT Directive, and so on). Three years later, in 1970, came the decision to give the EC its 'own resources'—a common EC fund as opposed to national budgets—by raising revenues based partly on farm levies but mainly on a proportion (up to 1%) of national VAT contributions. This system eventually proved inadequate, and under the Delors reforms of February 1988 has given way to a revised own resources system based partly on VAT and partly on a tax derived from a calculation of gross national product. This more fairly reflects each country's ability to contribute to the EC and, incidentally, creates difficulties for Italy because of the extent of the black economy, making the true Italian GNP almost unknowable. But even under the Delors package, VAT contributions remain a central part of the revenue system.

In 1977 the Sixth VAT Directive laid down the outlines of a common VAT base, yet so sensitive was the issue, and so great the resistance of national governments, that the directive contained a number of loopholes and exemptions, known in EC jargon as 'derogations'. On the other hand, the directive made it clear that such exemptions were only temporary, hence the subsequent cases in the European Court over whether exemptions granted to Britain on medical and social grounds were justified. At the same time, the EC decided to harmonize excise duties, beginning with cigarettes and tobacco, alcohol and hydrocarbon oils. By 1985 the White Paper was able to declare that 'the harmonization of indirect taxation has always been regarded as an essential and integral part of achieving a true common market'. Momentum had been lost between 1977 and 1985, it admitted, but this was due to 'the impact of recession on the economic policies of member states, and preoccupation with other problems'. Progress was now being resumed, 'and we must proceed vigorously if we are to achieve the target date of 1992'.

What are the technical arguments for VAT approximation? EC officials argue that if frontier controls are to be abolished so that people, goods and services can move about within the EC as if it were one country, this clearly affects those controls 'primarily designed to ensure that each member state can collect revenue in the form of indirect taxation'. Whether in the form of VAT or of excise duties, indirect taxes become part of the final price to the consumer. According to the White Paper:

> Different levels of taxation are reflected in different price levels. If the differences in level are substantial, the differences in final prices will also be substantial . . . We need to consider whether or not it would be practically possible, in the absence of frontier controls, for member states to charge significantly different levels of indirect taxation.

The Commission's own answer, unsurprisingly, is no, it would not. Under the Commission's draft Fourteenth VAT Directive—tabled in 1982 and eventually withdrawn in 1987, after much heated debate—EC states would all have had to shift to a system of 'postponed accounting' used in the Benelux states. Under this system, VAT accounting is done at inland tax offices rather than at frontiers. The Commission sought to meet member states' concerns by agreeing that 'some documentation' would still be needed at the border and governments would still have the right to check the movement of goods to prevent fraud. However, the Commission's basic principle remained that VAT incurred by a consumer should be deductible 'irrespective of the member state on which it has been charged'. Under a parallel proposal there would be a computerized central clearing house to ensure that VAT collected in the exporting state but deducted in the importing one was reimbursed to the importing state and not the exporting one. In the end, the Council of Ministers judged that the proposed clearing-house system was too unwieldy and too open to abuse. The Commission's position is that fraud and evasion could best be avoided if the current system of divergent VAT rates was replaced by a common one of approximated rates.

Similar arguments apply to the question of cross-border shopping. Because of the differences in VAT, and hence in prices, people in high-tax countries naturally cross where possible into neighbouring low-tax ones to reap the benefits. Cross-border shopping is particularly intense in Benelux, France and West Germany; on the Danish–German border; and between Northern Ireland and the Irish Republic. It applies less to Britain, because of the natural obstacle of the Channel. But arguably, Continental housewives would find it worth making the crossing if British VAT zero rates for 'basic products' were retained after 1992 in an otherwise harmonized EC, and mail order businesses would also benefit. Mothercare —to take one example—would be able to compete with an unfair (and highly lucrative) advantage over Continental mail order firms with a similar speciality in children's clothing and supplies.

Modification of the VAT proposals

In practice, as the fate of the Fourteenth VAT Directive shows, the Commission has found its arguments for harmonization fiercely opposed, and has moved to a policy of 'approximation' instead. This is a concession, but its outlines were already visible in the 1985 White Paper. This conceded that while excise duties could and should be harmonized—which is still the Commission's policy—VAT approximation need only be 'sufficiently close that the operation of the common market is not affected through distortions of trade, diversion of trade or effects on competition'. Opponents of VAT harmonization often point to the example of the United States, where variations exist between the federal states without any noticeable effect on what might be called the single American market. The

Commission took this argument and used it for its own purposes, holding up the American system as a model for an integrated Europe—adding, however, that cross-border tax variations must still be limited, with a proposed permitted divergence from the EC norm of plus or minus 2½%. Brussels also now acknowledges that VAT is only one element in the make-up of consumer prices, and that price is only one factor in consumer choice along with service, brand image and convenience: 'Retail markets are often tolerant of quite significant differences in prices.' A further problem admitted by EC officials is that Denmark and Ireland derive a larger proportion of their revenue from indirect taxation than most other EC states (16–17%, compared to around 10% in Britain or West Germany), so that major adjustments for approximation would give Copenhagen and Dublin budgetary problems (see Appendix 3).

Nonetheless, the Commission has remained determined to bring EC VAT rates broadly into line, whether under the banner of 'approximation' or 'harmonization'. It noted in the White Paper that VAT rates at present vary from zero (in Britain and Ireland) to a high point of 38% in Italy, with Denmark applying a standard rate of 22%.

In July 1987, after much internal discussion at the Berlaymont, Lord Cockfield, the Internal Market Commissioner, announced the Commission's 'approximation' proposals. VAT rates would be grouped into two broad bands: a standard rate of between 14% and 20% and a reduced one of between 4% and 9% on 'items of basic necessity'. The Commission, Lord Cockfield said, was ready to meet the 'particular difficulties' of Britain and Ireland over zero rating by considering temporary exemptions 'where these can be justified, for states for which the proposals could pose political, social or budgetary problems'.

The resulting reaction was, if anything, fiercer than that which greeted the Commission's earlier plans, largely because of the impact on zero rating. Not only would the abolition of zero rating affect lower income groups, the argument ran, it would also affect the economy as a whole, since nearly 30% of all consumer spending in Britain is accounted for by zero-rated goods—i.e. food, energy, children's clothes, water, newspapers, books and drugs. The then Paymaster General, Peter Brooke, declared: 'There is no question of our accepting anything that conflicts with the pledges the Prime Minister has given on our zero rates,' a reference to undertakings given during the 1987 election campaign. Shortly afterwards, Mrs Thatcher confirmed in the Commons that Britain would veto the VAT changes if they were put to the Council of Ministers. Nigel Lawson, the Chancellor of the Exchequer, has repeatedly told fellow EC Finance Ministers that the VAT proposal is unnecessary and unacceptable. Lord Young of Graffham restated the British view in *The Times* in July 1988. The Government's rejection of the VAT proposal was 'absolutely final', he said, adding: 'We are not going to harmonize.' Differing VAT rates did not affect competition, he argued—and if distortions did arise, they would, in any case, be corrected after 1992 by market forces. The new Scrivener proposals are the result of the Commission's efforts to meet such objections. But while the issue of VAT rates remains to be resolved, ministers have agreed on the means of collection, by maintaining the existing system of leaving VAT on goods and services in the country of consumption, despite Commission objections that this would entail retention of elaborate border controls.

The search for a compromise

The EC's influential Economic and Monetary Committee, composed of senior finance officials from the twelve governments, issued an interim report in April 1988. This sought to balance the opposing views on VAT, arguing that approximation along the lines advanced by Lord Cockfield can be combined with the 'market forces' line of reasoning. On the other hand, the Government's view has received support from leading experts, notably the Institute of Fiscal Studies, which in a report issued in February 1988 agreed that completion of the internal market did not require substantial changes to national VAT systems. The Institute suggested that instead of two broad VAT bands the EC should have common minimum VAT rates, or floors, allowing member states to set higher rates if they wished. It also took issue with the Commission's attempt to legislate for the good of the Community, declaring that if states with high tax rates suffered because of cross-border shopping they had only themselves to blame: 'It is not the business of the Commission to protect member states from the consequences of their own high indirect taxation policies.' It went on to argue that, as an island, Britain was less likely to be affected by cross-border shopping problems—an argument which may lose its force as cross-Channel traffic increases with the building of the Channel Tunnel.

A further compromise suggestion has come from the European Parliament. In July 1988 Alman Metten, a Dutch socialist MEP, proposed two broad VAT bands to replace those of the Commission, one ranging from zero to 6% or 9% and a higher rate of between 16% and 22%—in effect, taking account of the British–Irish zero rating problem and of Denmark's high standard rate of 22%. In October 1988 the European Parliament's committee on fiscal approximation approved this as an amendment to the Cockfield proposals. Ben Patterson, MEP for Kent West (who has himself proposed the retention of zero rating in a pamphlet entitled *VAT: The Zero Rate Issue*), welcomed the idea that zero rating should be a permanent part of the EC VAT system. On the other hand, critics of these compromise proposals argue that a system which tolerates variations of between zero and 22% can scarcely be called 'approximation' any more, let alone 'harmonization'.

The political and business climate in Britain remains suspicious of VAT harmonization, as is shown most vividly by reactions to the European Court's series of rulings on British exemptions under the 1977 directive. As noted earlier, the question of 1977 exemptions is, strictly speaking, separate from that of 1992 harmonization. Yet the two issues are, in a sense, linked aspects of the same basic drive towards harmonization—or approximation. In discussing the 1977 exemptions the White Paper made clear that they were (1) provisional only and (2) part of the wider process leading ultimately to harmonization: '. . .These derogations and social arrangements should ultimately be brought to an end . . . so that a common market permitting fair competition and resembling a real internal market may ultimately be achieved.' The 1977 directive itself stated that exemptions could be maintained until a date 'not later than that on which the charging of tax on imports and the remission of tax on exports in trade between the member states are abolished'. The date is not defined, but EC officials argue that it refers to the completion of the internal market—that is, 1992.

Rulings on the Sixth VAT Directive against Britain

The rulings arrived at by the European Court following cases brought against Britain by the Commission have certainly caused widespread concern in Britain. The rulings have come some ten years after the directive, but the wheels of EC justice grind slowly. In February 1988 the Court ruled that the VAT exemption granted in 1977 for the dispensing of spectacles and contact lenses could not be justified. Backbench Conservative MPs complained that an outside body was dictating to Parliament what taxes it could levy for the first time since the seventeenth-century ship tax. In June the Court caused another political row by ruling that the practice of either zero rating or exempting new commercial construction and certain services to industry (electricity, gas, protective clothing, sewerage, plus news services) was a further unjustified exemption (although it upheld the exemption for private domestic housing as well as for animal feedstuffs and livestock), leading to confusion in the media over whether Britain had 'won' or 'lost'. In the oral hearing in September 1987 the lawyer acting for Britain had argued that not all VAT exemptions in Britain were due to 'a funny Anglo-Saxon habit'.

Following the ruling on new construction, the standard British 15% VAT rate applies to non-domestic construction, and the sale of land for commercial property development, from April 1989. The Court allowed the continued zero rating of private housing, as opposed to commercial building, because Britain was entitled to pursue—on social grounds—'a policy of home ownership for the whole population'. The Government softened the blow to commercial building and services by refunding or partially refunding the extra cost for health authorities and charities, but private schools, hospitals and charities still expressed dismay. (To qualify for a refund the institution in question must be registered for VAT purposes.) Teddy Taylor, MP, giving voice to backbench feelings, recalled in a letter to *The Times* in June 1988 that when the Commons debated the

Sixth VAT Directive in November 1976, before its final adoption, the government of the day had repeatedly declared that the British right to retain zero rating was assured. The Court's ruling, Taylor said, was 'one more example of the wishes of the Euro-institutions to extend their powers and control at the expense of sovereign governments'. Responding to this and other charges that the Government had conceded sovereignty over taxation to the EC, Peter Lilley, Economic Secretary to the Treasury, pointed out that the ruling arose from the 1977 directive, in which the exemptions were not time limited, and that Britain had no alternative but to comply. The European Court is the Court of last resort.

The Cockfield legacy: the logic of approximation

There is, in other words, a clear link—although one not stressed officially —between the various VAT directives which have so far introduced partial steps toward VAT harmonization and the full Cockfield vision, which is seen by the Commission as the logical consequence and fulfilment of earlier directives. The departure of Lord Cockfield and the advent of a new Commissioner for the period 1989–92 signals a change of tone, with VAT harmonization pursued in a less adversarial style. However, the basis of the policy remains the same. If Britain agreed to partial harmonization in 1977, the argument runs, why should it not agree to the end result?

To some extent, the Commission has the new EC law on its side. The Single European Act specifically provided for VAT harmonization as part of 1992. The full passage of Article 99 reads:

> The Council of Ministers shall, acting unanimously on a proposal from the Commission and after consulting the European Parliament, adopt provisions for the harmonization of legislation concerning turnover taxes, excise duties and other forms of indirect taxation to the extent that such harmonization is necessary to ensure the establishment and the functioning of the internal market within the time limit laid down.

The time limit referred to is 1992: the argument therefore revolves around the phrase 'to the extent that such harmonization is necessary to ensure the functioning of the internal market'. Senior British officials continue to argue that it is not necessary: senior Commission officials in Brussels maintain that it is. Britain is not alone in taking its stand. France has also expressed strong reservations about VAT harmonization, largely because the broad bands proposed by the Commission are too broad, and would leave French businesses vulnerable to lower VAT rates levied in neighbouring West Germany. Both France and West Germany fear that VAT harmonization will force national governments to reshape their fiscal policies because of single market considerations rather than because of priorities set by governments themselves. Martin Bangemann, the new

West German Commissioner and former Economics Minister, is on record as stating that full fiscal harmonization can only come about after 1992, rather than before, since only after 1992 will the full effects of free competition in a frontier-free market become apparent.

The market approach and the Scrivener proposals

In September 1988 EC finance ministers met on the island of Crete, under the Greek Presidency, for one more attempt to find a solution on fiscal frontiers. Nigel Lawson, Chancellor of the Exchequer, unveiled a British plan under which there would be gradual elimination of restrictions on cross-border shopping, retention of differing rates of excise duty on alcohol and tobacco, and a postponed accounting system for VAT to reduce frontier controls. Market forces, he argued, would bring VAT rates into line after 1992. This was given a cool reception, and most ministers supported the Commission proposals in principle, while insisting that they be made more flexible.

This has duly occurred, with Mme Scrivener taking a more flexible line than Lord Cockfield. Instead of the Cockfield 'two-band' idea, the Scrivener proposals, formulated in April 1989 and presented to EC finance ministers at S'Agaró in Spain in May, suggest a minimum VAT rate for most goods of 15%, while 'socially sensitive items' not likely to be traded in quantity across borders could be rated at between zero and 9%. This is a victory for Britain, although only a partial victory, since the list of basic items is 'very limited', in Mme Scrivener's words, and far narrower than Britain would have wished. The plan includes the encouragement of cross-border shopping in the run-up to 1992, and 'case-by-case' negotiations on excise harmonization rather than a single rate. Mme Scrivener said she had taken the 'market forces' argument into account, moving Lawson to remark that a British dogmatist (Cockfield) had been replaced by a French pragmatist. A reduced and simplified clearing-house mechanism for VAT repayments to states would still be set up, but special arrangements would be made for cars (VAT paid in the country of registration), mail order sales (the seller to bill VAT at the rate of the country in which the purchaser resides), special equipment and local authority buying.

Nonetheless, EC states are required under the new proposals to begin harmonizing taxes by 1992, and Mme Scrivener regards the principle of tax harmonization as 'totally unchanged'. At the back of Treasury minds is the fear that the Commission will not rest there, and that Brussels will revive a forgotten 1975 plan for co-ordinating direct as well as indirect taxation. The 1975 proposal envisaged an agreed EC-wide direct taxation band of between 45% and 55%, the logic being that if European economies are to be integrated the taxation of both companies and individuals within nations becomes an EC concern.

Before leaving office, Lord Cockfield said that plans for corporate taxes, including a common rate for company profits and dividends, were 'still in the formative stage'. Mme Scrivener, complaining of the tendency for intercompany links to develop 'more between the US and Europe than between European countries', has revived four long-neglected EC proposals for: avoiding double taxation of dividends paid by a subsidiary in one state to its parent company in another state; deferring tax on company assets in cross-frontier mergers; giving Brussels the power to arbitrate between national tax authorities in disputes over transfer pricing practices involving multinationals; and fiscal consolidation of multinationals' profits and losses.

Checklist of changes

- VAT becomes only a part of the EC's own resources, together with a proportion of GNP.
- An approximation of VAT rates into two broad bands is proposed.
- Exemptions may be made for Britain and other countries where harmonizing VAT may be politically sensitive.

12 TRAINS, BOATS AND PLANES
Transport and travel in the single market

Before publication of the Internal Market White Paper the prospects for any significant progress towards the liberalization of the Community's heavily regulated air transport, road haulage, shipping and rail network systems—not to mention the creation of a genuine common transport policy—seemed negligible. Transport policy (or, more precisely, the lack of it) had become the single greatest failure of the EC. The architects of the European Community attached so much importance to transport as a means of promoting European economic integration that it was given its own chapter in the Treaty of Rome. Yet 30 years after the creation of the EC the highly prized goal of a coherent Community-wide transport policy still remained confined to the ever-receding horizon, with member states pursuing independent (and often conflicting) transport policies, united solely by their scant regard for the interests of the Community as a whole.

The failure of member states to deal effectively with the difficult issues involved in laying the foundations for a more efficient Community transport system has exacted a heavy toll. Community governments, businesses, employees and consumers have all had to bear the costs of fragmented, inefficient, poorly planned, unnecessarily expensive and environmentally insensitive transportation systems, while frequently being unaware or indifferent to the consequences of their actions. On the rare occasions that the *status quo* has been challenged, governments have all too often responded with the indignant defence that 'the traffic does flow'. So it may, at least most of the time, and especially if one is not trying to leave Heathrow in July or August, driving to work in the morning rush hour or bringing an articulated lorry through Italian frontier controls. However, as the Commission has been arguing for decades:

> If one takes a closer look it becomes apparent just how inefficient the conditions are. They make transport more expensive and in many cases slow down the integration of the Community.

Writing in *European Affairs* in autumn 1988 Stanley Clinton Davis, the then European Commissioner for Transport Policy, asked whether one could envisage a common policy for the free movement of products, services and citizens without a corresponding policy for the transport systems which carried them. Yet paradoxically:

Road transport continued to be controlled by a complex system of licences effectively isolating each national market from its neighbours; civil aviation policy operated on a purely national basis designed to protect the national flag carrier against allcomers—sometimes offering better terms to American or Singaporean carriers than fellow Europeans—with a whole web of agreements between governments and airlines. Each member state had its own maritime policy, and the railway systems maintained the pattern of arm's length co-operation which had reached its peak in the nineteenth century.

Even before the internal market programme made a fresh attempt to create a common transport policy, a series of developments had emphasized to member states the growing urgency of abandoning shortsighted national protectionist policies and embarking on concerted action to solve the Community's increasingly acute transport problems. Following the example of deregulation of the US air transport industry (which resulted in considerable increases in efficiency, substantial decreases in air fares and a significant expansion of the number of passengers), its European counterpart began to face growing criticism—principally from consumer lobbies —demanding an end to the air transport cartel which had kept air travel prices at extortionate levels for the few who could afford to pay and far out of reach for most European citizens.

Almost simultaneously, the absurdity of member state road transport policies, which effectively cut the Community's road network into twelve incompatible segments, was highlighted by a series of expensive and time-consuming blockages at frontier crossings during the early part of the decade and discredited by the flourishing black market in cross-frontier permits needed to transport goods into other member states. Likewise, following the contraction of the European steel industry, the decline in consumption of coal and iron ore left Europe's merchant marine fleets in a state of chronic overcapacity. This problem was further exacerbated by the growing tendency of the centrally planned and developing countries to exclude Community fleets from their domestic trade. Member states were thus presented with little option other than to look to the European Commission to protect the interests of their shipping fleets in trade negotiations with the Community's trading partners around the world.

In 1984 the European Parliament initiated legal proceedings against the Council of Ministers in the European Court of Justice for its failure to carry out the provisions in the Treaty of Rome calling for the creation of a common transport policy. To the embarrassment of the governments of the member states, the Court found that the Council had been negligent in its duties, and ruled that its defence—namely, that it had proved too difficult to agree on a common policy—was completely unacceptable. The Council was now under a legal obligation to overcome such obstacles, a task greatly facilitated by the ratification of the Single European Act and the introduction of qualified majority voting.

In addition to symbolizing the end of Britain's physical isolation from Continental Europe, the decision to build the Channel Tunnel opens up the possibility of bringing new life to Europe's ailing rail networks. The construction of high-speed rail systems between Europe's capital cities would at last enable these networks to compete effectively with air travel in speed, cost and comfort, thereby offering a commercial opportunity for Europe's historically indebted rail transport systems and helping to relieve some of the pressures faced by the air transport sector in the process.

Finally, the growth of tourism in Europe over the past 20 years (particularly in Britain, where the advent of the package holiday has had a profound effect on popular attitudes to Continental Europe) has helped to break down many of the traditional prejudices held by the peoples of Europe against each other. In 1985 140 million Europeans took at least one holiday, and over 20% of this total went to another member state. Three out of every four Britons have now visited at least one Community country, suggesting that the old Victorian adage—'fog in the Channel, Continent cut off'—has long been obsolete. Furthermore, Europe's cultural diversity, natural wealth and rich historical heritage are likely to prove a powerful magnet for the continued expansion of tourism in the decades ahead.

These developments have helped to focus attention on the urgent reforms needed to develop the Community's transport system, which, after all, makes a greater contribution to Community GDP than agriculture and which provides employment for millions of workers either directly or through other key sectors heavily dependent on it, such as the car, aviation, shipbuilding, construction and steel industries. Consequently, although only half-way through the internal market programme, and with much remaining to be done, the Commission had already made a number of impressive breakthroughs which had eluded Community politicians for decades.

The air transport sector

Because governments exercise sovereignty over their own airspace in a way similar to that enjoyed over their physical territory, entry into a national airspace has to be authorized by its respective government. Few governments, however, are equipped to carry out this function, and so they allocate the task to their national carriers (most of which are state-owned), who are empowered to negotiate terms governing capacity, fares, landing and take-off rights with other national carriers—subject to approval of member state governments. Out of a desire for a comfortable life, and in an effort to guarantee themselves a stable income, national carriers have traditionally granted landing rights to one foreign carrier in return for reciprocal landing rights in its country of origin. The two airlines have then entered into negotiations about flight prices and schedules and confirmed the deal by dividing the income generated between them on a 50–50 basis.

This formula was duplicated with the national carriers of every other country, thereby creating a powerful cartel throughout the international air transport industry which ensured the least possible competition between national airlines. Air fares were thus determined by cosy mutual agreements which deprived any new airline wanting to compete on somebody else's route the right to gain access to the market. The result, especially after deregulation of the US air transport sector, was that a passenger seeking the cheapest flight from, for example, London to Madrid would have to go via New York. Just as the railway networks were the pride of states in the nineteenth century, so the national air carriers became the symbol of state virility in the twentieth, and governments were reluctant to sanction any liberalization that might jeopardize the viability of their own airlines.

Admittedly, charter airlines are now firmly established, but they have done little to promote price competition between scheduled airlines, who still cater almost exclusively for the business traveller. Confident that their position was unassailable, the Community's national carriers had little incentive to introduce any change. In 1974, however, the first breach in the air transport sector's protected market was made following a ruling by the European Court of Justice that civil aviation was not exempt from the competition provisions of the Treaty of Rome. This ruling was given added force in 1986 in a case brought by the French travel agency Nouvelles Frontières, in which the Court confirmed that the Community's competition rules applied to the skies.

A bilateral agreement between Britain and the Netherlands in 1984, which opened up the market for new carriers, resulted in the introduction of cheaper fares between London and Amsterdam, and a 10% increase in passengers almost overnight. Flag carriers were soon forced to follow suit, but the arrival of discount fares was invariably surrounded by innumerable restrictions in an attempt to limit their effect on flag carriers' standard prices. Discount fares were merely a small hole in the cartel's dyke, but they were, nonetheless, the first significant erosion of the industry's power to set prices independently of market forces.

The combination of the Court's rulings, the determination of the Commission to create an internal market for transport in the air as well as on the ground, the emergence of small independent carriers challenging the dominance of the established airlines and the relentless assault on the air transport cartel by European consumer groups had finally put the Community's air transport industry on the defensive. In an attempt to drive home its advantage, the Commission made a two-pronged assault on the air transport sector by trying to agree an air transport liberalization package in the Council of Ministers while simultaneously threatening legal action against the Community's national carriers under Article 85 of the Treaty, should the negotiations fail. Once the national carriers had backed down and had recognized the authority of the Commission to enforce the competition rules, attention turned to the discussions between member states over price fixing, capacity and revenue sharing, in anticipation of the long-awaited arrival of the age of cheap air fares for millions of European travellers.

However, despite the furore raised by the airline companies, the changes demanded by the Commission could hardly be described as revolutionary. The main elements of the package provided for the abolition of the clauses in their bilateral agreements which formed the cornerstone of the air transport cartel (the so-called 50–50 deals), guaranteeing flag carriers only 45% of capacity for a two-year period, falling to 40% in the third year. It also sought to establish freedom of entry for new carriers on major routes, and to open up services between major hub and regional airports, and the introduction of discounts of up to 45% on normal economy class fares subject to certain restrictions. The proposals were very different from the creation of a European air space and the dismantling of the principle of bilateralism upon which the air transport cartel rested.

Consumer organizations, sceptical that acceptance of the package would lead to any significant reform of the structure of the European air transport industry, warned of a possible sell-out, and demanded that the Commission avail itself of the power conferred on it by the Community's competition rules. The Brussels-based consumer organization, BEUC, a consortium of consumer groups drawn from all over the Community, warned that: 'Whilst the gradual spread of lower fares continues, the resistance to any real change by the majority of scheduled airlines has now become so apparent that a satisfactory outcome in the Transport Council, without Commission and Court action, is impossible.' BEUC insisted that only the unimpeded freedom of new airlines to compete with established operators would open up the air transport sector to the rigours of competition, and demanded the full application of the Treaty's competition rules in place of the proposed 'watered-down agreement' being tabled by the Commission.

As member states gathered in Luxembourg in June 1987 for a crucial transport ministers' meeting the Commission was confident that the air transport liberalization package would finally get their approval. It acknowledged that its proposals were modest, and that the airlines would need time to adjust to a new competitive environment, but maintained that acceptance of the package would be a major first step along the road to more substantive reform.

However, just as the member states were about to put their signatures to the historic agreement an unexpected diplomatic row between Britain and Spain over whether Gibraltar Airport should be included in the package delayed the deal for months. Because the majority voting provisions of the Single European Act did not come into effect until 1 July, Spain was able to exercise a veto over the package. Señor Jesus Ezquerra, the Spanish minister responsible for conducting the negotiations with Britain over the status of Gibraltar, maintained that the land on which Gibraltar Airport was built was not ceded to Britain under the 1713 Treaty of Utrecht.

Portraying Britain as a neocolonialist power refusing to give up the ill-gotten gains of centuries past, Ezquerra insisted that Madrid could not sign an agreement covering Gibraltar without enshrining its present status in Community law, and demanded that Gibraltar be excluded from the deal. British ministers, infuriated at Ezquerra's decision to introduce a long-running bilateral dispute into a Community context, emphasized that Madrid had already accepted Gibraltar's status when it ratified Spain's accession agreement, and, for good measure, discreetly drew attention to Spain's Moroccan enclaves, Ceuta and Melilla, to demonstrate that one former colonial power was at least as bad as the next. However, Ezquerra could not be appeased, the deadline expired and the Commission was forced to redraft its proposals and present them to the European Parliament and the Council of Ministers, as required under the new procedures of the Single European Act. Only the consumers' organizations, which regarded the package as a betrayal of consumer interests in any case, had a kind word for Ezquerra.

When the package came up again for approval in December 1987 Ezquerra failed to put in an appearance, and the deal finally went through. Its provisions were more or less identical to those on the table in June, covering air fares, capacity sharing and market access, and the application of the competition rules to the air transport sector. Only services between member states were subject to the deal, while the application of the competition rules was limited to scheduled airlines alone. The package was the first effective inroad into the power of member states to control their scheduled airlines and introduced competition into what Commissioner Sutherland had once described as 'the most uniquely anti-competitive cartel in Europe'.

As of 1 January 1988, a common bilateral procedure for the approval of discount and deep discount fares became effective throughout the Community and a timetable established for the phasing out of capacity-sharing arrangements between the major airlines. Under the present timetable national carriers will be entitled to only 40% of route capacity by October 1989, and the Commission hopes that even this protection will be abolished by the 1992 deadline. Routes between most major hub and regional airports have been opened up, and procedures for applying Articles 85 and 86 to the air transport sector have also been established.

However, it is clear that the major airlines still regard the prospect of across-the-board lower fares as anathema. Despite the adverse effect of the lower fares charged by some of the smaller airlines on flag carrier profits, few have been forced to fundamentally overhaul their price structures. Indeed, most have done their utmost to resist reducing prices by trying to attract customers, especially business executives, with greater comfort and style. As Sir Colin Marshall, the chief executive of British Airways, said in an interview with *The Times* in October 1988: 'We are in business to make money. Low fares are available—at the back of the aircraft.' But greater competition in the post-1992 era could force many companies to trim their generous travel budgets, adding considerably to the downward pressure on prices.

As an indication of the Commission's determination to introduce greater competition in the air transport sector, the Belgian national carrier, Sabena, was fined £65,000 in November 1988 for refusing to give the Irish-owned air liner, Ryanair, access to its computer reservation system because the Dublin-based company was offering cut-price flights. The Commission's action followed a dawn raid on Sabena's headquarters the previous year, and was the first occasion on which the Community had exercised its new powers against an airline involved in anti-competitive behaviour.

As Community citizens were anxiously awaiting the arrival of the age of cheap air travel the Association of European Airlines (AEA), which represents 21 airlines responsible for approximately 90% of Europe's air traffic, began to issue a series of warnings about the shortcomings of the internal market programme. At its annual conference in Paris in April 1988 Karl-Heinz Neumeister, the Secretary General of the AEA, warned that the Commission's fiscal harmonization proposals would be a step backwards for the air transport industry. Once the internal market programme is completed, all intra-Community flights will be classified as domestic and therefore subject to VAT. However, Neumeister pointed out that the possibility of different rates within the lower 4–9% VAT band between member states would actually be a step away from a perfectly harmonized market, currently at 0%. Consequently, there was a need to maintain the zero rate or at least introduce a single rate throughout the Community.

Furthermore, Neumeister predicted that the abolition of internal frontier controls would require the expansion of the domestic sections of airports, while the introduction of new routes and more flights was likely to lead to a considerable expansion in demand, and yet few governments were planning to increase existing airport and runway handling capacity. Perhaps most important of all, the Secretary General drew attention to a major anomaly in the internal market programme which allowed member states to continue exercising sovereignty over their own air space (effectively fragmenting Europe's air space into twelve segments), a situation which was widely regarded as the major cause of the delays experienced by air travellers in the summer of 1988. In 1987 air traffic movements were already at levels forecast for 1991, and Neumeister predicted that the situation would only get worse until the member states overcame their traditional reluctance to relax control over their own air space:

> We would like to see an integrated European air traffic control system with co-ordinated plans, and at least working with the same standards. Perhaps we should give Eurocontrol the task it was originally designed to have: to co-ordinate and control the air traffic flows in Europe. Are we going to have the single market on the ground and still divide the skies?

In July 1988 the European Parliament accepted Neumeister's challenge by calling for the merging of Europe's air traffic control systems into a single Community network, under the authority of the Netherlands-based organization, Eurocontrol, which is already responsible for monitoring and predicting daily air traffic flows. Unfortunately, there was little to suggest that member states are prepared to accept the one remedy for freeing the Community's congested skies. Then in September, Paul Channon, the Secretary of State for Transport, gave the first indication that Britain was seriously considering the creation of a central unit responsible for flight planning in Europe. The issue was discussed by EC transport ministers meeting in Frankfurt in November, when the Commission formally proposed to member states that they create a single European air traffic control system based on Eurocontrol. By July the following year, when tens of thousands of tourists again faced lengthy delays at British airports, Community Transport Ministers agreed to a £40 million scheme setting up a centralized airflow management system based at Eurocontrol. However, while the new system will undoubtedly help to reduce departure delays, it is unlikely to be fully operational before 1992.

Meanwhile, the European Court of Justice had ruled the previous April that virtually all air fare price-fixing arrangements could be in violation of Community competition rules. Encouraged by a ruling which indicated that price-fixing arrangements on routes within member states (as well as those to non-Community destinations) were possibly illegal, the Commission announced three months later its intention to press ahead with phase two of the air-transport liberalization programme. The plan is based on an attempt to prevent member states from vetoing cut-price air fares proposed by airlines, and once implemented, should result in a considerable reduction in the cost of air travel around the Community.

Road transport and coastal trade

One of the most pervasive barriers to free trade in the Community is the technically illegal system of bilateral licences governing the European road haulage industry. Road haulage companies obtain the right of access to the roads of other member states on the basis of a licence obtained from its national department of transport. These, in turn, are arranged through a series of annual bilateral negotiations between member states, which determine the number of licences that are to be made available. In 1986, for example, West Germany granted 91,000 licences to Italian road haulage companies, while Italy granted 145,000 licences to West German ones. But the system has long been denounced, principally by Britain, as iniquitous, inefficient and one which protects the interests of the larger member states at the expense of their smaller neighbours.

Road haulage, which accounts for about £322 billion of intra-Community trade, is by far the most important artery along which trade between member states flows, and it is long overdue for reform. However, the Commission's proposals to create an internal market for road haulage were regarded by West Germany as a serious threat to its own heavily protected industry. The politically powerful West German road haulage lobby, fearful that much of its road haulage trade would slip away to its more efficient Dutch and Belgian competitors, adamantly opposed any liberalization before progress had been made on harmonizing the industry's operating conditions, notably lorry and fuel taxes and drivers' terms of employment.

Under pressure of legal action from the Commission, and a persistent refusal by Britain to accept anything less than the complete implementation of the Commission's liberalization proposals, the West Germans finally conceded at the Transport Council in Luxembourg in June 1988. The deal, which was widely seen as a major breakthrough for the internal market programme, committed member states to the complete abolition of quotas to Community and non-Community destinations by 1 January 1993, and required the Commission to specify the harmonization measures needed to ensure fair competition among road haulage companies by June 1991.

By the time the quota system is abolished, Community road haulage companies will be able to avail themselves of the freedom to make as many journeys as they like, anywhere in the Community. Far from increasing the number of articulated lorries on Europe's roads, the internal market in road haulage will automatically lead to a reduction of the number of empty lorries (estimated by the Commission to be around one in three), due to existing restrictions on trade conducted in other member states. Despite attempts by British road hauliers to obtain government approval for an end to the derogation which imposes a 38-tonne limit on lorries on British roads by 1992 (thus bringing them into line with the 40-tonne ceiling enforced in other member states), Paul Channon managed to retain the derogation until 31 December 1998, on the grounds that the government's bridge-strengthening programme would not be completed until that date.

Britain has, however, been less successful in convincing its partners of the need to abolish restrictions on Community ships trading along each other's coastlines. Britain, Ireland, Belgium and the Netherlands are the only countries that grant foreign vessels the unrestricted right to pick up and deliver loads between ports on their coastlines, known as coastal cabotage. Most of the Southern European states, fearful of increased competition, continue to reserve coastal trade for domestic shipping. If progress is not forthcoming Britain is likely to implement those provisions of the 1988 Merchant Shipping Act which grant it the power to demand reciprocal treatment.

Railways and the Channel Tunnel

The agreement between Mrs Thatcher and President François Mitterrand in 1987 to grant approval for the construction of a privately financed fixed link between Britain and France symbolized the end of Britain's physical isolation from the European mainland. More importantly, the Channel Tunnel (being built by Eurotunnel, and a consortium of British and French construction companies) and the decision to build a high-speed rail network linking London, Paris, Brussels, Amsterdam and Cologne will give Europe's ailing rail networks a much-needed opportunity to compete effectively with the air transport sector. Both projects should be completed shortly after 1992, enabling business executives and tourists to travel from London to Paris in 155 minutes and from London to Brussels in 178. BR is also expected to announce plans for so-called 'through services' from Paris and Brussels, via the Channel Tunnel, to Scotland and the regions. The new trains are expected to run on the existing east and west coast routes, providing services between London and Rugby, where the trains will divide for Birmingham and Manchester, and between London and Peterborough, before dividing for Leeds and Edinburgh. Yet while its Community partners are preparing to treat all travellers as domestic, Britain appears to be set on maintaining frontier controls, effectively depriving travellers of the substantial time savings gained by the investment of billions of pounds in the new transport infrastructure.

Plans are already well advanced for the construction of a £15 million frontier control facility at Waterloo Station, in defiance of the commitment under the Single European Act to create 'an area without internal frontiers'. Community nationals disembarking at London will be required to go through the traditional frontier control formalities, while coaches coming off the rail-only terminal outside Ashford in Kent will be emptied and their passengers and baggage examined. James Elles, MEP for Oxford and Buckinghamshire, described passing through the port of Dover as similar to going through an 'Eastern European border post', and asked why simplified procedures for the 'green channel', used at Heathrow and Gatwick airports, were not in operation at major ports—a situation which has only recently been rectified. Moreover, the Home Office is demanding that trains travelling beyond Waterloo devote about 10% of their capacity to frontier officials, who insist that they need the room to conduct baggage inspections and interview suspected terrorists, drug traffickers and illegal immigrants.

Some critics fear that Britain's refusal to dismantle internal frontiers could put between 30 and 45 minutes onto the time it takes to complete the train journey under the Channel, thereby eliminating one of the few competitive advantages surface transport has over air travel. The Home Office maintains, however, that checks will be efficient and streamlined, and that the delay to passengers will be minimal, and possibly 'even quicker than at airports'. However, business executives and tourists, already enthusiastic about the prospects for trouble-free travel in the internal market, are unlikely to accept government policy without protest.

But while Britain tries to adjust to the advent of the Channel Tunnel rail services, the European Commission is preparing the foundation of a European railway system for the 21st century. In November 1989, Karl van Miert, European Transport Commissioner, unveiled proposals for a radical restructuring of the European Community's national railway organizations, in an effort to break up existing monopolies, expand international passenger and freight services, and promote the construction of a transcontinental high-speed rail network.

Travel and tourism

Tourism now accounts for almost 5% of the Community's gross domestic product, is responsible for some 5.5 million jobs and is expanding constantly. An estimated 75% of Britons have visited at least one Community country, while the average Briton has visited 3.5 member states. The Community has spent millions of pounds developing a tourist infrastructure (holiday villages, pleasure harbours, ski-lifts and hotels) through the regional development funds and the European Investment Bank in an attempt to provide new employment opportunities and relieve some of the congestion in the more popular and overdeveloped resorts.

The Commission has also attempted to make life easier for tourists by introducing the Community passport, and producing brochures giving detailed information on existing border-crossing formalities, duty-free allowances and the availability of health care. Further publications listing places of interest such as museums and art galleries are in preparation, as are plans to produce a standardized classification of Community hotels (priced in ECUs) and a directive regulating the package holiday industry.

By 1992 millions of travellers and holidaymakers will be deprived of their duty-free allowances (now regarded as the legitimate booty of foreign travel) if the Commission's proposals on fiscal approximation are implemented. Yet the abolition of duty-frees is unlikely to be the unmitigated disaster predicted by the pro-duty-free lobby. Admittedly, Community-wide duty-free sales are estimated to be worth about £2 billion a year, and their demise, only as far as intra-Community travel is concerned, will have a significant impact on the revenues of short-haul ferries, charter airlines and regional airports.

However, everyone involved in the duty-free industry accepts that abolition is merely a question of time, and are already planning ways of compensating themselves for lost revenues. British ferry companies are planning to introduce a new generation of floating department stores for cross-Channel shoppers. Built from modified roll-on–roll-off ferries, the offshore superstores are likely to make extensive use of franchises, similar to those already in operation at most Community airports, to sell a wide selection of discount consumer products.

James Hannah, Sealink British Ferries' corporate communications director, is convinced that there are great opportunities for skilful marketing to a captive audience. Pointing to the success of franchising operations at airports, Hannah said that:

> Dublin Airport, for example, is now selling more black silk lingerie than many major High Street stores. It's quite a phenomenon. I suspect it's the only chance businessmen get to buy their wives a gift.

These sentiments are also shared by Graeme Dunlop, managing director of P&O European Ferries, who told *The Times* in an interview in June 1988:

> We are making our plans now on the assumption that the European internal market will be a reality in 1992. If we are going to survive, it's the only prudent course to take.

Despite the generally optimistic prospects for the European tourist industry, greater mobility throughout the Community has brought with it the serious and growing problems of hooliganism and drunken rowdiness. These are by no means confined to British tourists, although the reputation is. During her visit to Spain in September 1988 Mrs Thatcher felt compelled to apologize to Felipe Gonzalez, the Spanish Prime Minister, for the behaviour of the small minority of British holidaymakers who have been responsible for disfiguring many Spanish resorts in recent years. Mrs Thatcher made it clear, however, that the Spanish authorities had her personal support in taking severe action against the troublemakers. It may eventually be necessary to consider a Community initiative designed to temporarily deprive those Community nationals unable to behave responsibly in other member states of the right to travel in the internal market, perhaps through the issue of EC identity cards, withdrawable in the event of damage or nuisance to property or persons.

Checklist of changes
- The European Commission's determination to create an internal market for air transport will further erode the restrictive practices of the European air transport industry.

- There will be increased freedom of entry for independent air carriers on major European air routes.
- Services between major and regional airports will be progressively increased.
- National carriers seeking to restrict competition from the new independent carriers will find themselves subject to substantial fines imposed by the Commission for violating the Community's competition rules.
- The availability of discount fares can be expected to multiply as a result of increased competition from the new independent carriers.
- In an effort to ease the congestion in Europe's crowded skies, pressure for a single integrated European air traffic control system will result in the creation of a central unit responsible for flight planning in Europe.
- There will be an internal market for road haulage following the abolition of the system of national quotas for the road haulage industry.
- European road haulage companies will have complete freedom of destination within the Community.
- Coastal trade will also be opened up to free competition.
- Duty-free allowances for travellers will come to an end following the harmonization of member states' varying rates of indirect taxation.

13 TELEVISION WITHOUT FRONTIERS

Broadcasting and satellite technology in 1992

Of all the internal market directives contained in the White Paper pro-
ramme, few have aroused as much passion as the European Commission's efforts to create a single market for satellite broadcasting without
frontiers. Supporters of the Commission's unprecedented entry into the
television broadcasting sector have characterized the initiative (in imagery
similar to that used in Hollywood's portrayal of the last days of General
Custer) as Europe's heroic last stand against the twin assault of American
cultural imperialism and Japanese technological dominance, and the only
real hope of saving Europe's ailing cinema film and electronics industries
from extinction.

This vision of the Community's predicament is not shared by everyone. Some member states, principally Britain, Denmark and West Germany, have, from the outset, insisted that there was no compelling case for
Community legislation in the field of satellite broadcasting and have
challenged the competence of the Commission to legislate on cultural
matters. Many of the new English-language satellite companies have
endorsed the Commission's broad objectives, but are deeply opposed to
the way in which it has set about putting them into practice. Finally, over
the past few years there have been many prophets of doom, predicting
that the age of satellite broadcasting will destroy civilization as we know it
by submerging national values and culture in a tidal wave of smut,
pornography, gratuitous violence, low-budget soap operas and game
shows, manipulative advertising and, to cap it all, US-style television
evangelists.

Passion aside, the Community is confronted by a series of wide-
ranging changes in the audiovisual sector which it can do nothing to
prevent. The rapid pace of technological change in the field of telecommunications has already conferred on satellite broadcasters the ability to
ignore national boundaries and reach audiences of continental proportions. The so-called 'footprint' of satellite transmissions cannot be held
up at national border controls for inspection by customs officers before
being granted or refused permission to enter.

However, because of the great variation in national regulations governing television broadcasts, particularly on advertising, programming
and public morality, the technical ability of the new satellite companies to
reach large numbers of people is constrained by their legal obligation to

respect the differing regulations of the various member states. Unless satellite broadcasters comply with national regulations, the cable companies who relay the satellite transmissions into our homes can be effectively prohibited from doing so. Even in the case of direct broadcasting by satellite (where viewers can pick up transmissions themselves after installing the necessary receiving equipment) the member states are capable of preventing transmissions which violate national law through the Community's legal system and, theoretically, by the use of sophisticated jamming techniques.

If the extraterrestrial technological advances are not to be stillborn as a result of divergent terrestrial regulations, twelve national systems must be replaced by one set of common rules governing satellite broadcasting. Addressing the Independent Broadcasting Authority on the sensitive question of advertising regulations in April 1985, Dr Ivo Schwartz, the Commission official responsible for overseeing the Community's satellite broadcasting initiative, said:

> Given the reality of communication satellites and continental wide cable television, as well as the imminence of direct broadcasting by satellite, the Commission believes that it is essential to institute as quickly as possible a minimum of rules for European advertising within which the providers of commercially supported programmes may freely operate. Such limited approximation will make it possible that from then on, only the rules of the country of transmission shall apply to cross-border advertisements.

The same principle would also be applied to the European content of programming schedules, public morality and the protection of minors.

However, the Commission maintains that the audiovisual challenge faced by the Community goes far beyond the mere legal mechanics of creating a single unified market for satellite broadcasting. Europe is also confronted by a series of cultural, scientific, technical, industrial and commercial challenges, in which the United States and Japan clearly have the advantage. The Commission has forecast that somewhere in the region of 200 new satellite channels could be available by the 1990s. The very rapid growth in the number of broadcasting hours available is already beginning to generate an almost insatiable demand for new programming material, which European countries are unable to satisfy at competitive prices. Similarly, the expansion of satellite broadcasting has already begun to create new markets for transmission equipment and potential mass markets for receiving equipment. These new markets could provide a great stimulus to Europe's electronics industry, creating thousands of new jobs in the process. However, many EC and national officials fear that, unless the Community is able to respond to these challenges, the benefits of a single market for satellite broadcasting will be enjoyed only by film studios in Hollywood and consumer electronics companies in Tokyo.

Television without frontiers

The challenge to the Community's competence to legislate in the field of satellite broadcasting was effectively undermined following the adoption by all member states of the Internal Market White Paper, which made explicit reference to the need to create an internal market for cross-frontier television broadcasting. Furthermore, the Commission was able to point to its obligation under Article 3 of the Treaty of Rome, requiring it to approximate national laws 'to the extent required for the proper functioning of the common market', and Articles 59–62, which prohibit member states from exercising their supervisory powers to restrict trade in goods and services on a discriminatory basis. As 'services' include television broadcasting, these articles collectively confer on the Commission the authority to propose legislation regulating satellite broadcasting between member states.

They also provide the legal basis on which the satellite broadcasters themselves, even in defiance of the wishes of national governments, can demand access to audiences throughout the Community. However, member states retain the legal right to impose non-discriminatory restrictions on foreign and domestic broadcasters in the interests of public policy, security and health, or because of the need to protect copyright, until such times as the various national laws had been harmonized. As a result, by the time the satellite broadcasters had acquired the technical ability to reach European-wide audiences it was not only incumbent on the Commission to provide the necessary regulatory framework for them to do so but had also become a race against time to put this framework in place before or shortly after the satellite stations were operational.

The urgency of this task was emphasized by the collapse of Europa-TV in November 1986. A group of networks from five member states had combined in an attempt to launch the first public broadcasting service as an alternative to the growing number of private, commercial stations. Using the latest technology for dubbing and subtitling, Europa-TV transmitted multilingual broadcasts to some 5 million homes in the Community. But after running up debts in excess of £25 million, the Netherlands pulled out, and the initiative came to a halt. According to the testimony given by a Commission official to the House of Lords Select Committee on the European Communities in 1987:

> Europa-TV faced formidable difficulties obtaining access to existing cable networks because of conflicting advertising regulations in West Germany, Belgium, Ireland, Denmark and even in its host country the Netherlands. It failed because it could not generate sufficient advertising revenues.

Following publication of the Commission's 1984 Green Paper on television without frontiers and extensive consultations with member states (including the various professions involved in the television industry), the Commission tabled a draft directive on satellite broadcasting in June 1986, later revised in March 1988. Behind the proposed legislation lay the conviction that the Community was more than merely an organization of states; it was also a union of peoples. The emergence of cross-frontier television broadcasting would reinforce the creation of the internal market by providing companies with access to a single market of 320 million consumers through satellite advertising. However, it also contained the rather visionary notion that new communications satellites would also provide the means by which the peoples of Europe would become more familiar with each other as a result of exposure to their different television cultures, thereby reinforcing (or, perhaps more realistically, at least making people aware in the first place) that they shared a common economic and cultural identity.

The directive is designed to enable satellite broadcasters to transmit programmes anywhere in the Community without restriction or interference from other member states provided that they meet certain minimum requirements governing the European content of programming, the organization of advertising breaks, copyright protection, public morality and the protection of minors. The directive also applies to ground-based broadcasters if their transmissions can be received in neighbouring member states. Lord Cockfield attached particular importance to the directive, regarding it as the 'flagship' of the entire internal market programme, and called for prompt action by the member states to implement the proposal which was already a year behind schedule. However, the draft legislation met with bitter opposition when ministers first discussed it in March 1988. From the outset, Britain had objected vigorously to any attempt to introduce programme quotas. Ministers made no secret of their conviction that the proposal was one of the most élitist and paternalistic documents ever produced by the Commission. It was denounced as an example of 'European cultural imperialism', and Britain felt that it had no alternative but to put all its hopes for a more liberal satellite broadcasting system on the rival convention being drawn up by the 21-member Council of Europe in Strasbourg.

Quotas, advertisements and copyright

Within three years of the March proposal being adopted, all satellite broadcasters would have been required to reserve at least 60% of their air time for feature films made in the Community or in association with members of EFTA and the Council of Europe. The proposal has nothing to do with abolishing barriers to the free movement of television across frontiers. In fact, it purposely sets out to achieve the exact opposite. Its overriding objective is to stimulate the European film industry by protecting it from foreign competition and providing it with a guaranteed part of the European market. The Commission maintains that such action is necessary because:

> Frequent warnings are heard about the dangers of the cultural domination of one country by another in motion pictures, although this is not a problem between member states. As for the production of television programmes within the Community, no individual member states are predominant. Statistics on the films broadcast on television in member states show that the proportion of films from other member states is regrettably small. However, most of the films shown come from a single non-member country, the US.

The main source of such warnings are the French and Italian film industries, who are already facing difficult times and fear that they would have to close if they were forced to compete with their American counterparts. Writing in the spring 1988 edition of *European Affairs*, Jack Lang, the National Secretary for Culture and Youth in the French Socialist Party, while paying tribute to the achievements of the American film industry attacked the view expressed by Britain that the new satellite broadcasting companies should be allowed to decide for themselves what proportion of their broadcast material came from within or outside the Community. Lang insisted that:

> At a time when Europe, the cradle of Western civilization, loses control over one of the main areas in which contemporary culture is being made, the audiovisual, one can no longer react aesthetically to such liberal or ultra-liberal ideologies. Reality demands that concrete steps be taken as quickly as possible.

By which he meant quotas.

In defence of the proposal, Lord Cockfield maintained that the quota plan was not so much anti-American as pro-European. Commission officials, however, acknowledge that the 60% quota would present severe difficulties for specialized film channels, and have indicated that a limited number of derogations or exemptions could be incorporated into the directive. However, such concessions have done little to allay the anxieties of satellite and ground-based broadcasters, who fear that the Commission is asking them to drink a cup of hemlock in the name of the defence of European culture.

In 1987, for example, the BBC screened 709 feature films, of which 409 were made in the United States. Both Sky Channel, owned by Rupert Murdoch, and SuperChannel, now owned by Richard Branson in association with an Italian company, are also heavily dependent on US feature films. The same applies to every other English-language satellite station planning to launch new stations, even the non-English-language ones showing dubbed or subtitled US films. Whatever the critics of the US film industry may say, American feature films are extremely popular all over Europe, and the attempt to restrict them to 40% of the European market would deprive the new satellite stations of the large-scale audiences and advertising revenues needed to make them economically viable. After all, what one cannot see on television one can usually pick up in a High Street video shop.

The Commission argues that Britain's opposition to the quota plan is dogmatic, and points out that the Independent Broadcasting Authority (IBA) already accepts the principle of quotas by requiring 86% of all programmes on ITV and Channel 4 to come from Community sources. However, Britain insists that this is a regulation enforced by the IBA, and apart from specifying that a 'proper proportion' of all broadcast material should be Community sourced, broadcasters should be free from government or Commission interference to decide what that level should be. The problem faced by the Commission, however, is that it is not self-evident what a proper proportion means. Twelve member states would produce twelve different definitions, effectively creating a new barrier to satellite broadcasting across frontiers. At the same time, no amount of compulsory screening will make European-made films any more popular.

The Commission's proposed regulations on satellite advertising have received a considerably less hostile reception from most member states. The directive establishes a maximum threshold of 15% a day or 18% an hour of total programming time which can be allocated to broadcast advertising. Any station transmitting above these thresholds can be prohibited by the member states. Governments retain the right to impose more stringent conditions on domestic broadcasters serving national audiences if they so wish. The directive no longer requires broadcasters to group advertisements at the end of programmes, as required in the 1986 version. Under the terms of the revised directive they are granted the option of broadcasting commercial breaks in concentrated blocks or periodic slots, provided that the 'integrity' of programmes is maintained and as long as programmes are not interrupted excessively. Advertisements must not fall below prevailing standards of decency or exploit the immaturity of minors.

Britain seems to be quite content with the directive's provisions on broadcast advertising, in contrast to those incorporated into the Council of Europe's convention on satellite broadcasting. The government had originally agreed with the convention, primarily because of its opposition to the Community's proposed quotas and in the hope that it would prove to be a more liberal regulatory system. However, to the consternation of Downing Street, the West Germans, urged on by domestic press barons who do not want to see their advertising revenues jeopardized by competition from the new satellite television stations, were able to insert into the draft convention a provision requiring satellite broadcasters to bunch commercial breaks in a 'block' at the end of programmes. Consternation turned to exasperation in the summer of 1988, when the West Germans, without success, tried to have the same restrictions that were incorporated into the draft convention also applied to the draft directive.

Britain, as well as the other member states opposing this provision, is not obliged to sign or ratify the Council's convention. Yet too many refusals to sign undermine the entire purpose of the agreement, as individual member states would be forced to embark on bilateral negotiations with their European neighbours. Long before the convention was due to be ratified in November 1988 it was clear that the proposal was deadlocked.

Although ministers were unable to reach a consensus on the convention, at the Stockholm meeting there was a considerable narrowing of the differences of opinion between Britain and West Germany on advertising breaks. Britain appeared ready to accept that 'serious' programmes should not be interrupted more than once every 45 minutes, while West Germany seemed content with allowing more frequent advertising breaks for less serious programmes. Nevertheless, France still expressed grave reservations about allowing too much imported US broadcast material into the Community, and seemed to be determined to hold out for a quota of at least 50% of all programmes broadcast to be of Community origin. With agreement still out of reach, ratification was postponed until June 1989. The Commission, however, saw the impasse over the convention as an opportunity to rewrite their own draft directive and regain the initiative in the rivalry between the two organizations to create Europe's satellite broadcasting system for the twenty-first century.

In the summer of 1988 Commission officials let it be known that a plan to split the draft directive in two was being given serious consideration. The scheme would enable the Commission to deal separately with the issues of programme quotas and advertising regulations. If accepted, it would mean that the Commission could press ahead with issuing a directive on satellite broadcast advertising for an industry whose development was outstripping the ability of Community and national legislators to regulate it, while allowing the vexed issue of programme quotas to be given a reduced priority for EC Cultural Affairs Ministers to sort out at their leisure. However, officials realized that the major obstacle in the way of the proposal would be the objections of France and Italy, who appeared to remain adamant over their demand for Community quotas.

Gradually, however, it began to occur to the French authorities that quotas and advertising restrictions could mean the end of the new satellite companies. If broadcasters could not transmit the kind of material likely to attract mass audiences, and if restrictive advertising regulations forced the advertisers to seek other outlets, then there would be no new satellite stations, and certainly no new money with which to stimulate the output of the ailing European film and audiovisual industry. In February 1989, EC trade ministers (taking their cue from the Rhodes summit meeting) managed to agree on a compromise on the controversial issue of quotas, allowing satellite broadcasters to transmit a 'majority' of European-made programmes 'where practical', thereby eliminating Britain's objection to the imposition of legally enforceable quotas. Unfortunately, the compromise began to unravel in June, due to last-minute reservations by Paris. The issue fell to France to resolve during its Presidency of the Council of Ministers.

In October, during a ministerial meeting in Luxembourg, the seemingly interminable wrangle of cross-frontier broadcasting regulations was finally laid to rest. On a majority vote, the ministers agreed to the 50 per cent European programming restriction, and at the same time accepted that legal imposition of the quota was a 'political' measure, and thus legally unenforceable. Welcoming the agreement, Richard Dunn, chairman of the ITV Association said: 'ITV does not believe the directive will have a detrimental effect on our current practices in terms of advertising, programme content, and origin. We can certainly live with it.' The US, however, immediately expressed its hostility to the measure, and announced its intention to bring the issue before the disputes panel of the General Agreement on Tariffs and Trade.

The Commission believes that the existing system of copyright protection is also a potential barrier to the free movement of programmes across frontiers, and wants to replace it with one that allows satellite and cable companies to broadcast or retransmit any programme after two years, while ensuring adequate remuneration for copyright holders. The Commission argues that once a programme has been placed in the public domain in one member state, copyright regulations should not be used as a method of preventing it from circulating around the other member states. According to one Commission official: 'Once you have taken the fundamental decision to market your service, you cannot rely on national frontiers—in this case through intellectual property rights—to divide the market.'

The system would operate on the basis of voluntary contractual agreements between the copyright owners and broadcasters, sponsored by the individual member states. Broadcasters would have an automatic right to a licence on the copyright if terms could not be agreed within the two-year period. However, anyone broadcasting a programme before the two-year period had expired, or with the intention of depriving the copyright holders of their legitimate remuneration, would be liable to court action in the appropriate member state. The Commission acknowledges that without a system for providing authors, performers and copyright holders with equitable remuneration there would be a detrimental effect on the very industry responsible for generating the programmes needed to fill the new programme schedules. Consequently, copyright must be adapted to reflect the needs of the modern audiovisual age. Britain, however, has opposed the initiative on the grounds that copyright cannot be considered a barrier to trade.

Quantity versus quality

If the Commission's estimates are realized and there are some 200 new television stations by the 1990s what will they be broadcasting into our homes? Not enough new material is being produced to fill the existing satellite stations' schedules with new programmes, and many critics fear that an excessive proportion of what we get when the new stations are operational we will probably have seen already, and much of the remainder will be cheap imported soap operas, game shows and serials from the United States, which we will not want to watch in any case. Many fear that the age of satellite telecommunications will represent a giant step forwards for technology, matched only by a giant step backwards for culture. Fearing the worst, they have predicted the end of the expensive quality programmes like *The World At War*, *Upstairs Downstairs* and the various wildlife documentaries, and because of the competition for advertising revenue, broadcasters will be compelled to fill their air time with popular and inexpensive off-the-shelf reruns of programmes like *Blankety-Blank*, *Dallas* and *Chips*. In short, satellite broadcasting will become little more than 'chewing gum for the eyes', and will probably turn us all into vegetables.

It is precisely this anxiety that has prompted the Commission to advocate the introduction of quotas in an effort to stimulate the European film and audiovisual products industry. Having created a single audiovisual market, the Commission wants to have sufficient European products to fill it with, and 'ensure that the new televisual media continue to reflect the Community's cultural diversity and richness, and that the large market does not simply operate to encourage a search for the audiovisual lowest common denominator'. However, there is no guarantee that the Commission's attempts to provide a stimulus for Europe's film and programme makers will prove successful. The French have never shown much of a liking for West German serials, Holland is only going to have a very limited interest in Portugal's news and Britain is unlikely to get too enthusiastic about Greek game shows. Even if some magic formula was found that overcame such national dispositions, it would be many years before there was sufficient material to satisfy the needs of the proliferating satellite television stations.

However, the experience of satellite broadcasting to date, while hardly a triumph, is far from being the unmitigated disaster the pessimists had predicted. Admittedly, the launch of SuperChannel was greeted with almost universally poor reviews, and the lack of late-night advertising forced it to reduce its transmissions from 24 to 20 hours a day. During the summer of 1988 most of its programme schedules were made up of old ITV–BBC reruns like *Some Mothers Do 'ave 'em*, *The Professionals* and *Spitting*

Image. However, it has also shown some of the great classics of television from the 1950s like *The Twilight Zone*, while its nightly 30-minute European news broadcast (now, sadly abandoned) was thoroughly professional, with a breadth of outlook often lacking in British television news programmes.

Similarly, Sky offers a mixture of the high- and lowbrow. Its 1988 summer schedules were filled with many childhood favourites like *Dr Who*, *Lost in Space* and *Fantasy Island*. It has bought in a number of old US programmes like *Hawk*, *Wanted Dead or Alive* and *Hogan's Heroes*, which put many of America's more recent offerings to shame. Sky has also broken new ground with its *Earth Watch* environmental programme and its current affairs programme *Roving Report*. Since linking up with the Arts Channel, viewers have also been able to see a broad selection of classical music, opera and jazz—albeit after midnight. Many adults have objected to what they regard as excessive amounts of music broadcast by both channels, now running in the region of 10 hours a day—a criticism not shared by the Community's teenagers.

The calibre of advertising, by any standard, is atrocious, and is in desperate need of improvement. Nothing much could be done for washing-powder advertisements, which seem unable to break out of the traditional formula in which a housewife compares a new version of the old brand-name to an unnamed rival and decides to go for the newly packaged old washing powder which, as a result of successive unexplained biological breakthroughs, is now washing clothes nuclear-white. Such advertisements are undoubtedly destined to remain appalling, no matter what language they are in. However, for Britain's advertising companies, who, in the words of one observer, have already managed to send the nation to work on an egg and succeeded in getting a respectable proportion of British holidaymakers onto the beach before the Germans, the European advertising market could provide new, interesting and potentially rewarding challenges.

The arrival of the age of satellite television is not going to be a second Renaissance. Indeed, the anticipated widespread appeal of satellite broadcasting may be wholly misconceived. Viewers in the Netherlands already have no less than 21 stations to choose between, yet the two main channels account for almost 90% of the audience, and the situation is similar in the United States, where cable stations have been operating for many years. Indeed, most evidence suggests that family viewing times are declining in the face of competition from video cassette recorders, and the new television satellite stations are likely to find it difficult to win back this audience. It is doubtful whether audiences will be able to cope with 20 satellite stations, let alone 200. After a few years of rapid expansion in which a multitude of channels will be available on our screens, the industry is likely to be faced with a shakeout in which only a handful are likely to survive.

Meanwhile, the Commission has begun to adopt an increasingly militant line against Eurosport, the joint venture between Murdoch's News International Corporation and the BBC, on the grounds that it could 'restrict and distort competition within the Community'. The Commission's action follows a complaint lodged by W. H. Smith, the High Street newsagent, which also has satellite television interests in Screen Sport, Eurosport's rival.

W. H. Smith complained that it has been deprived of the ability to buy broadcasting rights for key sporting events—such as the February 1989 Frank Bruno–Mike Tyson fight—by the European Broadcasting Union (the international organization which effectively controls coverage of major sporting events), as it has granted all such rights to Eurosport. Given the Commission's determination to ensure that competition prevails in the new satellite television sector, the exclusive arrangement between News International and the EBU could well be broken up.

High-definition television

In contrast to the argument over programme quotas and advertising regulations, the Community acted swiftly, and decisively, to avert a potentially devastating technological challenge from Japan. Because of increased competition from some of the newly industrialized countries in the Far East, Japanese electronics companies took the decision in the early 1970s to abandon the market for traditional television sets to their more competitive neighbours and concentrate on producing a new generation of high-definition television sets (HDTV) that would offer the viewer 35 mm picture quality and stereo sound. In 1985 Japan submitted its production standard for HDTV to the world broadcasting organization, the International Radio Consultative Committee (CCIR), as the first step in an attempt to get its production standards adopted as the world standard.

The implications of Japan's attempted *démarche* were lost on no-one. If Japan succeeded in getting its standards adopted as the world standard, Japanese electronics companies would have pulled off one of the biggest coups in the history of consumer electronics, enabling them to dominate the industry well into the next century. Moreover, Europe's 140 million television sets would have been made obsolete overnight, as they would be unable to receive the new HDTV transmissions.

At the CCIR annual assembly in Dubrovnik in May 1986 European electronics companies argued against Japan's all-or-nothing approach towards the introduction of new technical standards for the next generation of television sets, and put forward the case for a more evolutionary transition to HDTV which would be compatible with existing receiver sets. Europe's leading consumer electronic equipment manufacturers promptly joined forces under the Community's Eureka telecommunications research and development project in a bid to perfect the new

HDTV technology before the Japanese begin to introduce their version in 1990.

Meanwhile, the Council of Ministers has adopted a directive on common technical standards for transmitting direct broadcasts by satellite (known as the Mac-packet family of standards) with the intention of avoiding the current situation in terrestrial broadcasting in which the market is divided by the two competing systems of technical standards, PAL and Secam. The Mac-packet family will provide 35 mm picture quality and stereo sound, and give satellite broadcasters control over access to programmes in a potentially lucrative single unified market for transmission and receiving equipment.

The joint venture between Rupert Murdoch and Alan Sugar, the chairman of the Amstrad consumer electronics company, will produce satellite dishes for around £250 that are capable of receiving Murdoch's new satellite television stations launched at the beginning of 1989. Although they will only be capable of receiving transmissions in PAL it is widely expected that they will be upgraded to receive HDTV signals once the market takes off. British Satellite Broadcasting, whose shareholders include Granada, Pearson, Virgin and Anglia TV, and which plans to launch three new satellite stations at the end of 1989, and the consortium led by Robert Maxwell and W. H. Smith, which is planning to launch some seven additional satellite stations before 1990, will use the new Mac-packet family of technical standards.

Checklist of changes

- There will be considerable expansion in the number of satellite television channels available to viewers.
- Satellite broadcasters will have the right to transmit television programmes anywhere in the Community, provided that they meet certain minimum requirements.
- Broadcasters will be obliged to reserve a specified quota of their air time for feature films made in the Community.
- Television advertisers will have the option of grouping commercials into blocks or slots, and will be required to abide by prevailing standards of decency.
- Satellite and cable companies are expected to have an automatic right to broadcast or retransmit any programme within two years of original transmission, as long as adequate remuneration for the programme copyright holder is provided.
- Viewers will benefit from a considerable improvement in picture quality and sound, following the introduction of high-definition television.

14 RICH MAN, POOR MAN
Regional aid, the North–South divide and Britain

One of the main purposes of the 1992 process is to reduce the disparities between rich and poor regions of the EC. The aim, simply put, is to ensure that the integrated market of the Twelve develops harmoniously or cohesively. Hence the jargon words 'cohesion' or 'convergence' for the 1992 policy of averting a North–South divide, or a 'two-speed Europe', in which Britain, France, West Germany, the Benelux nations and Denmark reap the benefits of the single market while the 'Southern' group of nations—Greece, Spain, Portugal, parts of Italy (notably the Mezzogiorno) and Ireland—are left behind. There are opportunities for British and other North European firms to take part in 1992 modernization projects in the Southern countries, and hence to benefit from regional grants given to the Southern nations. Regional policy in the run-up to 1992 is in the hands of a British Commissioner, Bruce Millan.

To some extent, however, to speak only in terms of the North–South split and deprivation in backward Southern areas is misleading. Partly on British insistence, 'cohesion' has become more than a policy for redressing the North–South balance through use of the EC 'structural funds'—the regional and social funds. It also refers to efforts (including use of the structural funds, which are to be doubled by 1992) to develop depressed urban regions in the Northern countries, not least the rundown industrial areas of Britain. The North–South divide, in other words, runs within individual nations as well as across Europe as a whole. One market research company (Mintel) suggests in a recent report (*Mintel Regional Lifestyles Report 1988*) that European integration in 1992 and the arrival of the Channel Tunnel could increase the affluence gap between North and South in Britain, with the South-east in particular benefiting disproportionately from the business boom the single market is expected to produce.

Cohesion: reducing regional disparities
The aim of 1992 is to bring all areas of the EC up to a high standard of living and economic growth, largely by raising extra revenue and distributing it around the Community on the basis of priorities decided by successive EC summits and implemented in detail by the European Commission. Whether throwing money at the problem in this way will prove effective is a moot point: as with any aid programme, there is ample scope for abuse or misuse. Widespread fraud in the Southern countries—especially Italy and

Spain—where agricultural funds are concerned does not offer an encouraging example, and the Commission lacks the resources or the powers to carry out adequate inspections to ensure that funds are properly used. On the other hand, the regional and social funds already have a record of achievement, and British citizens are often unaware that motorway schemes, youth training programmes or urban regeneration projects have been funded wholly or partly by the EC.

The commitment to 'cohesion' pre-dates the 1992 programme but has been given added impetus by the single market. In its current form it stems not only from the original Cockfield 1992 programme but also from the Single European Act. The Commission has always been conscious of the North–South problem, and Delors has made 'cohesion' something of a personal crusade. The 1985 White Paper referred to the issue in its introduction in the following terms:

> The Commission is firmly convinced that the completion of the internal market will provide an indispensable base for increasing the prosperity of the Community as a whole. The Commission is, however, conscious that there may be risks that by increasing the possibilities for human, material and financial services to move without obstacle to the areas of greatest economic advantage, existing discrepancies between regions could be exacerbated and therefore the object of convergence jeopardized. This means full and imaginative use will need to be made of the resources available through the structural funds. The importance of the funds will therefore be enhanced.

Shorn of Eurospeak, this conveys the Commission's fundamental worry that money and resources will move towards the more prosperous North in the EC after 1992, with the Southern states—and backward regions—unable to stand up to cross-border competition. This anxiety has also been strongly expressed by the Southern countries themselves, not least by Greece—which held the Presidency of the Council of Ministers in the second half of 1988—and Spain, which had the Presidency in the second half of 1989. As a consequence, many 1992 directives (for example, the directive on the liberalization of financial services by July 1990) contain exemptions for the Southern states, to allow them a 'breathing space'. Other exemptions originate from the accession terms negotiated by the Southern countries. On the other hand, all these exemptions are provisional, and it is assumed that in due course (in the later 1990s, perhaps) the Southern economies will be strong enough to co-exist with other European economies in a frontier-free commercial environment.

Increasing the structural funds

To achieve this, the EC 'structural' funds are being increased, so that the

Southern states and backward regions can benefit from greater investment and—with the aid of the regional and social funds—stage an economic recovery. The White Paper referred, rather coyly, to the importance of 'enhancing' the funds. What the Commission really wanted, however (and achieved at the important Brussels summit of February 1988), was to increase the funds substantially, and even to double them—a proposal resisted at first by Britain and other states but eventually agreed as part of the Delors reform package which followed the Single European Act and 'cleared the way' for 1992 legislation.

Even the Act avoids direct reference to a 'doubling' of the structural funds. The relevant section (Title Five) notes that

> In order to promote its overall harmonious development, the Community shall develop and pursue its actions leading to the strengthening of its economic and social cohesion . . . In particular, the Community shall aim at reducing disparities between the various regions and the backwardness of the least-favoured regions.

To achieve this, the EC states undertook to co-ordinate their economic policies in such a way as to avoid a North–South split, although it was not altogether clear what this meant in practice. More immediately, the EC was committed under the Act to making better use of the three 'structural funds': the European Agricultural Guidance and Guarantee Fund; the European Social Fund; and the European Regional Development Fund (ERDF), as well as loans from the European Investment Bank. Article 130c outlined the purpose of the regional fund in particular: 'The European Regional Development Fund is intended to help redress the principal regional imbalances in the Community through participating in the development and structural adjustment of regions whose development is lagging behind, and in the conversion of declining industrial regions.'

So far so good: but the Act went on to authorize the Commission to submit 'a comprehensive proposal to the Council, the purpose of which will be to make such amendments to the structure and operational rules of the existing structural funds as are necessary to clarify and rationalize their tasks in order to contribute to the achievement of the objectives . . . and to increase their efficiency'. In practice, Delors and the Commission wanted nothing less than to double the funds so that 1992 could go ahead without major disruption and the further creation of regional imbalances.

The European Regional Development Fund

The structural funds had been operating for ten years before the 1992 process began. Yet oddly enough, the need to redress regional imbalances to prevent one part of the EC developing faster than another (or rather, to bring more backward regions up to the higher levels of development) was not foreseen in the Treaty of Rome, which has no separate clause on regional problems. The preamble refers to the need for the EC to 'ensure harmonious development by reducing the differences existing between the various regions', and in the 1960s there were plenty of examples of backwardness—in the low-subsistence agriculture of the Italian South, in depressed coalmining regions in Belgium and the Ruhr, and in central France. Some funds were channelled through the European Investment Bank (EIB).

However, the ERDF was only created in the mid-1970s, after the Six had grown to Nine with the addition of Britain, Ireland and Denmark in 1973. Britain, although not one of the underdeveloped regions on a par with the Southern states, did (and still does) have important areas of both rural and, above all, industrial decline, including Northern Ireland— which is still singled out as a high-priority area for regional aid under the 1992 programme, partly with the political aim of promoting harmony between the conflicting Ulster communities. Denmark had a poor region in Greenland—it subsequently left the EC after a local referendum; and the Republic of Ireland, for its part, had a low per capita income and added to the weight of what was to become the 'Southern bloc' with the entry of Greece in 1981 and Spain and Portugal in 1986.

What had started as mainly a 'rich man's club' in 1957 had become a much more diversified Community by the 1970s and 1980s. It quickly became apparent after 1973 that the 'less favoured' EC regions were either backward rural areas with high unemployment levels and poor communications and transport, largely in the South, or—no less important to Britain, West Germany, France and Belgium—regions which were formerly thriving centres of traditional industries, such as iron and steel, but which had increasingly fallen on hard times because of changes in global trading patterns and competition from outside Europe, with a consequent cost to Europe in unemployment, economic decline and social malaise.

However, the allocations made to member states under the regional fund, set up in 1975, were not universally regarded as fair or just. The practice was (and is) that member states propose projects—a new motorway, inner-city developments, irrigation schemes—and the Commission decides which projects are worthy of the most support. Both public authority and commercial projects can qualify. However, in the early days the Commission took the view that each country should have a part of the regional aid funds, even if Country A's depressed regions were far better off than those of Country B. In practice, it is true, most of the aid between 1975 and 1985 (one eighth of the EC budget) ended up in the regions which arguably needed it most: the Italian Mezzogiorno; Greece; Ireland; Britain (including Northern Ireland); and the French overseas departments, which also count as EC territories.

The allocations, however, needed adjustment, and at the time of the 1992 White Paper in 1985 the rules were changed to give each country a maximum percentage of the regional fund budget rather than a fixed annual quota. The maximum percentage of the ERDF budget allocated to Britain was 19.31% and the minimum guaranteed 14.48%. This compares favourably with the 9.96% upper limit allocated to France, the 3.40% given to West Germany and even with the 10.64% allocated to Greece or the 14.20% for Portugal. Only Spain and Italy had higher allocations than Britain, with upper limits of 23.93% and 28.79%, respectively. Following the Brussels agreement of February 1988 the Commission proposed a new system under which it would reserve to itself 15% of the structural funds to ensure a fair redistribution of wealth, while issuing 'indicative allocations' for the remaining 75%. In practice, 'indicative allocations' have been equivalent to the old quotas, which remain informally in force.

The Southern states also benefit from a separate fund known as the Integrated Mediterranean Programmes (rather amusingly abbreviated to IMP), which derive from the accession terms negotiated by Greece, Spain and Portugal and which benefit selected Mediterranean regions through a system of grants and loans (the French Mediterranean regions also receive IMP funds).

In addition, the European Social Fund—which, unlike the regional fund, was included in the terms of the Treaty of Rome—has the principal aim of encouraging job creation in areas of high unemployment, partly through retraining schemes. The Fund's importance has grown together with unemployment, so that it now accounts for almost the same proportion of the EC budget as the regional fund. The Government's Youth Training Scheme, for example, was established with help from the EC Social Fund—although again, not many people are aware of this. The Fund also helps to retrain employees unfamiliar with new technologies, migrant workers and women whose families have grown up and who return to full- or part-time employment only to find that techniques and work patterns have changed.

The February 1988 Brussels Agreement

The key question as 1992 approaches is whether the Commission and Council will succeed in further developing these funds to prevent a North–South division, or whether the less-advantaged regions will fall further behind as free competition benefits those economic sectors most prepared for it. The decision to double the structural funds by 1992 has certainly improved the chances of avoiding a 'two-speed' Europe. Taken in February 1988, it appears to have surprised even those—like Delors—who had sponsored the proposal. On the other hand, the increase in regional and social spending is directly related to the Delors package's overhaul of EC finances. Europe can only spend more on its regions because it is increasing the revenues coming into central EC funds while at the same time cutting back on farm spending under the Common Agricultural Policy, despite protests from EC farmers and farm ministers.

The decision, in other words, only came after the Northern countries, with Britain heading the campaign, had insisted that extra regional spending was a luxury the EC could only afford once other expenditure (above all, farm support) had been brought under control. The Commission, for its part, recognized that budgetary reform was needed if the 1992 programme—regional aid included—was to be based on a 'sound economic footing'.

The process of bringing EC spending under control to allow for greater regional aid, and the framework programme for technological research, has dominated the past four years, just as the preceding four had been overshadowed by the question of the British budget rebate. The crisis really came in June 1987, at the Brussels summit marking the end of Belgium's EC Presidency, when Mrs Thatcher demanded 'good housekeeping' in the EC before budgetary increases for 1992 could be contemplated. Chancellor Kohl of West Germany declared Bonn's willingness to increase the regional and social funds by up to 50%, but Mrs Thatcher declared that the CAP had to be curbed first, and there was, in any case, room for improvement in the way the existing structural funds were administered. 'The EC is not a mechanism for redistributing wealth, it is a common enterprise for producing it' was her spokesman's terse comment.

The result was a 'Maggie versus the Rest' summit, in which Mrs Thatcher held out against a compromise package because it lacked budgetary rigour, arguing—correctly—that she was 'doing the Community a service'. At Brussels, Mrs Thatcher was mocked by Jacques Chirac, the French Prime Minister, for taking a 'housewifely' view of the budget. A senior British diplomat at the EC subsequently compared Mrs Thatcher —rather more admiringly—to a nanny: 'She says to the others, if you don't eat your porridge up now you'll have to eat it cold tomorrow.' The alternative, Britain insisted, was EC bankruptcy as expenditure continued to exceed revenue.

On the eve of the next summit, in Copenhagen in December 1987, France and West Germany suggested a compromise, allowing states to escape farm spending cuts 'in exceptional circumstances'. Sir Geoffrey Howe, the then Foreign Secretary, replied on Britain's behalf that there was no point in filling the proposed spending deal with loopholes 'like a motheaten sock'. The British solution lay in strict ceilings on farm output, known as 'stabilizers', coupled with a West German-backed scheme for taking land out of production (set aside, and an altered revenue system, as devised by the Commission, to include a GNP tax), provided that there was no consequent alteration for the worse in the British budget rebate agreed in 1984. In the end, Copenhagen failed, but the debate was better tempered, and the leaders moved closer to agreement, with the summit vowing to take action when it reconvened in special session in Brussels in February 1988, under West German chairmanship.

The extraordinary Brussels summit, when it met, was on the verge of breaking up several times, with French leaders taking a hard line against farm cuts because of the impending French presidential election and Mrs Thatcher still insisting that the regional funds could not be increased by more than 50–60%. Chancellor Kohl, after allowing the summit to drift, held separate talks with his fellow leaders—'confessionals' in EC jargon —to break the deadlock. In the final negotiation Chirac went one better (or worse) than his earlier 'housewife' epithet when, late at night on the second day, he shouted a crude French word (*couilles*) across the table at Mrs Thatcher after she had accused him of holding up the deal by going on interminably about non-arable products.

In the end, the February 1988 summit reached an historic deal. With last-minute concessions on all sides—not least from Mrs Thatcher—it finally reformed EC finances along the lines of the original Delors plan, thus not only allowing for a doubling of the structural funds by 1992 but also 'clearing the way for 1992' as a whole, in the Prime Minister's own words. The Brussels agreement included:

1 An overall increase in the EC budget from £31 billion in 1988, to £37 billion in 1992, with revenues based not only on VAT but also the GNP tax (the resulting mix producing revenue equivalent to 1.9% VAT);
2 Preservation of the British rebate, which Mrs Thatcher said had saved British taxpayers £3 billion over three years;
3 Legally binding limits on cereals and other crops, with the proportion of farm spending in the budget to decline from two thirds to 56% by 1992; and, above all,
4 A rise in the structural funds to £9.5 billion a year by 1992, or over a quarter of the budget, with most of the new aid going to Portugal, Ireland, Spain and Greece.

Britain and the structural funds

Since the Delors reforms, the argument has mainly been over the official definition of a 'less-developed region' and of a 'depressed industrial area', defined in the summit conclusions as an area with unemployment higher than the Community average. There is concern over the Commission's interpretation of this to mean that the very poorest EC regions should be developed first to help them to cope with 1992. The Commission proposed giving most of the new money to 'Category One' regions, in which per capita income must be below 75% of EC average (with only Northern Ireland among the British regions therefore qualifying for high-priority Category One). The Government objected in the Council that other British regions deserved special treatment—rural Wales, the Highlands and Islands of Scotland (which officials had hinted would be Category One), parts of Devon and Cornwall, and inner-city 'black spots' in London, Liverpool, Manchester and elsewhere.

In late 1988 a further difficulty arose over British objections to public spending being taken into account in the allocation of structural funds. The Commission, for its part, does not want to see member states using regional funds as an excuse to cut public spending.

British special pleading—accompanied by special pleading from other countries—has had some effect, partly because the logic of earlier regional grant awards supports the British case. The Highlands alone received £100 million over the first ten years of the ERDF, with EC cash supporting projects like the new Perth-to-Inverness trunk road. Neither Scotland nor Whitehall was keen to lose this support. The Government aim was (and is) to maintain a situation in which Britain was a major recipient of structural funds, and especially ERDF cash. According to figures published by the Commission, in the first ten years of the ERDF Britain was near the top of the league of aid recipients, with over £3 billion in aid. The initial Commission list of regional aid recipients in March 1988 gave the whole of Greece, Ireland and Portugal as 'Category One' regions, together with regions of Spain and Italy, Corsica, the French overseas departments and Northern Ireland. However, Britain has since been given assurances that other of its regions—including both rural areas and those of industrial decline—will benefit substantially from the new funds, up to Britain's allotted ceiling, even if they are in Category Two rather than Category One. Under the new criteria, Category Two covers areas of industrial decline, defined as areas where there has been higher than average unemployment for more than three years, or where there has been an 'observable fall' in industrial employment.

In the spirit of 1992 Kent County Council has joined forces with the regional Council of the Pas de Calais (Nord) to apply to Brussels for £1 billion worth of aid over a ten-year period to help develop the infrastructure on both sides of the Channel for the Channel Tunnel. On the other hand, under the new criteria neither Kent nor the Pas de Calais qualifies as a high-priority depressed region in terms of regional aid—although both qualify for Social Fund cash.

In other words, the new approach to the expanded structural funds —concentrating resources on the most backward areas—still gives rise to concern in Britain. The Government has put forward plans for including areas of 'high deprivation' such as Merseyside and Strathclyde in future EC aid allocations to Britain. Some areas (Cornwall is one example) have even launched their own campaigns to ensure they do not lose out in 1992. Cornwall received £125 million worth of aid from the ERDF between 1975 and 1985, but the decline of tin mining and other local industries has brought continuing high unemployment.

Helping the North to help the South

On balance, the doubling of structural funds by 1992 will benefit Britain as well as the Southern countries. Whether it will succeed in achieving Delors' aim of averting a North–South split in the integrated European market remains to be seen. One often-overlooked aspect of the increase in structural funds is that British and other 'Northern' companies can benefit from aid granted to the 'Southern' countries by entering into joint ventures which have the approval of Brussels and which draw on regional fund allocations. This is a particularly attractive proposition to companies which specialize in development aid projects in underdeveloped economies but which have been adversely affected by problems in the Third World, such as indebtedness or the decline in oil revenues. EC officials argue that many Southern countries in the EC will have to turn to Northern companies for help in development, since the funds they are likely to receive under the social and regional fund reforms will exceed the capacity of local industry and commerce to meet the challenge (for example, in construction). It is already becoming clear, however, that to benefit from 1992 joint ventures in the South, British companies would do well to have close arrangements with local firms in Spain, Greece, Portugal or Southern Italy, and will probably gain the most benefit if they have a local subsidiary.

The DTI—which has a projects and export policy division dealing with 1992 joint ventures—has warned that other North European countries such as West Germany or the Netherlands will not be slow to seize this 1992 opportunity. Will the tables eventually be turned, with Southern EC companies which benefit from increased EC aid becoming strong enough to challenge Northern European firms on their home ground under the rules of the single market? In the short run it is unlikely, but if the integrated market develops after 1992 to the benefit of the South, the North may find its present superiority under challenge, not least from countries like Spain, which have a policy of economic dynamism backed by a great desire to prove to the rest of the EC—and the world at large—that they are part of a modern European economy and culture. If skills, labour and plant—including high-tech industries—move South in the integrated market, Spain and Portugal, and perhaps Southern Italy, could become the European equivalent of the American Sun Belt.

Not all scenarios are so optimistic. At Madrid in June 1989, Bruce Millan, the Commissioner for regional development, said structural funds reform was 'off to a good start' and 'going pretty well to schedule'. He outlined a possible stark alternative to Southern enrichment, however, saying the Commission had serious doubts about 'further concentration of resources in major central conurbations' in rich Northern areas because of pollution, traffic congestion and poor housing. The Commission, Millan said, wanted 'a more centrifugal view of Europe' in the 1990s because of the danger of a cycle of decline in less-developed and depressed industrial regions if economic expectations were not met and then fell. The rich areas, from southern England to northern Italy, would be unable to sustain the pressures of migration from a declining South, and the 'rich centre' would then itself fall into a cycle of overcrowding and decay. To avoid this, the regional funds needed yet more cash, and new technology and market economics must be exploited to show that peripheral regions could be just as competitive as central regions. EC regional programmes would focus on transport, the environment, telecommunications, energy, steel and ship-building.

Checklist of changes

- Community regional funds will be increased and made available to poorer areas of the EC to enable them to achieve a higher standard of living and increased economic growth.
- Social funds are now being used to help with youth training, and retraining in new technology will be expanded.
- Most of the new funds will go to 'Category One' regions, for which only Northern Ireland qualifies in the UK, but rural regions and areas of urban decline also qualify for aid.
- UK and other North European companies will be able to draw on regional funds for investing in Southern EC states.

15 COLDITZ EUROPE?

Protectionism and global trade

Complete and effective implementation of the internal market programme will have a number of profound implications for the global economy and for the Community's world-wide trading partners. The gradual removal of Europe's internal barriers to trade will create the single largest advanced industrial market in the world. An integrated European economy could act as a major stimulus to world trade or it could become a major obstacle in the path of such expansion. Decisions about who has access to this market, and on what terms, will affect millions of people, from the humble banana producers of the Caribbean to the giant trading houses of the Far East, all of whom depend on a healthy and expanding trading relationship with the European Community for their livelihoods.

The ink on the Internal Market White Paper was barely dry before some observers had begun to complain. The European Commission found itself accused of turning its back on the world by planning to increase trade between the member states at the expense of business with their traditional trading partners, and of scheming to restrict access to the internal market to only those countries that granted the Community reciprocal access to their own domestic markets in return.

From Australia to Latin America and Japan to the United States, many were alarmed at the prospect that, as Europe's internal barriers began to crumble, they would be replaced by a unified external one designed to limit the benefits of the internal market to a new 'Fortress Europe'. Business executives began to express anxieties that, once the external barrier was in place, the Community would have the power to dictate who should be let in and who should be kept out.

These fears were increased by a series of articles in some of the world's leading business publications predicting the worst. In May 1988 the influential Hong Kong-based *Far Eastern Economic Review* ran as its cover story an eight-page account of how Europe was preparing to steal the initiative from the dynamic, newly industrialized countries of the Pacific Rim, and bring the centre of gravity of international trade back to the Old World. Warnings that 'the Fortress Europe of such simple protectionism as national quotas could give way to a complex citadel of Europrotectionism, enshrined in Community-wide quotas, a generally stiffer trade policy, and less liberal policies towards outside investment' almost seemed calculated to confirm the international business community's worst fears.

At the same time, the European edition of the *Wall Street Journal* —published just as the controversial trade bill with protectionist clauses was passing through the US Congress—predicted that the next frontier of protectionism would be found emerging from the borders of Europe. It insisted that the combination of the EC's historical record, especially the Common Agricultural Policy, which it called 'a black hole of protectionism', and the growing pressure from European car manufacturers, financial institutions and other industrial sectors for Community help in the face of external competition would turn the internal market programme into one of the most restrictive initiatives ever implemented by a regional trading group, precipitating a new and vicious round of trans-Atlantic trade wars.

Much influential US opinion concedes that the European Commission, along with the GATT, is one of the leading advocates of free trade in the international community, yet remains convinced that, without any legislative power of its own, the Commission would soon fall victim of the protectionist instincts of member states. However, US attitudes to 1992 are by no means uniform. For the giant corporations like IBM and Caterpillar, who have regular access to the Commission, the internal market programme is seen as a great opportunity. For the small and medium-sized exporting companies, whose access to information about the Commission's activities is considerably more limited, the fear of being excluded from the internal market is very real. Such anxieties have undoubtedly been increased by political rhetoric and alarmist newspaper reports, such as that in the *Wall Street Journal*, which reminded its readers that 'Protectionism is as much a part of the European business climate as the three-hour lunch'.

A new strategy for external trade

Much of the blame for such visions can be attributed to the Commission. The Internal Market White Paper failed to address itself adequately to the vital issue of the external implications of the 1992 programme. The whole question was neatly averted with a passing reference to the necessity of replacing the separate national import policies with unspecified 'temporary measures'.

Under Article 115 of the Treaty of Rome, member states are granted the right to impose quantitative restrictions against each other on imports from third countries. They are also empowered to inspect intra-Community trade in order to establish the origin of a given import, and thereby prevent what is known as trade deflection, the ability of external exporters to gain access to the protected market of one member state via the unprotected market of another.

However, a central part of the internal market programme is the abolition of frontier controls, and as Article 115 relies on these to monitor intra-Community trade from third countries, it will have to be gradually phased out. The White Paper, however, gave no indication of how the Commission intended to deal with the problem posed by the different policies member states have adopted towards third-country imports. Will the restrictions on, for example, imports of cars adopted by one member state (whether through quotas, tariffs or voluntary export restraints) have to be adopted by every other member state? Will the member state in question have to abolish its national restriction and bring it into line with everybody else? Or will there be some sort of compromise between the two extremes? If so, what will be the level and nature of Community protectionism on 1 January 1993?

These were the kinds of questions being asked by the international business community when the Commission began to give the first indications of the strategy on external trade it was in the process of evolving. In his various addresses, Willy de Clercq, the then Commissioner for External Relations, began to make much use of the word 'reciprocity', indicating that external trade relations were to be based on the principle 'You scratch my back and I'll scratch yours'. On one occasion de Clercq said bluntly, 'If our partners want to take advantage of our integration, and profit from the dynamism it will create, they will have to co-operate with this effort and be determined to open up their markets on equivalent terms', effectively confirming the worst suspicions of business executives around the world. In a keynote speech in London in July 1988 de Clercq attempted to dispel some of the fears prompted by his earlier comments.

> The Community is already the world's largest trading partner. Our exports of manufactured goods represent 26% of those of the OECD countries, compared with 14% for the United States, and 17% for Japan. Our share of world exports of services is even greater. As a result, we have a vital interest in the maintenance of a worldwide liberal trading system.

Having reaffirmed the Community's commitment to an open trading system, de Clercq then went on to outline three principles that would guide the Commission's external trade policy in the run-up to 1992 in practice. In the first place, he acknowledged that the internal market programme would automatically lead to the reinforcement of the external identity of the EC as a result of the phasing out of Article 115. However, he insisted that the Community would adhere to its commitments under the current round of trade-liberalization talks being held in Geneva under the auspices of the GATT not to introduce any new protectionist barriers.

He also made it clear that as the GATT does not yet cover trade in services, the Community saw no reason why the benefits of internal liberalization 'should be extended unilaterally to third countries'. Asked what this meant in concrete terms, the Commissioner illustrated the point by saying that any American or Japanese bank already resident in one member state would not be allowed to expand into other member states, unless Community banks were granted the same privileges in return.

Britain is especially unhappy about the use of reciprocity as a means of securing access to foreign markets, as this is likely to invite retaliation which could harm British interests, particularly in the financial services sector. In August 1988 Sir Nicholas Goodison, the former chairman of the London Stock Exchange, expressed Britain's fears by warning the Commission that any attempt to put a 'ring fence' around European financial markets would 'lull Europeans into a false sense of security'.

Finally, de Clercq confirmed that the wide divergence between the import arrangements of the twelve member states would have to be eliminated. In most cases, import restrictions could be abolished without difficulty. However, he insisted there were a number of 'hard-core cases' where abolition would cause considerable hardship in some member states, and that national protective measures would have to be replaced by 'appropriate measures at Community level' for a transitionary period.

Shortly thereafter, the Commission gave the first indication of its plans for one of these so-called hard-core cases. These call for the complete abolition of all the fiscal and technical regulations fragmenting the European car industry and a severe restriction on state subsidies. The Commission also proposes to replace the quantitative restraints imposed on Japanese car exports by Britain, France, Italy, Spain and Portugal by a Community-wide ceiling of one million units per annum until 1992, in order to give European manufacturers time to adjust to the new climate of international competition. The Commission maintains that this is the only way that member states could be cured of their addiction to quantitative restrictions in the car sector.

The proposal represents a compromise between the two extremes of outright abolition and permanent Community quotas outlined above, and was even seen by some as the model solution for all other divergent national import arrangements. But the question of what level of access to grant Japanese car exporters proved to be so politically sensitive between those favouring a high degree of protection and those in support of a more liberal import system that the Commission was forced to postpone repeatedly the publication of the Community's strategy towards Japanese car imports. By August 1989, Japanese car manufacturers were still awaiting some indication from the Commission about the likely extent of EC protectionism in this sector. If the Commission opts for a high level of protectionism it is likely to be the subject of considerable criticism. For those economists who have argued that the objectives of the internal market—in terms of the promotion of competition through innovation, industrial restructuring and economies of scale—necessarily entail an open disposition towards the world economy, it is a step in the wrong direction. Protectionism has rarely encouraged manufacturers to become more competitive in the past, and there is no reason to assume that it will do so now. Regardless of what member states say today, they are likely to oppose the abolition of the car imports ceiling when the deadline expires.

Despite his protestations to the contrary, in the eyes of many critics de Clercq's three principles collectively constitute a violation of the spirit of the GATT. That system, which has been struggling to overcome the increase in protectionism throughout the world, is based on the principles of non-discrimination and multilateralism. By contrast, the de Clercq system of international trade asserts its commitment to multilateralism where possible, but makes no attempt to hide its readiness to revert to discrimination and bilateralism where necessary. Admittedly, the GATT does not yet cover trade in services, but the willingness of the world's largest trading bloc to show its strength in a pursuit of its own self-interest does not bode well for the future of an international trading system, already under severe strain from the increasing temptation of nation states to resort to bilateral solutions to trade difficulties.

The main reason the Internal Market White Paper had not dealt effectively with the problems posed by the strengthening of the Community's external identity was that it was an entirely new area of Community competence, in which definitive policies are still in the process of being formulated. In September 1988, however, EC external relations policy underwent a major transformation following a ruling by the European Court of Justice, which conferred on the European Commission the right to take legal action and impose fines on non-Community companies that violated EC competition laws.

The decision was the first to grant the Community powers in the highly sensitive area of extra-territorial jurisdiction, and was seen by legal experts as one of the most important rulings by the Luxembourg-based court —effectively granting the Community global jurisdiction. The ruling followed an appeal by a group of wood-pulp producers from the United States, Canada and Finland against punitive price-fixing fines levied on their exports to Community manufacturers in 1984.

The producers (most of whom are based outside the EC) initiated legal proceedings against the Commission on the grounds that it had no authority to interfere in the activities of companies operating outside the EC. In a preliminary ruling earlier in the year, the court said that the Commission did have the power to take action against non-EC companies engaged in price-fixing or market-sharing conspiracies if it believed that 'free competition within the Community would be affected'. The ruling was based on the highly controversial US 'effects doctrine', granting American authorities the power to regulate foreign companies whose activities outside the US have a damaging impact on domestic ones.

However, in what legal experts interpreted as an attempt to avoid the potentially divisive issue of infringing the sovereignty of other nation states the final judgment made no reference to the so-called effects doctrine. Instead, the court based its decision on the consequences of external activities inside the Community, arguing that 'the decisive factor is the place where the agreement is implemented'. The court found that 'where wood pulp producers sell directly to the Community and engage in price competition in order to win orders from those customers, that constitutes competition within the common market'.

At the time, observers acknowledged that the distinction between price-fixing agreements and their place of implementation was little more than a legal fiction, but it did enable the court to avoid dealing with the effects doctrine. Morever, the implications of the decision were far-reaching, as the Commission can now exercise jurisdiction over the supply of all raw materials to the EC.

The European Free Trade Association

Few countries outside the European Community have been forced to think harder about the external implications of the internal market programme than the six-member EFTA. Formed in 1960, following ratification of the Stockholm Convention the previous year, EFTA was basically a reaction to the creation of the EC three years before. The EC and EFTA reflected the two conflicting visions of Europe's future which were fighting for ideological ascendancy in the immediate post-war period. The first saw Europe moving in the direction of economic and political union, with supranational institutions in a federation of states, while the second had the more modest ambition of creating a loose commercial association, thereby enabling its members to preserve their traditional economic relations with other parts of the world.

Despite initial rivalry and suspicion, each survived to become the other's most important trading partner. Following the implementation of the 1972–3 free trade agreements between the two trading blocs, the volume of two-way trade flourished. In 1986, 25% of EC exports went to EFTA countries (more than the Community's exports to the United States or Japan) while 50% of EFTA exports went to the EC. Overall trade was valued at £120 billion. All seemed rosy—until the Commission published the Internal Market White Paper. Now, the Community's drive for economic integration by 1992 could mean the end of EFTA.

Composed of the six small but highly industrialized countries— Austria, Finland, Iceland, Norway, Sweden and Switzerland—EFTA is currently struggling to define its identity in relation to its larger and more powerful regional neighbour before the 1992 deadline expires. Will EFTA be allowed to preserve intact its privileged access to the Community's internal market? If so, will the member states be prepared to enact the same legislative programme of physical, technical and fiscal harmonization measures being implemented by the EC in order to be able to avail themselves of the Community's largesse? If not, will the organization break up as some or all of its members join in the headlong 'rush for Brussels'?

Prior to the publication of the White Paper, the two halves of Western Europe had already been moving in the direction of increased economic co-operation. At the first ministerial meeting between the two groups in Luxembourg in April 1984 they announced their intention to create by the 1990s a 'European Economic Space', made up of all 18 nations. The most tangible expression of this rather vague rhetoric to date has been the inclusion of EFTA in the Community's Single Administrative Document arrangement for simplifying the amount of documentation required for the cross-frontier transportation of goods.

At the first ministerial meeting between the two organizations since the announcement of the White Paper programme, held in Brussels in February 1988, the two groups reaffirmed their commitment towards the creation of a common economic space and identified a number of areas for further co-operation, including common rules for technical standards, rules of origin and greater openness in the field of public procurement and state aids. However, by the time de Clercq met EFTA ministers in Tampere in June it was already clear that the Community was determined to impose strict limits on the extent to which EFTA could benefit from the creation of the internal market.

De Clercq, with a remarkable tendency for formulating principles in batches of three, enunciated another set of guidelines around which the Community's relations with EFTA would be organized:

1 Priority to internal market considerations over EFTA at all times;
2 The preservation of EC sovereignty to make decisions regardless of the extent of co-operation with EFTA; and
3 The maintenance of a balance of advantages and obligations between the two groups in any agreements made between them.

In addition, de Clercq told the EFTA nations that they must recognize 'that there is a difference between the European economic space and the internal market, and only member states can expect to participate fully in the internal market'.

De Clercq's three principles may well have come as a shock to EFTA members, but the indications had been obvious for some time. Like most organizations, the Community's resources of time and manpower are limited, and any endeavour to incorporate EFTA into the internal market programme would divide the Community's attention from the primary task in hand. Equally, EFTA was free to mirror Community harmonization legislation if it so wished, but having done so, it could not then expect to veto or influence any subsequent decision by the Community to alter or amend any part of the programme in any way it saw fit.

Finally, the Community insisted that it was entitled to benefit as much as EFTA from any closer association between the two trading blocs. This particular issue had already become the source of considerable friction within the Community. A number of the Southern member states, anxious that they would not be able to compete with the more advanced economies of EFTA, had complained bitterly about the Commission's granting favours to rich non-member states instead of doing more to help the poorer member states. Spain, particularly, accused EFTA of seeking a free ride on the EC by wanting preferential access to the benefits of the internal market while remaining free of the financial burdens imposed on member states, such as the cost of the CAP. Indeed, this feeling is so strong that British Conservative MEPs openly refer to EFTA as EFRA—the European Free Ride Association.

Consideration has been given to the possibility of EFTA making financial contributions to regional development in the Community's poorer regions by way of compensation for the privileges of access to the internal market. Much of the controversy has since been taken out of this issue following the decision by the Council of Ministers during the February summit meeting in Brussels to double the structural funds to some £9 billion by 1993, most of which will go to the poorer member states.

The idea of paying a premium to the Community in exchange for certain privileges neatly encapsulates many of the dilemmas faced by EFTA nations in the run-up to 1992. Because of its determination to preserve its sovereignty over decision making the Community could not permit EFTA to say how the money was spent. However, ceding the power of decision making to Brussels represents a fundamental loss of sovereignty, far more serious than anything sustained by members of the Community—who at least play a part in the decision-making process. Such problems have already caused a debate in many EFTA member states (particularly Austria, which formally applied for membership in July 1989, and Norway, which is expected to follow suit in the near future) about the possibility of accession to the EC. However, while the Community could not possibly embark on yet another round of accession negotiations prior to 1992, it has accepted EFTA's initiative, announced after its summit meeting at Oslo in March 1989, to improve economic and institutional ties between the two blocs.

In November, Frans Andriessen, the new External Relations Commissioner, announced plans for a new round of EC–EFTA talks, designed to create a "common economic space" between all 18 countries, thereby extending the benefits of the single market to the Six without undermining the autonomy of existing EC institutions. The talks, which began in 1990, are expected to last a year, and will attempt to establish a new institution capable of reconciling any disputes that arise between the two. In addition, East European states—assuming multi-party democracy is eventually introduced—could also apply for EFTA membership, and any existing EC member state which wanted to opt out of the integration process, such as Britain, could leave the Community and join EFTA.

The United States and Japan
Most American business executives, accustomed to thinking about the EC

in terms of Eurosclerosis (a wasting disease attributable to endemic labour rigidities, rampant protectionism, an elemental fear of competition and, of course, the proverbial three-hour lunch) have been caught off-guard by the Community's version of *perestroika*. The initial reaction to the internal market programme was one of profound scepticism, but that has since given way to the conviction that the EC is in the process of erecting a giant industrial version of the CAP.

It took the US Administration over three years to make its first official response to the Community's internal market programme. That reaction finally came in August 1988, in an address given by Peter McPherson, a deputy secretary of the US Treasury Department, to the Institute of International Economics in Washington, DC. McPherson's speech betrayed a deep ambivalence towards the goals of the 1992 programme. On the one hand, he welcomed the Community's new initiative to the extent that it would help to promote economic growth in the EC, increase the demand for US exports and thereby help to reduce the US trade deficit, which had reached a staggering $170 billion in 1987. However, he gave a clear warning that the process of internal liberalization must not succumb to the temptation for greater external protection. If in abolishing the divergent import arrangements of individual member states the Commission opted for a common commercial policy that reflected the demands of its more protectionist members, McPherson left the Community in no doubt that the United States 'would respond'. Turning to the vexed issue of reciprocity, he insisted that any attempt to implement such a policy would provoke a serious deterioration in transatlantic trade relations.

The problem yet to be resolved lies in the conflicting approaches taken by each trading bloc to external trade. The Community's insistence on reciprocity appears, on the surface, to be quite innocuous—if you grant us access to your market we will grant you access to ours. What could be more equitable? However, it fails to acknowledge that in countries like the United States there are stringent regulations governing interstate trade and commerce. US banks, for example, are not free to operate in any state they choose. The Community's demand for reciprocal treatment would mean revising federal and state banking laws to allow European banks greater privileges than those enjoyed by US ones. Hence the US Administration's insistence on the principle of national treatment, whereby foreign companies are governed by the same rules as domestic companies.

However, while warning the Community that 'the creation of a single market that reserves Europe for the Europeans would be bad for Europe, bad for the United States and bad for the multilateral economic system' McPherson had little to say on the Omnibus Trade Act, just then approved by the US Congress. This grants the President powers to employ sanctions against countries running chronic and persistent trade surpluses with the United States. The EC, for example, had a large $21 billion surplus with the US in 1987, and would seem to be a prime target for US retaliation.

The Trade Act is a clear indication that the United States has decided to take a more aggressive approach in attempting to reduce its trade deficits with its major trading partners. However, predictions that the move is the first step in a transatlantic trade war, possibly leading to the dissolution of the Atlantic Alliance, seem to be little more than an exercise in hyperbole. As one senior US official said:

> The US trade bill is nowhere near as onerous as it once was. Similarly, 1992 is not going to turn out to be Armageddon. Trade negotiators are sensible people who are not going to go around slashing each other's wrists. The international trading system is simply too important to sabotage.

Indeed, many Europeans have expressed fears that the large US and Japanese companies will be the primary beneficiaries of the completion of the internal market. Many US corporations have been operating in Europe for decades (a few for considerably longer), and most are often more at home with the European way of doing things than companies from individual member states. De Clercq, however, has dismissed these fears as groundless, and insisted that:

> There is no *a priori* reason to suppose that the subsidiaries of American or Japanese companies operating in the Community will do better or worse than European-owned companies. Europe will be neither a fortress nor a sieve.

Europeans have yet to be convinced.

Nevertheless, the protectionist debate has continued unabated. Indeed, by the summer of 1989, mutual recrimination between Washington and Brussels over the issue reached the level of a transatlantic propaganda war. Publication of the US National Trade Estimates Report in May, which singled out the Community for a host of restrictive practices, was matched two days later by the publication of a 41-page report by the Commission accusing the United States of more or less the same thing. However, as Commission officials were quick to point out, while the EC report merely described US protectionist practices, the US report triggered those provisions in the 1988 Trade Act which set in motion potential retaliatory action. But despite continued attempts by the Commission to convince foreign trading partners the Community will not retreat behind a protectionist wall, many, particularly the US and Japan, remain profoundly suspicious of Brussels' intentions.

The US approval of the internal market programme (albeit with reservations) has been echoed by the Community's other major trading partner, Japan. During a major speech at the Mansion House in London in May 1988 Noboru Takeshita, the former Japanese Prime Minister, issued an unprecedented call for the strengthening of relations between Japan and the Community in an effort to remedy what he described as the 'weak link' in the US/EC/Japanese economic triangle. Displaying some of the growing concern in Tokyo over the protectionist tendencies inherent in the internal market programme, Takeshita also said that the Community had a responsibility to maintain an open stance towards the global economy as 1992 approaches.

Takeshita's concerns were more than academic. The EC has registered a series of bilateral trade deficits with Japan in recent years (which exceeded £14 billion in 1987), and the Commission has reacted by persuading the Japanese government to accelerate the opening up of its domestic market to Community imports and by inaugurating a severe restriction on imported components destined for Japanese manufacturing facilities located inside the Community.

During the past three years the Commission has imposed a series of large anti-dumping duties on Japanese goods, including dot matrix printers, electronic typewriters, photocopiers and electric scales, produced by so-called 'screwdriver plants'. The Commission argues that its action is justified, because Japanese companies are trying to evade the Community's anti-dumping duties on imported finished products by building manufacturing facilities inside the EC and then supplying them with Japanese-made components at low prices.

GATT rules allow countries to impose anti-dumping duties on products sold at below the cost of production where such action is causing hardship for domestic manufacturers, but the Japanese insist that the Commission has taken no account of the difficulties they face locating reliable Community component suppliers in the period immediately after a new manufacturing facility has been established in a member state. Moreover, the Japanese emphatically deny that they have been importing components at prices below those being charged in the Japanese market in an effort to secure an unfair advantage over Community producers, and have appealed to GATT's anti-dumping panel to pass judgment on the legitimacy of the Community's action.

The issue is likely to remain highly sensitive and politically charged. A number of member states are making great endeavours to obtain Japanese investment to help reduce their levels of unemployment. Britain, particularly, has been competing with some of its Community partners to become Japan's gateway to Europe, and is distinctly unhappy about the way the Commission's anti-dumping policy has developed. Alternatively, many industrialists insist that Japanese screwdriver plants are undermining the foundations of local industry, and are a major contributory factor to the very unemployment problem they purport to resolve.

In October 1988, for example, the French government made public its determination to impose restrictions on exports of the British-made Nissan *Bluebird* car in order to protect French car makers from Japanese competition. Initially (and unofficially) the Commission indicated that such action would be illegal under the free circulation of goods provisions of Article 30. Although, as a result of intense diplomatic pressure from France, the Commission was forced to 'rephrase' its assessment of the French plan, there seemed little doubt that once France appeared before the European Court of Justice it would be forced to back down. The row was, however, illustrative of the deep reluctance on the part of member states to subject their national industries to increased competition.

Yet if the logic of the internal market programme is to be applied systematically, European industrialists have little option but to adjust to the effects of competition from Japanese companies, or indeed any other foreign competitor. Assuming that Japanese companies are not increasing their penetration of European markets by unfair means, European producers must become equally competitive or accept that they lack any comparative advantage in particular manufacturing sectors, and divert their resources to those areas where they can compete more effectively. In the words of one leading economist, where the Community lacks comparative advantage, protection is costly.

At the end of the European Council meeting in Rhodes in December 1988 the EC issued a communiqué on 'Fortress Europe', in an effort to convince the United States and Japan that they would not be discriminated against as a result of the abolition of internal barriers to trade. The communiqué asserted that: 'The internal market will not close in on itself . . . 1992 Europe will be a partner not a Fortress Europe'. Mrs Thatcher had argued for a reference to the internal market programme serving as a model for the rest of the world in the interests of free trade, thereby thwarting attempts by Mitterrand and Gonzalez to give greater prominence to the concept of reciprocity. However, there could be little doubt that the communiqué was as much a reminder to EC member states of the Community's commitment to free trade as an attempt to appease Europe's major trading partners.

The Soviet Union and Eastern Europe

Complementing both the Community's attempts to liberalize its internal market and EFTA's efforts to make sure that it is not excluded from the economic benefits liberalization is expected to create, the Soviet Union and Eastern Europe have also opened up a new chapter in relations between the two estranged halves of Europe. At a ceremony in Luxembourg in June 1988 the EC and the Soviet-led state trading organization Comecon signed a declaration of 'mutual recognition', thus ending almost 30 years of unremitting enmity between the two trading blocs.

Although described by Lord Plumb, the President of the European Parliament, as 'destined to change the map of Europe', by itself the agreement will alter little other than the tone of EC–Comecon relations. The declaration, which was signed by Hans-Dietrich Genscher, the West

German Foreign Minister, de Clercq, on behalf of the European Commission, and Vyacheslav Sychov, the Soviet Secretary of Comecon, commits the two trading blocs to little more than a formal acknowledgement of each other's existence.

The declaration nonetheless represents a significant breakthrough for Mikhail Gorbachov, who is credited with overturning the traditional Soviet policy of hostility to the EC by manoeuvring Comecon (which groups the Soviet Union, East Germany, Poland, Czechoslovakia, Hungary, Bulgaria, Romania, Mongolia, Cuba and Vietnam) towards accepting the normalization of relations on terms approved by Brussels. Prior to the Luxembourg Declaration, Comecon had refused to recognize the EC on the grounds that it was the economic arm of the Nato Alliance.

Hitherto, Moscow was determined to retain tight control over East European trade by demanding that the Community conduct all trade accords through Comecon. However, because Comecon is not a supranational body it has no authority to negotiate international trade agreements on behalf of its members, Brussels refused to deal with what it called a 'phantom organization', and insisted that bilateral trade accords must run parallel with bloc-to-bloc recognition.

The overriding objective of Gorbachov's new approach is to lay the foundations for a significant increase in trade across Europe's ideological divide, in the expectation that Community finance and technology will be attracted east, providing a much-needed stimulus to the ailing Soviet and East European economies. In 1987 EC exports to Comecon were valued at £12.7 billion, while Comecon's exports to the Community totalled £16 billion. Considering the size of the two trading blocs, the volume of bilateral trade is comparatively small.

Two months after the declaration was signed, the Soviet Union, East Germany, Czechoslovakia, Hungary, Bulgaria and Poland had entered into formal diplomatic relations with Brussels. Simultaneously, the EC signed a wide-ranging trade agreement with Hungary, in which most of the Community's quantitative restrictions on Hungarian exports will be phased out by 1995. Moreover, during a meeting of the 24 Western countries in Brussels in September 1989, Hans-Dietrich Genscher, the West German Foreign Minister, added impetus to the current process of democratization in Poland and Hungary by suggesting that Eastern Europe could eventually become part of the European Community. Such rapid progress is, however, unlikely to be repeated with the other East European countries, at least until their economies have gone much further down the path of economic reform.

But the rapid pace of the democratization process in Eastern Europe, and particularly the tearing down of the Berlin Wall in November 1989, has provoked an anguished debate over whether it is possible to reconcile the Community's attempt to 'deepen' the relationship between existing member states by accelerating the integration process, with the desire—most notable in West Germany—to 'broaden' the Community's relationship with Eastern Europe—especially with East Germany—in the hope that the two Germanies will eventually be re-unified.

With little other than raw materials to export, the Soviet Union is far more interested in an economic co-operation agreement than the standard EC 'off-the-shelf' trade accord. However, de Clercq has made it clear that the extent and nature of such co-operation will depend very much on what the Soviet Union can offer the Community in return. High on the agenda is a considerable improvement in access to the Soviet market for West European companies and reform of Soviet maritime policies which reserve the great majority of Soviet seaborne trade for its own merchant marine. However, even assuming that Gorbachov is prepared to go this far, European business executives, hoping to take new opportunities in the East, will have to wait until the more fundamental problems of currency convertibility and the repatriation of profits are resolved before their expectations are realized.

The Third World

Most developing countries are able to export specified amounts of their manufactured produce to the EC with a partial or total reduction of Community customs duties through an arrangement known as the Generalized System of Preferences. However, the 66 members of the African, Caribbean and Pacific group of nations (the so-called ACP states) are granted quantity-free access for their exports under the provisions of successive five-year trade accords known as the Lomé Conventions. The Third Lomé Convention is due to expire in 1990, and negotiations for a Fourth Lomé Convention were initiated in October 1988 and are expected to last for about 18 months.

In contrast to trade accords conducted with the most economically advanced nations, the Lomé Conventions are not based on the principle of reciprocity, and represent one of the Community's most important mechanisms for promoting economic development in the Third World. They are regarded by the Third World, however, as a modest attempt to give ACP countries a guaranteed market for their exports, increase hard-currency earnings and thus reduce the burdens imposed by heavy external debt.

However, because of the internal market programme and the necessity of creating a common commercial policy towards third-country imports the current round of Lomé negotiations are likely to be of particular importance to ACP members. Many of these countries have benefited from preferential access to particular markets of EC member states. The Windward Islands, Jamaica and Belize, for example, have been able to export bananas to Britain under extremely favourable terms for decades. Under the proposed new harmonized external trade arrangements preferential treatment on a national basis will have to be eliminated. It seems

likely, however, given the Community's record on Third World development, that some formula will be devised which will preserve the privileges
enjoyed by ACP countries, albeit on a Community-wide basis. However,
the October decision to reduce grants in the Community's export guarantee programme for imports from developing countries appears to have
confirmed fears that the Commission is shifting its attention to Eastern
Europe at the expense of the Third world.

Checklist of changes

- The abolition of internal barriers to trade will be accompanied by
  a strengthening of the Community's external identity.
- National import quotas, such as those that currently exist for cars,
  will be gradually phased out and replaced with Community-wide
  quotas, at least until European manufacturers have been given
  sufficient time to adjust to international competition.
- The European Commission intends to use the principle of
  reciprocity to gain access to the markets of its major trading
  partners, particularly in the field of financial services.
- Although the six members of EFTA will continue to enjoy a
  privileged trade relationship with the Community, they will not
  be permitted to participate in Community decision-making
  processes to the same degree as member states.
- There is likely to be an increase in the number of US and Japanese
  companies locating themselves in Europe in the expectation that
  the Community will create protectionist barriers after 1992.
- There are also likely to be further increases in the number of
  anti-dumping duties imposed on foreign companies, principally
  those in the Far East, which the Commission believes are
  increasing their penetration of European markets by unfair means.
- The Community will experience a significant development in
  economic ties with Eastern Europe in the short-term, which could
  increase dramatically in the years ahead.

16 ARMS AND 1992
Defence and security in a united Europe

As Europe becomes more closely integrated, can a common European defence policy be far behind? The Single European Act certainly provides the basis for a common security policy. Although 'security' is a wider and more political term than the purely military concerns of 'defence', the two concepts overlap. Both have been given a new urgency by rapid developments in Eastern Europe, which have altered Western perceptions of the Soviet threat and have led the US to re-consider its military commitments to Europe within NATO. Together with new hopes come new concerns for the West: what if Gorbachov were to offer to remove Soviet forces from East Germany provided NATO forces withdraw from West Germany—in essence, bartering the GDR for the highest price Moscow can get? This could have the effect of limiting EC unity to the economic sphere, just as it is evolving into a political and—potentially—a defence union.

The member states of the EC have so far shown little inclination to make decisive steps towards a European defence union of the kind which was tried and found wanting in the 1950s. The consensus among defence experts is that a joint defence policy can only come after political union, and would need an act of collective political will to combine the differing defence interests and technologies of the European states. Three NATO countries, moreover—Iceland, Turkey and Norway—remain outside the EC. Nonetheless, giving 1992 a defence dimension is the subject of growing debate both in Brussels and in defence and foreign affairs institutes around Europe, while the prospect of sharing military costs through European co-operation in armaments design and manufacture is a politically attractive proposition.

As it happens, moves towards a common defence or security policy coincide with a rethink of values and strategy within NATO 40 years after the Atlantic Alliance was founded, with talk of the need for a new 'transatlantic bargain' and for Europe to contribute more to its own defence. This trend gained impetus when the Europeans found themselves not consulted by the United States at the time of the Reykjavik Reagan–Gorbachov summit in 1986, and were forced to take the question of European defence interests more seriously. All this coincides with 1992.

Yet of all the 1992-related issues, defence is the one with the most problems. These include the traditional reluctance of the EC to involve itself in defence matters, partly because of Irish and Danish reservations; American distrust of all moves towards a separate European defence identity; and (at present) lack of support among many Europeans for a greater defence effort at a time when East–West tensions appear to be easing after the Gorbachov reforms and the signing of international disarmament treaties such as the INF Treaty on intermediate nuclear weapons. Nonetheless, it is clear that security and military-related issues will be very much on the post-1992 agenda.

Arguably, the process of creating a common defence or security identity has already begun. When EC Foreign Ministers assembled for their semi-annual informal meeting at the seaside resort of Nyborg in Denmark in October 1987 one of the main items on the agenda was Gorbachov's speech at Murmansk, offering the West a pact on the partial demilitarization of seas in the Nordic area. The offer was considered and rejected, on the grounds that it merely reiterated a long-standing Soviet proposal, and would not materially add to Western security. However, it is worth noting that the EC was discussing an East–West defence and security issue. The Foreign Ministers have no power formally to accept or reject a Gorbachov proposal; this one just happened to be made on the eve of their meeting in the EC's only Nordic member country—Norway having rejected membership in 1972. Nonetheless, the EC has increasingly debated East–West issues, and this is hardly surprising since all EC states except Ireland are members of NATO. Nine of them—including Britain—belong to the Western European Union (WEU), the hitherto moribund European defence organization which was founded in 1948 and which has more recently become the focus of efforts (so far with only limited success) to lay the basis for a modern European defence policy in the 1990s.

One difficulty is the lack of any obvious forum for the evolution of a supranational defence policy. If an integrated Europe is to have an integrated or partially integrated European defence, such a joint effort could be organized through the WEU (which has somehow still not pushed itself into the forefront of the debate five years after its revival began); through bilateral defence co-operation, with the Franco-German Defence Council as a model; as the European pillar of NATO, perhaps with the present Euro-Group of European Defence Ministers and officials acquiring an expanded role; or by the EC itself.

EC security and foreign policy

Although political logic points to the EC acquiring a defence responsibility (and Jacques Delors, President of the European Commission, is keen that it should) the EC option is, apparently, the least likely and the least feasible. Of the Twelve, Ireland is neutral and a non-NATO member; Greece, although in NATO, has taken a maverick line more favourable to both the Soviet Union and radical Arab states than that of other Western nations; while Denmark—also a NATO member—inclines towards neutralism, and has a sizeable minority opposed to Denmark's membership of both the EC and NATO. On the other hand, the Nyborg meeting took place under Danish chairmanship. It was attended by the Irish Foreign Minister, who—unusually—did not find an excuse for leaving the room when the Gorbachov proposal was raised.

The question of formulating a defence or security policy is directly related to—indeed, grows out of—the EC's history of gradual, often crab-like moves towards a joint foreign policy, culminating in the growing importance of the EC foreign policy structure known as 'European political co-operation' (EPC), or (somewhat inelegantly) POCO. Political co-operation meetings are usually held at Foreign Minister level, with the assistance of Foreign Ministry political directors responsible for POCO co-ordination. Discussion of security issues in this context is justified by the reference in the Single European Act to the need for 'closer co-operation on questions of European security' within the political co-operation framework.

With or without a security dimension, the record of EC co-operation in foreign policy has been mixed. EC states remain divided over how they should proceed towards 'closer co-operation' in security, as well as over the difference between what is meant by 'security' and what is meant by 'defence'. The concept of a defence union to accompany economic and political union raises fundamental issues of national sovereignty, since defence and foreign policy—like taxation—are normally considered the prerogative of national governments and therefore 'no-go' areas for the EC.

European political co-operation

'Political co-operation' is a relatively recent invention, with its origins in the Davignon Report of 1970 rather than in the Treaty of Rome. Viscount Davignon of Belgium (later an EC Commissioner) was asked by The Hague EC summit of 1969 to put together a team of senior Foreign Ministry officials (he was himself in the Belgian Foreign Ministry at the time) to report on ways of increasing EC co-ordination in foreign policy. Despite objections on grounds of national sovereignty, the Davignon Report recommended the 'harmonization' of foreign policy views and—where possible—joint decisions on matters affecting the foreign policy interests of Europe as a whole. A number of countries, led by France, opposed the idea on the grounds that whereas individual states had foreign policy interests, Europe as a whole did not. Nonetheless, the proposal was adopted, with provision for twice-yearly meetings of EC Foreign Ministers to tackle 'political co-operation' questions.

Subsequent events provide an object lesson in the way in which harmonization proposals tend to be agreed by the EC, with member states entering reservations which eventually become eroded or apparently irrelevant. Initially, France made sure that a rigid distinction was drawn between 'political co-operation' meetings—held in the member state holding the Council of Ministers' Presidency—and normal EC Councils. At first the distinction was strictly enforced: long-serving EC officials recall that Foreign Ministers used to hold their regular sessions in Brussels or Luxembourg and then depart, with their staffs, for the country holding the Presidency in order to put their 'political co-operation' hats on. Eventually, however, this practice came to be regarded as wearisome and unnecessary, and the situation became confused, making such elaborate arrangements seem quaint or redundant. French opposition declined after the death of de Gaulle, and it become common for Foreign Ministers to mix normal EC business with foreign policy (most often, by discussing foreign policy matters over lunch). More recently, East–West issues and matters related in one way or another to defence, security or the common fight against terrorism have come onto the agenda, thus completing the original Davignon vision. 'It is simply not realistic to expect EC Foreign Ministers, who may have just come from a United Nations meeting in New York, a Western economic summit or a NATO Council to confine themselves to the EC budget' one senior diplomat in Brussels argues: 'They are bound to carry on discussing issues of vital concern to the West and to Europe in particular—and increasingly that means defence issues.'

Under the Single European Act a political co-operation secretariat was set up in Brussels to help the Foreign Ministry of the Presidency country to co-ordinate foreign policy. The Foreign Minister of the Presidency country speaks for the EC as a whole in the United Nations (UN). In theory, at least, the Twelve work out a joint line on international issues at the UN and vote together in the UN General Assembly: and the EC takes a common line on human rights and related issues at the Vienna European Security (CSCE) conferences. EC summits and Foreign Councils make declarations on global issues, from Afghanistan to the Middle East, and EC Foreign Ministers hold regular meetings with their counterparts from regional groupings—the Gulf, Central America, ASEAN, etc. These declarations have sometimes been influential: the 1980 Venice summit declaration on the Middle East is still remembered in the region because of its implicit suggestion that the Palestine Liberation Organization (PLO) should take part in the peace process, provided that it recognized the right of all states in the region (Israel included) to live within secure borders.

The EC has also taken limited sanctions against various states in an attempt to use its political and economic power for agreed European aims: against Libya and Syria over terrorism, for example, and against South Africa over apartheid. However, such sanctions have tended to be modified in practice, and have had mixed results (EC sanctions against Argentina in support of Britain during the 1982 Falklands War eventually failed completely).

As 1992 approaches it is entirely possible that, far from a defence union emerging from a joint foreign policy, the impetus may work in reverse, with the EC finding its foreign policy identity only when a joint defence effort is finally consolidated. Apart from trade issues such as Third World and Japanese dumping, there is still no pressing reason forcing the EC towards a common stance on most world issues. Foreign policy, for the most part, still rests on perceived national interests. Splits in Europe over how to deal with Iran and the hostage crisis in the Lebanon provide a case in point, with nations disagreeing on whether and how to deal with hostage takers. Britain and France still have world roles and links which echo past glories and responsibilities; West Germany looks to the East, and hopes that the problem of German re-unification can be resolved in the context of overall European unification, a prospect that unsettles its allies (as well as Moscow); Spain, Italy and Greece all have special links with the Arab world and the Mediterranean; Denmark is attracted to the Nordic states, and Danish ties with Scandinavia are formally acknowledged by the EC (for example, in allowing Denmark to maintain special trading and border arrangements with its Nordic neighbours). Developing a common foreign policy is a political minefield politicians do not rush to enter.

NATO and the American presence in Europe

A common European defence, by contrast, is more obviously (and can be more convincingly represented as being) in the general interest of Europeans. It is already firmly emphasized because of a growing movement in the United States—not least in Congress—to oblige 'the Europeans' to assume more of the Western defence burden—'roles, risks and responsibilities' in NATO jargon. In fact, the European members of NATO already contribute 90% of NATO's manpower in Europe, and almost the same percentage of the Alliance's tanks, artillery and combat aircraft. Nonetheless, American demands for a larger European defence effort reflect a general rethink in the Western Alliance and genuine American resentment over the extent of the US commitment to European defence.

There is no question of a US withdrawal, or a lessening of Washington's commitment to Europe. Yet troop levels could be reduced, and, as the US Presidential campaign in 1988 showed, it has become common in the United States to argue that although the depth of American involvement in European defences was justified after the Second World War, the world has moved on in the past four decades. This has been reinforced by Gorbachov's unilateral reductions in conventional arms, announced by him at the UN in December 1988. In 1988, the North Atlantic Assembly declared in its report *NATO in the 1990s* that a 'new transatlantic bargain' had to be struck. The European response has been to look for ways of meeting the American demand for fairer 'burden sharing' within NATO while at the same time exploring avenues towards a joint European defence—sometimes, paradoxically, to the alarm of the United States, which wants Europe to pay more for its own defence but does not relish the thought of a European defence body emerging as a counterweight or alternative to NATO itself.

West European—especially West German—susceptibility to the Gorbachov 'charm offensive' has caused much anxiety in Washington (and in

London), and the rapturous reception (dubbed 'Gorbymania') given to the Soviet leader in Bonn in June 1989 did nothing to allay fears of NATO disunity. On the other hand, President Bush did much to reassure the European allies and consolidate NATO by his performance at the Brussels NATO summit at the end of May 1989, when he matched Gorbachov's deftness in arms control by putting forward a proposal acceptable to all NATO members for conventional troop cuts, coupled with a compromise on eventual negotiations on short-range nuclear weapons (although tensions on this issue remain between Bonn and other allies). Bush subsequently pressed home his advantage in visits to Poland and Hungary, calling for a 'Europe whole and free', with the removal of the Berlin Wall, 'a brutal monument to the failure of Communism'. Bush also did much to recement US ties with West Germany on Ostpolitik, calling in a speech at Mainz for the encouragement of democracy in eastern Europe and East –West co-operation on pollution as well as 'a less militarized Europe'. In July Gorbachov replied, in an address to the Council of Europe in Strasbourg, that there could be 'no European unity' based on an attempt by the West to dismantle Communism, but it was an 'outmoded stereotype' that Russia had hegemonistic designs on Western Europe or wanted to 'decouple' it from the United States. He added: 'What we have in mind is a restructuring of the international order in Europe which would put common European values in the forefront and make it possible to replace the traditional balance of forces with a balance of interests.'

At their Malta summit in December 1989 Gorbachov and Bush moved toward a strategic nuclear arms treaty. Bush spoke of a 'new era' in Soviet–American relations while Gorbachov said: 'We are leaving behind the epoch of Cold War.' Even before Malta the usually hawkish Richard Cheney, the US Secretary of Defence, noted that the US wanted to 'take advantage' of reduced Warsaw Pact spending by making cuts of its own, while remaining alert to the possibility that Kremlin policy might be reversed. Cheney was reported to have ordered a study of possible cuts totalling 180 billion dollars in the fiscal years 1992–94, equivalent to an annual reduction in military spending of 5%. US proposals for a limit of 275,000 troops in Europe per superpower would mean the withdrawal of 30,000 US soldiers (out of 320,000) and some 300,000 Soviet soldiers. Some Pentagon sources suggest even bigger US cuts to help Bush reduce the huge US budget deficit.

When Mrs Thatcher met Bush at Camp David before the Malta Summit, she was at pains to stress the continuing Soviet threat, and urged the US to keep a 'substantial presence in Europe.' She warned against 'excessive euphoria' over change in the Soviet bloc, and called on NATO to maintain and modernize its forces, including short range nuclear weapons, as agreed at the NATO May 1989 summit. Yet when Hans Dietrich Genscher, the West German Foreign Minister, visited Washington in November 1989, his officials said this was now irrelevant, since the short range missiles were aimed at Poland, Hungary and East Germany. 'What do we need the missiles for—to bomb Lech Walesa?' was one West German comment.

In his Thanksgiving Day address Bush assured the Europeans that 'even if forces are significantly reduced on both sides—a noble goal indeed—we will remain in Europe as long as our friends want and need us.' Nonetheless, pressure for reduced defence spending in Britain and Europe is strong in the new climate. Quite apart from Polaris/Trident, the UK spends £300 million a year to maintain 67,000 troops and airmen in West Germany, and an extra 3000 in Berlin.

In Brussels, at the end of November 1989, NATO Defence Ministers affirmed 'the high priority we attach to the continuing US commitment to the defence of Europe.' The ministers noted that Soviet tank production had been cut by half, but said the Warsaw Pact still had 'well-equipped forces which outnumber those of the West . . . Unprecedented changes in the East give rise to the hope that a more secure military balance at lower levels of forces can be achieved,' the NATO statement said. 'But at a time of rapid change . . . our defence requirements must be assessed against the realities of Warsaw Pact capabilities.' Addressing the NATO allies in Brussels after Malta, Bush said: 'The US will remain a European power,' adding, 'we must not blur the distinction between promising expectations and present realities.'

The Western European Union

Given the present drawbacks of developing an EC defence dimension, attention has tended to focus on the WEU, which groups together Britain, France, West Germany, Italy and the Benelux countries, plus—following enlargement on 15 November 1988—Spain and Portugal. All nine countries are also in the EC, making the WEU potentially something close to the defence arm of the EC (although neither the EC nor the WEU would accept such a description).

The WEU was founded by the Treaty of Brussels in 1948 (the founding members were Britain, France, Belgium, the Netherlands and Luxembourg), and expanded in 1954 when West Germany and Italy joined. The 1950s were not a propitious time for European defence efforts, however, as is shown by the fate of the proposed European Defence Community (EDC), which was set up in 1952 by France, West Germany, Italy and the Benelux states but collapsed when the French National Assembly voted against ratification of the EDC Treaty two years later (West Germany joined the other Western nations in NATO shortly afterwards).

Unlike the abortive EDC, the WEU survived, with offices in both Paris and London, but lay dormant until it was revived in 1984 at Foreign Minister level. It has since been further strengthened under a triple impulse:

1 The need to create a closer European defence identity at a time
  when the superpowers are concluding far-reaching disarmament
  agreements directly affecting European interests;
2 Common European interests in areas outside Europe, notably the
  Gulf, with its vital oil supplies to Western Europe (less vital to the
  United States); and
3 The fact that two European powers, Britain and France, have
  independent nuclear deterrents which could be used for European
  as well as national defence but are not yet included in the terms of
  reference of any wider international arms control process.

A key move in the development of the WEU came in March 1987, when
Sir Geoffrey Howe, the then Foreign Secretary, in a speech to the Institute
of International Relations in Brussels called for a European defence
strategy, with the WEU headquarters moved from Paris and London to
Brussels. This proposal (much resisted by the French) would bring the
WEU institutions closer to NATO—and to the EC. Sir Geoffrey, like all
leading European statesmen, stressed Europe's continuing need both for
the protection of NATO and for the security provided by the US nuclear
umbrella—and the 350,000 US troops stationed in Europe. European
defence moves would not lead to the transatlantic 'decoupling' Moscow
was aiming at, Sir Geoffrey declared, but, he added, Europe had to face the
fact that it no longer dominated American thinking. Washington believed
that, nearly 40 years after post-war reconstruction, the Europeans were
prosperous enough to assume more of the defence burden.

Bilateral defence co-operation

In this analysis, a European defence policy could be based on a strengthened European conventional defence effort against the background of a
more equal balance of East–West forces, if the new Warsaw Pact–NATO
talks in the Vienna CSCE framework succeed, plus the deterrent provided
by the British and French nuclear forces, at present under national control,
and, in the British case, assigned to NATO. Thinking of this kind has been
encouraged by the development of limited forms of cross-border defence
co-operation, notably Anglo-French and Franco-German. In his Brussels
speech in 1987, Sir Geoffrey Howe noted that France was moving tenta-
tively away from the notion of a 'national sanctuary', protected by the *force
de frappe*, and towards the concept of a nuclear force for the protection of
both West Germany and France, and possibly of Western Europe as a
whole.

Other bilateral moves include exploratory Anglo-French talks on
nuclear co-operation (for example, joint targeting of the sovereign nuclear
deterrents) and the formation of a joint Franco-German military brigade.
This brigade, part of the 1988 Treaty renewing the 1963 Elysée Treaty, is
based at Boblingen, near Stuttgart, with 4000 men plus light tanks and

artillery. French and West German forces have also held large-scale manoeuvres in Bavaria. The Atlantic Assembly's report *NATO in the 1990s* went further, and suggested building on the Franco-German example to form a European brigade drawn from the national armed forces of Europe. Such moves are clearly partly designed to coax France back into the orbit of Western defence structures, if not into the integrated military structure of NATO, which the French left in 1966. Bonn has been reassured by Mitterrand's statement that French short-range missiles are not aimed at West Germany, and that the Hades missile (which can reach every West German city) may not be upgraded for three years, until after the next West German elections in 1991. There are also moves towards Anglo-German bilateral co-operation within NATO, although such co-operation falls short of the Franco-German link and no Anglo-German brigade is envisaged at present.

The WEU platform on European security

In October 1987, at The Hague, the WEU launched its 'Platform on European Security Interests'. 'Platform' was (and is) intended to sound less grandiose than 'Charter'—the original title of the WEU declaration —and therefore less likely to antagonize Washington. However, the WEU Platform marked an important step forward by laying the foundations for future joint European defence, with specific reference to EC integration. It said:

> We recall our commitment to build a European Union in accordance with the Single European Act, which we all signed as members of the European Community. We are convinced that the construction of an integrated Europe will remain incomplete as long as it does not include security and defence.

The Brussels Treaty founding the WEU, the declaration said, had far-reaching obligations to collective defence (more so than the NATO Treaty), and marked 'one of the early steps on the road to European unification'.

The WEU declaration noted that, despite the Gorbachov era, there had been no lessening of the Soviet armed build-up, and Europe remained vulnerable to superior Soviet conventional, chemical and nuclear forces. Partnership with the United States remained vital, with the transatlantic alliance resting on 'twin pillars'. However, 'specific European security interests' had to be taken into account by the superpowers in arms control deals—a reflection of European alarm at being left out in the cold and not consulted when Reagan and Gorbachov came close to negotiating substantial arms cuts at the Reykjavik summit in 1986. Above all:

> We see the revitalization of the Western European Union as an important contribution to the broader process of European

unification. We intend therefore to develop a more cohesive European defence identity . . . We shall ensure that our determination to defend any member country at its borders is made clearly manifest by means of appropriate arrangements: improve our consultations and extend our co-ordination in defence and security matters; see to it that the level of each country's contribution to the common defence adequately reflects its capabilities; aim at a more effective use of existing resources, *inter alia* by expanding bilateral and regional military co-operation; and concert our policies on crises outside Europe in so far as they may affect our security interests.

The last provision has given rise to what is perhaps one of the most effective aspects of WEU 'revitalization': the use of the WEU as an umbrella organization for the co-ordination of European activities in the Gulf, notably minesweeping and other naval actions by British, Dutch and Belgian warships.

Obstacles to a joint European defence

On the other hand, as 1992 approaches it remains unclear what is meant in reality by 'a more cohesive European defence identity'. Nation states remain reluctant to pool national resources in so sensitive an area as defence. There can be few more potent symbols of nationhood than a country's armed forces. The formation of a European brigade, let alone a European army, is as fraught with difficulty as the formation of a European police force to combat crime and terrorism in a border-free Europe.

Bilateral defence co-operation is complicated by tensions between the Western allies—for example, between West Germany and most other NATO allies over the modernization of short-range nuclear forces remaining after the removal of medium-range weapons under the INF Treaty (Bonn's anxieties arising from the fact that short-range battlefield nuclear forces are deployed on West German soil). European publics remain sceptical about the need for a greater defence effort at a time of East–West détente. Defence expenditures vary widely from one country to another, with the military budget amounting to 4.7% GDP in Britain, 4.0% in France, 3.0% in West Germany, 2.2% in Italy and 2.1% in Denmark. Britain, for its part, continues to place high value on its military co-operation with the United States. Anglo-French talks on British use of a French air-launched 'stand-off' nuclear missile to replace ageing British freefall nuclear bombs have run into difficulties because the French ASMP rocket, used on Mirage fighters, has a range of 150 miles rather than the 300 miles Britain wants, and does not have radar-foiling 'Stealth' technology of the kind developed in the United States.

Britain has clearly a key role in the field of defence. Although both Mitterrand and Kohl have cultivated links with Moscow—Kohl with an 'ice-breaking' visit to Russia in October 1988 and Mitterrand the following month—Mrs Thatcher is seen as a key European figure in East–West relations, and she could be central at a time of transition in superpower relations, as Russia adjusts to President Bush rather than President Reagan. However, Mrs Thatcher's views—as expressed in Bruges in September 1988—have hardly encouraged hopes of a joint European defence policy. Instead, she stressed the need to 'maintain the US commitment to Europe's defence', while adding that the WEU could be strengthened provided that it was not 'an alternative to NATO'. This echoed the Prime Minister's earlier warnings against 'substructures' within NATO.

The impetus towards co-operation

For all these difficulties, the impetus towards a common European defence is strong, and the question of how to achieve greater 'cohesion' is certain to be high on the post-1992 agenda. David Greenwood, Director of Defence Studies at Aberdeen University, argued in the June 1988 issue of the *NATO Review* that the transatlantic partnership is 'unhealthily unequal': the fact that American power and technology dominates NATO breeds 'European resentment', while the bearing by the United States of what it sees as a disproportionate share of the burden of defending the West fosters 'American disenchantment'. Western Europe, Greenwood suggests, must develop not only a more assertive personality but also more durable defence structures, for three purposes:

1 Co-ordination of policy;
2 Co-operation in arms procurement; and
3 Collaboration in defence industry production.

The case for intra-European co-operation in arms procurement is particularly compelling, since 'no country in Western Europe can afford the price of self-sufficiency in weapons research, development and production'. NATO has a procurement agency in the form of the Independent European Programme Group (IEPG), and projects such as the Euro-Fighter testify to the growing importance of collaborative projects. However, NATO officials want far more weapons harmonization, with a common defence research programme and a central register of defence requirements to match defence industry production and development. Greenwood concludes that the EC should 'promulgate a defence–industrial policy in the name of the Single European Act and in parallel with its policies for civil industry and technology'.

François Heisbourg, director of the International Institute for Strategic Studies (IISS), also believes that constructing an effective 'European pillar' of NATO would be 'a logical corollary to ventures leading to the creation of a single unified European market after 1992' (*The Times*, 8 July 1988). Yet, as he points out, Franco-German military co-operation, co-ordination of the European naval presence in the Gulf and the adoption of the WEU Platform in 1987 are still fairly modest achievements, given the scale of the problem. Moreover, West Germany, a key member of both the EC and NATO, has its own strategic and economic interests, preoccupied as it is with Central Europe and 'the other Germany'. France, while it acknowledges the existence of a general European 'strategic area', still resists defence harmonization or integration into the NATO structure, while Britain sees its defence role as separate from that of Europe, partly because of transatlantic ties and partly because of a long tradition of island defences against the very Continental powers now involved in 1992 integration. British defence planning also has a global role—albeit a much-reduced one—an echo of great imperial power. Britain, in Heisbourg's analysis, 'would appear to be in a position to take a leading role which it does not seem to be exploiting to the full'.

Defence and European political union

The impetus towards European defence need not weaken the transatlantic alliance, which has so far survived tensions not only in defence matters but also in trade and finance, with US–European strains arising over protectionism and the dollar and over regional conflicts. Transatlantic tensions will not go away, especially if (as the 1988 group of US experts' report *Discriminate Deterrence* suggests) US interests gradually move away from Western Europe and towards other regions of strategic interest to Washington. However, Europe remains central to US thinking.

The main problem lies within Europe itself, not least in a reluctance to face up to the consequences of a weakening of US nuclear protection after INF, the possible reduction of America's troops stationed in Europe and the cost of self-reliance. There is still insufficient common ground on defence between France and Britain, and between the two European nuclear powers and West Germany, which, because of its ties with the East, favours short-range nuclear reductions linked to progress on conventional and chemical weapons in the Vienna talks.

A convincing collective European defence policy, like an effective joint European foreign policy, can only come about when Europe is fully integrated both politically and economically. A European Defence Union, in other words, will be possible when the 1992 process is completed: it is unlikely to precede it.

This need not, however, prevent the European nations from now making preparatory moves towards greater co-operation in arms procurement and other defence fields, thus laying the foundations for some form of closer defence integration to accompany other aspects of the 1992 phenomenon. In the end, in defence as in the political, economic or technological fields, Europe will progress as far and as fast towards union as its publics and politicians want. Both the United States and the Soviet

Union meanwhile will watch closely and—for different reasons—anxiously to see how the defence dimension of 1992 develops in practice. An integrated Europe of 320 million people not only has the potential to challenge the superpowers and Asia in trading terms, it also contains within it the basis of a powerful and technologically advanced defence bloc—provided that the political will is there to bring it about.

17 YALTA TO MALTA AND BEYOND: REDRAWING THE MAP?

Eastern Europe, German reunification and the EC

In Western Europe, 1992 promises to make already successful economies even more prosperous. In Eastern Europe, by contrast, statues of Lenin and hammer and sickle symbols are being thrown on the scrap heap—and the East is looking to the West for its political and economic models. In a manner and speed which would astonish the EC's founders, what began as an enterprise of Six, then Nine and now Twelve may come to embrace all or most of the continent. The future of Europe is 'a question now posed in the broadest terms since the end of the Second World War,' *The Times* said in an editorial entitled 'Germany and Europe' in November 1989, as the Berlin Wall started to crumble. The dramatic developments in Eastern Europe, and especially in East Germany, since the latter half of 1989 have given the debate on Europe and 1992 a new focus. From the River Elbe dividing the two Germanies to the frontier with Turkey, the 'other Europeans' have risen with remarkable speed and determination to throw off—in a largely bloodless revolution—the Communist system imposed on them four decades ago.

This re-opens the question of what we mean by 'Europe', and of what is to be the link between the EC and its Eastern European neighbours in the changed political landscape, especially as the two Germanies move toward a new relationship, if not German reunification. Britain, France, West Germany and the Commission in Brussels all have different priorities, with Mrs Thatcher urging caution and using the upheaval to try and slow down economic and monetary union within the EC; Mitterrand arguing that a fast pace of integration will help anchor Bonn more firmly in the Community; Kohl striving for German unity while insisting that West Germany is not veering toward neutralism; and Delors seeking a common line based on fast EC integration, with EC aid to Eastern Europe made conditional on reforms which might make the East Europeans part of the EC 'family', particularly Poland and Hungary, whose reform record has long departed from Soviet-style centralization.

On the edges the two superpowers watch closely. In the USSR, increasingly reverting to its role as a European power, Gorbachov supports East European pluralism, while opposing German reunification, maintaining Communist one-party rule within the Soviet Union itself (although in an editorial in *Pravda* in December even the 'leading and guiding role' of the Communist Party was brought into question), and trying to keep nationalist separatism in the Soviet republics under control. President Bush, for his part, wants the EC to 'take the lead' so that the US can scale down its military commitments with confidence. As Bush put it on the eve of the Malta Summit: 'I do not share the concern that some European countries have about a reunified Germany, because I think Germany's commitment to the Alliance is unshakeable.' At his Malta summit with Gorbachov in December 1989, Bush clarified that re-unification was possible, but only in the context of close EC integration, and provided West Germany remained firmly within the EC and NATO. Delors agrees: Europe is in a 'state of flux' so the EC must 'reinforce its cohesion'.

Malta did not seek to redraw the map of Europe as defined at Yalta in 1945: some kind of belated reordering of the post-war shape of things could begin at the Helsinki Conference ('Helsinki Mark II'), proposed for 1990 by Gorbachov during his visit to Rome at the end of 1989, to 'overcome division' and 'deepen integration'. At his historic encounter with Pope John Paul II in the Vatican on 1 December, on the eve of Malta, Gorbachov spoke of the need to find 'solutions to common European problems' based on 'respect for people's national, state, spiritual and cultural identity'. This was 'an indispensable condition for the stable international environment which Europe and the world need to cross the historic watershed and attain a new period of peace'.

The assumptions which have underpinned the post-war world, includ-ing the carve-up at Yalta by Stalin, Churchill and Roosevelt, the Allied victors over Nazism, have certainly been thrown into question. The suspicion of many in the US and Britain is that Moscow's long-term aim is the dismantling of the two post-war military power blocs, NATO and the Warsaw Pact, with the West paying the price in the form of a neutralized Germany. Moscow is certainly playing the reunification card astutely, with Bonn's sensitivities in mind; when Hans Dietrich Genscher, the West German Foreign Minister, visited Moscow in December 1989, Soviet leaders said the Soviet Union was prepared to discuss German unity 'in the spirit of new thinking', but that the Kohl plan (see below) was 'tantamount to dictating to East Germany, a sovereign state, how it should develop relations with the other German state.' On his visit to Italy before Malta, Gorbachov said history would decide the question, and history could not be pushed. Western defence experts argue that as long as some kind of East-West division persists, NATO and the Warsaw Pact are still needed to maintain security, and as channels of communication on security and disarmament.

The euphoria which greeted the exhilarating sight of young Germans from East and West sitting atop the once-feared Berlin Wall on 10

November, hacking away whole chunks of it, has thus given way to more considered rethinking on Europe. The tidal wave of 'people power' in East and Central Europe requires a long-term EC strategy linking 1992 integration to the mapping out of a future Europe in which non-EC nations from both EFTA and democratized Soviet bloc countries are somehow involved in the single market. The EC-EFTA ministerial meeting in December, which authorized negotiations in 1990 on an EC-EFTA link-up, was a potential step in the direction of a redefinition of the single market.

This prospect, and its impact on 1992, dominated both the special EC Paris summit eight days after the Berlin Wall was breached, and the Strasbourg EC summit in December. The same questions dominate the debate in 1990: will the changes in Eastern Europe so preoccupy Bonn that West Germany's attention is distracted from the 1992 process as it focuses on 'the other Germany'? Will Britain use the upheavals in the Communist world to slow down 1992 integration in fields such as monetary union, on the grounds that the EC should wait and see how Europe develops before making further progress? And will the East Europeans themselves want to have a close relationship with the EC of Twelve, or even join it in a broad, historic European Union? Beyond these issues lies the fear, expressed from France to Poland, that a united Germany or 'Fourth Reich' would revert to the militaristic tendencies of the past. A less emotional but no less real concern is that a new German economic giant of 80 million people would upset the European balance, at present based on the Anglo-French-German triangle.

At their summit meeting in Strasbourg in December 1989, EC leaders attempted to alleviate these anxieties by in effect exchanging approval for German reunification for agreement to hold an inter-governmental conference in December 1990 to discuss moves towards economic and monetary union. President Mitterrand, eager to bind West Germany even closer to the Community, came up with a formula which satisfied German national aspirations, while at the same time committing Bonn to the next stage of European integration. Brushing Mrs Thatcher's objections aside, the summit communiqué endorsed the principle of German reunification, providing such moves were 'peaceful, democratic, and honoured existing treaties,' set the date for the inter-governmental conference needed to revise the Treaty of Rome, approved the creation of a new European Development Bank to assist East European economic reconstruction, and gave its seal of approval to the controversial European Charter of workers' rights. At the end of the summit President Mitterrand declared: 'Henceforth there are no longer two halves of Europe acting in the shadow of two great powers.'

Concern over German national aspirations had surfaced among West European leaders even before the Berlin Wall was breached. EC leaders could hardly be indifferent to the sight of overwhelming popular demand for change engulfing discredited traditional Communist leaderships from

Sofia to Prague, Warsaw to Budapest, forcing once feared and hated Politburo hardliners to give way to reformist leaders, make deals with opposition parties and promise free elections. In Poland, the first non-Communist government since the Second World War took office in August 1989, with the Solidarity-backed Catholic journalist Tadeusz Mazowiecki as Prime Minister.

In Budapest, the government abandoned the term 'People's Republic', and the Communist Party reconstituted itself in October 1989 as a democratic Socialist party, announcing multi-party parliamentary elections for late 1990. In Czechoslovakia, galvanized by the return of Alexander Dubček from oblivion, massive crowds succeeded in ousting the hardline leadership in Prague and extracting a commitment to elections coupled with the relinquishing of the Party's monopoly of power. In the words of Gennady Gerasimov, the Kremlin spokesman, the 'Brezhnev Doctrine', used to justify the 1968 invasion of Czechoslovakia to 'preserve socialism', has been replaced by the 'Sinatra Doctrine'—letting East Europeans 'do it their way'.

Yugoslavia, which went its own way long before other East European states, with a federal system and economic self-management, is of special concern to the EC: 40% of Yugoslavia's exports go to the EC, which is worried by the country's hyperinflation and $17 billion foreign debt. In November, EC foreign ministers discussed aid to Yugoslavia and approved new trade deals with Poland and Hungary, eliminating all EC barriers against Polish and Hungarian exports from 1990, with the Commission empowered to negotiate access to EC markets for steel and textiles from the two countries. Frans Andriessen, the External Relations Commissioner, said events in Poland, Hungary and Czechoslovakia were a 'cause for rejoicing throughout Europe'.

The heart of the matter remains Germany, and Germany's place in Europe. East Germany had a special relationship with the EC before 1989, through its low tariff deals with West Germany. But the growing exodus of young East Germans through gaps in the crumbling Iron Curtain, notably through Hungary, put the German question high on the EC agenda. On 10 September, Hungary opened its border with Austria to let 30,000 East German refugees through to the West. In October, thousands more left by special trains after taking refuge in West German embassies in Warsaw and Prague, and in November the exodus became overwhelming, accompanied by huge street protests in East Berlin and Leipzig. Erich Honecker was removed as East German leader in October and his successor, Egon Krenz (who resigned in December), faced with mounting protests and a mass of East Germans voting with their feet, took the desperate gamble of throwing open the border on 9 November, rendering redundant at a stroke the 'Anti-Fascist Protection Barrier', on which over a hundred East Germans had died trying to escape after its erection in 1961, and which Honecker had vowed would last a hundred years.

Early in November Martin Bangemann, the senior West German EC Commissioner and former government minister, himself born in East Germany, attacked suggestions that West Germany sought to recreate 'Mitteleuropa'—in effect, a powerful, reunited Germany. Bangemann, who held talks with Krenz in East Berlin on the implications of 1992 for East-West German trading relations, also criticized Mitterrand and Delors for indicating that 1992 integration should proceed even faster because of the challenge posed by East European democratization. Hans Dietrich Genscher appealed in Budapest on 24 November for the closest possible East-West integration, remarking: 'There is no capitalist German nation or socialist German nation but one united German nation.'

Sir Leon Brittan, Britain's senior EC Commissioner, appears to endorse this, and Delors' argument that 'Europe' denotes a 'family' which ultimately goes beyond the Twelve. Giving the Granada lecture at the Guildhall on 7 November, Sir Leon said expressing anxiety about German reunification would not prevent it taking place: 'Indeed, if Germany's partners give the impression of being opposed to reunification, this will only increase what is at present a small risk—that some in Germany may be tempted to see reunification on the basis of doing a unilateral deal with the Soviet Union, involving the setting up of a new unified German State outside the Community.' Opposing reunification would 'make it more likely to occur in the form we would least want'. By accepting a unified Germany, the EC would be making the kind of 'imaginative and far-sighted step it had taken by accepting West Germany into the EC in the first place as an act of post-war reconciliation', Sir Leon declared.

But how deep does democratization in Central Europe go, even given the vestiges of pre-war democracy which persist in Central European culture? To what extent have the East Germans developed a separate identity in the past forty years? At the heart of the EC debate on Eastern Europe lies the question of whether the EC should wait until the dust has settled before deciding on a firm policy, or should it rather attempt to consolidate and influence East European reforms by stepping in at the beginning of the democratization process to offer economic aid with political conditions attached. If the latter, should East Germany be singled for special attention, as Delors suggested before the special EC summit in Paris? The dilemma arose when Douglas Hurd, the Foreign Secretary, visited Berlin on 16 November, and agreed with Genscher that East Germany should not be given any special links with the EC before it holds free elections.

Commenting that the East German people themselves had 'opened up the Wall by their constant pressure for reform,' Hurd made clear that the privilege of special association with the EC had to go hand-in-hand with political reforms 'equally in each of the (East European) countries'. Delors' view that the East Germans were 'part of our family' and should be drawn closer to the EC, ahead even of Poland and Hungary, was rebuffed not only by London but also by Bonn. Theo Waigel, the West German Finance Minister, told the *Suddeutsche Zeitung* that it was not enough for West German consumer goods to fill empty East German shelves—there must be a restructuring of the East German system, with joint East-West German commissions to modernize East Germany's antiquated transport, communication and energy sectors.

The extraordinary Paris Summit of November 1989—convened so hastily that no 'position papers' were prepared—agreed that the dilapidated economies of Eastern Europe deserved EC support—provided the move toward democracy continued. Over dinner at the Elysée Palace, the Twelve decided to 'co-operate by all available means toward creating healthier economies (in Eastern Europe) in exchange for a verified return to democracy, respect for human rights and the calling of free and secret elections', in the words of President Mitterrand. Mrs Thatcher backed this up, commenting: 'It is important that practical help should be in return for proper democracy.' The summit made EC aid to Poland and Hungary dependent on progress in talks between Warsaw and Budapest and the International Monetary Fund, noting that if a deal with the IMF was reached, the EC could release a $1 billion 'stabilization' loan to Poland and a 'bridging loan' of the same amount to Hungary. Kohl, reflecting the more urgent West German perspective, declared: 'We are under enormous time pressure if the reforms are to succeed . . . If reforms in Poland and Hungary should fail, this would have unpredictable consequences for the whole of Europe.'

Much will depend on the post-Malta superpower relationship, and the attitude of Moscow and Washington to events in Germany. As the Paris summit leaders departed, Henry Kissinger, the former US Secretary of State, predicted that the reunification of Germany would be 'unavoidable' within ten years. But despite Soviet ambiguity on the issue, Viktor Karpov, the deputy Soviet Foreign Minister and former arms negotiator, told a West German weekly that Bonn must 'take into account the real situation: the existence of two sovereign German states and their places in the European political system.' The Gorbachov leadership clearly remains wary of the kind of strong, united Germany which has posed such an awesome threat to Russia in the past. At the Malta Summit, Gorbachov declared: 'We have to abide by realities. In Europe today there are two German states.' Mrs Thatcher agrees: the question of re-negotiating Europe's borders, she said at Paris, was 'not on the agenda'. The borders 'should stay as they are, and all military matters must continue to be conducted through NATO and the Warsaw Pact' she added.

Nonetheless, as noted in the previous chapter, democratic reform in the Soviet bloc has altered perceptions of the Soviet threat, and thus changed the arms control agenda. Dick Cheney, the US Defence Secretary, noted even before Malta that the US was able to consider 'significant' cuts in its defence spending because of a drop in Warsaw Pact spending. But a reduced US commitment in Europe is only possible for Washington if a thoroughly integrated EC provides a solid bastion of strong, well-defended democracy, allowing West and East Germany to forge a new relationship across what was once the Iron Curtain. At both Paris and Strasbourg, Kohl sought to meet this challenge with a compromise formula: 'We are all aware that the union of Europe within the European Community has priority today more than ever' he declared. 'Indeed, it is one of the preconditions for reform in Eastern Europe.' During his historic visit to Poland in November 1989, at the time of the breaching of the Berlin Wall, Kohl told an audience at the Catholic University at Lublin that 1992 must have a 'strong East European dimension', and that German unity 'must be on the agenda' in some form. Poles, he said, should surely understand more than most that 'the historic unity of a nation cannot be artificially destroyed. Any policy based on the division of a nation is ahistorical, without credibility, and therefore without a future.'

The Germany of today was not the old Germany of dark excesses, he said, but a Germany of democratic and Christian values, of which the EC integration process was a guarantee. 'We want European union, the United States of Europe' Kohl declared firmly. 'The EC was, is, and will stay open for other democratic countries in Europe—Warsaw, Moscow, Prague, Budapest and Vienna are as much a part of Europe as Brussels, London, Paris, Rome, and of course, Berlin.' The EC must 'approach with imagination and flexibility those Central and East European states which are embarking on deep reforms of their politics, economy and society'.

Yet Kohl's reference to 'dark excesses' strikes a chord, even causes a shiver in those parts of Europe whose present borders are the result of cruel and barbaric rule by Nazi and Stalinist totalitarianism. The democratization of Eastern Europe has not only raised the question of borders, it has thrown up the even deeper question of whether the process of integration in Western Europe, founded on common democratic values, can be extended to the rest of Europe, perhaps even to Moscow, where such values have often had only shallow roots.

As Donald Cameron Watt, Professor of International History at the LSE, put it in *The Sunday Times* on 19 November, freer travel across East-West borders opens up a vision of Europe as 'a total free trade area', with 'its peoples living together in comparative amity, free from fear of war or violence, its security forces reduced to the minimum to combat civil and international crime, the frontiers open, and the public, not excluding salesmen and investors, travelling freely'. Yet Europe was still obsessed with memories of '1870, 1914 and 1939'. As the Soviet empire crumbled, old national frictions were emerging: the Hungarian minority in Romania, the German minority in Silesia, the Albanians in Yugoslavia. Transnational management and planning were certainly needed to tackle the legacy of Stalinist governments which had polluted and impoverished everything they touched. Yet 'within French and Polish hearts, at levels much deeper than reason, talk of German reunification stirs images of the Gestapo . . . of the midnight knock on the door and the sealed train to the death camp. Pessimism sees ahead of us a Central Europe no longer dominated by the long shadows of 45,000 Soviet tanks or 1400 Lance missiles, but still divided, disappointed and embittered with ancestral memories and hatreds.'

Lord Callaghan, the former Labour Prime Minister, sounded a similar warning in the House of Lords debate on the Queen's Speech on 22 November: the Cold War, and Moscow's iron grip on Eastern Europe, had 'kept many of Europe's ancient antagonisms and feuds in the deep freeze'. The loosening of that grip could mean 'the Balkanization of Eastern Europe, for some of those countries do not have long experience of the conventions and constraints that a democratic system imposes'.

Behind the challenge for the EC in rethinking 1992, in other words, is the question of whether the process of integration started by Monnet and Schuman, and taken up by Delors, will prove equal to the weight of European history, a history in which rivalry and bloodshed have figured more often than co-operation, with a consequent cost in human pain and division. In the near future, as the Strasbourg summit indicated, the EC watchword is likely to be caution coupled with encouragement of reform.

When Kohl appeared at the Berlin Wall as it was breached he declared exuberantly 'Long live a United Germany', adding: 'This is a great day for German history. We are and will remain one nation and we belong together. Step by step we must find the way to our common future.' His subsequent emphasis, however, has been on the 'step-by-step' approach. Launching his ten-point plan for a German 'confederation', Kohl told the Bundestag that while the 'unity of the Fatherland' was of concern to all Germans, West Germany had to 'close ranks with our allies'. It would be a 'fatal error to slow West European integration' because of developments in the East. German problems could only be solved 'under a European roof'. But the GDR could not join the Community before 1992 at the earliest: 'If you look at what we have still to do [in the EC], you will see that GDR membership is not feasible until 1992 is completed.'

The Kohl plan, unveiled on 28 November, offered a three-stage process: first, free elections in East Germany and a free vote on reunification; second, the setting up of pan-German commissions on economic matters; and third, some form of 'confederation', with West Germany staying in the EC and NATO, and East Germany staying in the Warsaw Pact. Kohl laid down no timetable, declaring 'We are not daydreamers, German unity cannot be achieved overnight'. Even so, Moscow accused him of trying 'to push the recently-begun process of renewal in the GDR in a nationalist direction'. Europe, the Kremlin said, preferred stability to 'the destruction of territorial political structures', and the German question could only be solved as part of a broader process of overcoming the division of Europe.

East German leaders were also critical, indicating that many East

Germans would prefer to retain some of the socialist features of the GDR. Some East Germans fear that Kohl's plan would end in the virtual annexation of East Germany by its richer and more powerful Western neighbour. As Gorbachov told Bush at Malta, German reunification is at best a distant prospect. It will nonetheless be the uninvited guest at every debate on Europe and 1992 from now on, forced onto the agenda by a tide of history which neither the superpowers nor the architects of EC integration had anticipated.

The overthrow and execution in December 1989 of the Romanian dictator Nicolae Ceausescu, following a popular revolt supported by the Romanian Army, serves to underline the way in which apparently immoveable Communist regimes have crumbled, and with them old certainties about the European order. The events in Romania were all the more remarkable because of tacit approval for the revolt given by Moscow. Even the Soviet attitude to German reunification appears fluid: on his historic visit to Brussels as 1989 gave way to 1990, Eduard Shevardnadze suggested that neutrality and the de-militarization of the Germanies were Soviet conditions for unity. Hope for a peaceful future certainly dominated the extraordinary cross-border New Year's party celebrated by Berliners from East and West at the newly re-opened Brandenburg Gate at the start of 1990.

Already, the Bank for International Settlements in Basle has detected a major shift in lending by Western banks toward Eastern Europe and away from other areas such as Latin America. Investors are focussing on West Germany as the likely locomotive for economic regeneration in the East. In the long term, the question is not only whether East European countries can achieve political stability, but also whether given an injection of market forces they will prove able to match the growth rates of the West. If they do, the result could be a Greater Europe combining the 320 million people of the EC with the 400 million of Eastern Europe and the Soviet Union, giving Greater Europe a total GDP twice that of the United States by the early part of the next century. If all goes well—and it could still go disastrously wrong—the centre of gravity of world trade could be about to shift back to the Old World from the New.

CONCLUSION
Britain, 1992 and European union

For Britain, the upheavals in Eastern Europe make the question of British committment to EC integration more imperative—not less. As Anthony Sampson argued in the December issue of *Newsweek*, Britain remains torn between the idea of Europe as a close association of nation states, and the rival concept of a Community in which sovereignty is shared and nationalism is contained. The East Europeans, Sampson points out, want to be part of the Community, and admire its dynamism, yet also want to assert their national identities as 'the natural response to their liberation from Soviet domination.' The opening up of Eastern Europe is a profound historic change, with important consequences for Germany. It also confronts Britain, in sharper than ever form, with the question of whether the British preference is an old-fashioned 'Europe of Nations' or an integrated United States of Europe. The EC, Kissinger has said, 'cannot survive if the Germans see it as a device to thwart unification.' But Britain holds the key to a balanced Europe, since a thoroughly committed Britain, together with France, Italy, Spain, could surely contain even a powerful Germany: 'Indeed, the strongest argument for Britain's wholehearted participation in the 1992 process is the need for Britain's political experience in establishing an appropriate balance within the European Community.'

The debate over 1992 can be presented too much in terms of Britain versus the Rest. All EC nations have their views on 1992, all have hopes and fears. The French, like the British, are resisting the approximation of VAT rates through directives rather than market forces, partly because Paris prefers VAT to income tax as a source of revenue. France, Spain and other countries are as concerned as Britain about the need to control drugs, terrorism and crime after 1992. West Germany is worried about the impact on previously highly protected sectors such as transport and insurance, and is anxious that the EC should not lose sight of the fact that 'Europe' embraces East as well as West Europe. Most EC countries, moreover, have a far worse record than Britain when it comes to observance of EC law and the Treaty of Rome.

Even the stereotype of the insular Briton, unable to speak European languages and secretly wanting to draw up the Channel drawbridge, has its Continental counterpart. Anyone who has observed West German tourists in Spain or Italy will note that German capacity for speaking foreign languages is not much greater than our own. On many Continental trains, passport and customs checks are minimal already. Yet anyone taking a train from France to Italy, or from Italy to France, along the Riviera

Coast, having to change at the border and pass through customs only to find that trains on either side of the border do not connect, will reflect that the French and Italians also have a long way to go before they regard one another as part of the same internal market. There is even the danger that, contrary to the idealism of its founders, the EC will degenerate into xenophobia as nationalist feelings come to the fore in a belated reaction against 1992.

Nationalism and European identity

In her speech on Europe at Bruges in 1988 Mrs Thatcher poured scorn on the idea of an 'identikit European personality': 'To try to suppress nation-hood would be highly damaging . . . Europe will be stronger precisely because it has France as France, Spain as Spain, Britain as Britain, each with its own customs, traditions and identity.' Yet Jacques Delors, at the opposite end of the Euro-spectrum, also acknowledges that national traditions will persist long after 1992, and as a Frenchman could hardly do otherwise: 'Naturally there is the question of national identity' he told *Le Monde* in July 1988.

> But in my concept of Europe the French will remain French, France will still be France. Quite simply, the French will also belong to a second country called Europe.

This is in line with Lord Cockfield's theory that the creation of a United Europe is analogous to the creation of the United Kingdom. Scots, Welsh and English owe fundamental loyalty to the United Kingdom, pay taxes to its government and are ready, if necessary, to don a uniform and defend it, yet they do not cease at the same time to owe often intense regional loyalty to Scotland, Wales or a region of England. There is no reason, in this view, why they should not in future owe a triple loyalty: to region, country and Europe as a whole.

Far from being in retreat, regional and national feeling appears to be intensifying in West and East Europe, from Scotland to Estonia. However, in theory at least, Western Europe's kind of integration can contain such pressures. The Scottish National Party even advocates an independent Scotland within a barrier-free EC. In response, Leon Brittan, the senior UK Commissioner, said in *The Times* on 19 November 1988 that if a majority of Scots want to go their own way within the EC they should be allowed to do so, since although Scotland would 'suffer by separation from the rest of the UK', self-determination is a fundamental right.

It is, in any case, questionable to what extent the British are 'anti-European'. Opinion polls conducted by Euro-Barometer, the EEC's own polling organization, consistently show a majority of British respondents in favour of some form of European unification. A MORI poll published in *The Mail on Sunday* on 25 September 1988, shortly after the Bruges speech, produced similar results, with a majority of those questioned favouring unity up to and including a single currency, a result which suggests that anti-EC rhetoric is not necessarily a vote winner. As Christopher Huhne observes in his monograph on *The Forces Shaping British Attitudes Towards the EC* (Centre for European Policy Studies, Brussels, CEPS Paper No. 23, 1985), Britain is an island, 'but an island with a long tradition of trade and exchange with the continental mainland . . . the degree of foreign travel, the increasing willingness to learn other European languages and the opinion poll evidence all suggest that the British people's attitudes would be unfairly characterized as isolationist'.

For that matter, Mrs Thatcher herself is not an isolationist. At Bruges she said:

> We British are as much heirs to the legacy of European culture as any other nation. Our links to the rest of Europe, the continent of Europe, have been the dominant factor in our history . . . And let me be quite clear: Britain does not dream of some cosy, isolated existence on the fringes of Europe. Our destiny is in Europe, as part of the Community.

Britain is inextricably enmeshed in the economic and political machinery of the EC, and plays a major role in it. After the February 1988 summit, where Britain compromised on structural funds and farm limits—with David Williamson, the new British Secretary General of the Commission and a Thatcher confidant playing a key role—Frans Andriessen, Vice-President and Farm Commissioner, writing in *European Affairs* in 1988, wondered whether Mrs Thatcher's 'accommodating attitude' heralded 'a more fundamental swing of the UK towards Europe'.

The appalling behaviour of British football hooligans on the Continent, and the drunken rampages of young British 'holidaymakers' in Spain, reflect a contemptuous and ignorant attitude towards fellow Europeans as well as personal inadequacy and social malaise at home. On the other hand, the modern generation of professional-class Britons is far less influenced by stereotypes of 'Continentals' than previous generations, and more likely to view Europe in terms of business and money market opportunities. The modern approach is relatively hard-headed and unsentimental, unimpressed by narrowly 'nationalist' values. To a degree, Mrs Thatcher's rhetoric masks the fact that the Prime Minister herself has taken a full and exhaustive part in EC decision making, often improving the end result by leavening wilder EC proposals with common sense and experience. The internal market programme and the Single European Act both bear British hallmarks, not least in the emphasis they place on deregulation. As the *Wall Street Journal* rightly put it in an elaborate headline on 7–8 October 1988): 'Thatcher May Berate EC But She Leads UK Into Ever Deeper Role: Cantankerous Pose Increases Her Clout, Although She May Be Risking Isolation'. It added: '1992 Goal—Made in Britain?'

Britain, the EC and pooling of national sovereignty

Nonetheless, Britain is the country widely perceived in Europe as being the most resistant to European integration. The history of Britain's relationship with the EC (late application, rejection, accession, renegotiation, budget rebate squabbles) has produced a Europhobia in which Britain's natural reaction to EC proposals tends to be 'no' rather than 'yes but'. This is reinforced by the fact that, as an island race, the British do not feel culturally European; by ties with the United States and the Commonwealth; by a continuing global defence policy; and by the role of sterling as a world currency.

There is therefore a trend in British opinion, also reflected in Mrs Thatcher's approach, which fears that instead of the Prime Minister's preferred vision of 'willing and active co-operation between independent sovereign states', something more like a 'European superstate' will emerge. The Commission promotes symbols of European nationhood —the EC flag, the European anthem (Beethoven's *Ode to Joy*)—when in reality the process of forming a European identity has barely begun. To suggest, as the Commission has in newspaper advertisements, that all Europeans should share in the glory of medals won by the Twelve at Olympic games is counterproductive, since national feeling is expressed above all through sport, and will continue to be long after 1992.

Yet 1992 and the Channel Tunnel will, between them, bring great psychological changes, as the British adjust to having an 'umbilical cord' tying them to the Continent. There is already a breed of business executives who commute across the Channel, and British property developers are moving into the Pas de Calais and the Boulogne area. After 1992, this kind of cross-Channel fertilization will be common.

Does this make it inevitable that something approaching a United States of Europe will come about, as a natural consequence of 1992? Mrs Thatcher thinks not: others believe that union of some kind is both inevitable and desirable. The case has been most forcefully put by Chancellor Kohl of West Germany, who, as a Christian Democrat, is ideologically aligned with the Conservative Party but who reflects West German enthusiasm for European integration. In a speech in Brussels in October 1988, Kohl spelled it out as graphically as he could, without mentioning Mrs Thatcher by name. He spoke in favour of the 1992 'social dimension', under which trades unions would become involved in the 1992 process and employees' rights would be harmonized, perhaps through an EC company statute (dismissed by the UK at an internal market council in Luxembourg in October 1988 as 'irrelevant').

Kohl said that fiscal harmonization was indispensable in 1992; as for the fight against crime and terrorism, he called for a European police force along US lines, adding: 'I know this idea has far-reaching consequences, but the nature and size of the challenge we face leaves us no choice.' On defence, Kohl suggested the eventual creation of a European Army, although this would require 'a pragmatic approach and much patience'. Finally, the loss of sovereignty involved in 1992 would be counterbalanced by a gain in pooled sovereignty jointly exercised. Similar views were expressed by Ciriaco de Mita, the Italian Prime Minister, when he met Mrs Thatcher at Lake Maggiore in October 1988. While Thatcher reiterated opposition to a European Central Bank ('I do not expect to see it in my lifetime, or if I'm twanging a harp, for a long while after'), de Mita remarked:

> The idea that Europe can be nothing more than an economic entity without political power is absurd. Transfer of sovereignty will become increasingly necessary.

Michel Rocard, the French Prime Minister, on 24 October 1988 also told the *Financial Times* that he was a 'federalist': 'If we are not federated within 20 or 30 years our generation will be guilty in front of the world.' Mrs Thatcher's view of the EC as a confederation of nation states was 'archaic'. When presented with the Charlemagne Prize at Aachen, together with Kohl, in November 1988, Mitterrand defined the EC goal in 1989 as 'one currency, one culture, one social area, one environment'. Speaking alongside President Bush in Mainz in May 1989, Kohl declared: 'For us Germans, political union is not a distant vision. I would very much like to see it achieved by the end of the century.'

'Socialist central control' and the European superstate

The process outlined by Kohl, de Mita, Mitterrand and other leaders does not quite add up to a United States of Europe—but it is a step along the road. This adds force to Mrs Thatcher's post-Bruges observation that she had been accused of attacking a prospect which did not exist—the European superstate—when in fact it did. This is crucial to the whole 1992 debate: is Mrs Thatcher 'tilting at windmills', as even some in her own party have put it, or is she resisting very real attempts by her fellow EC leaders to make 1992 into a platform for outright political union?

Part of the problem is that neither the phrase 'an ever-closer union' laid down in the preamble to the Treaty of Rome nor the goal of 'European Union' enshrined in the Stuttgart summit declaration of 1983 have ever been properly defined. This gives room for conflicting interpretations, including, in Mrs Thatcher's case, the 'nightmare' of a 'socialist' and 'collectivist' European superstate run from Brussels (in part, a reaction against union power), 'consensus politics' and pre-Thatcher Conservatism of the 'wet' variety as much as anything describable as 'socialism'. At the Conservative Party Conference in Brighton in October 1988 the Prime Minister gave the formula a new twist: 'We haven't worked all these years to free Britain from the paralysis of socialism only to see it creep in through the back door of central control and bureaucracy from Brussels.' She repeated this formula during the 1989 European election, telling the Scottish Conservative Party conference that Labour wanted 'the socialist utopia that mercifully we have been spared in Britain: they are all for devolving power to Brussels. If they can't get socialism in by the front door—and they can't—they'll get it in by the back—if they can'.

The choice, Thatcher said, was between two Europes—'one based on the widest possible freedom for enterprise, and one governed by socialist methods of centralized control and regulation'. The choice is not, however, a real one. The 'social dimension' would involve the law in employer–employee relations, but few Continental leaders, whether of the left or right, would regard this as 'collectivist'. Most Continental systems rest on a political culture of consensus, so that Kohl (for example) presides over a Centre–Right coalition which accepts worker participation in industry (*Mitbestimmung*) as much as the opposition Social Democrats do. The effect of 1992, West German industrialists believe, will be to reduce overprotection of employees rather than the reverse. All EC leaders are committed to free-enterprise capitalism, as is Delors, even though he is a French socialist by origin. As Joe Rogaly wrote in the *Financial Times* on 19 May 1989: 'Margaret Thatcher has an enemy clearly in her sights and is fighting it with every ounce of her ferocious energy. But the enemy is largely a figment of her imagination: a sinister Brussels conspiracy to impose corporatist and Marxist principles on Britain.'

To some extent, generalized attacks on 'rule from Brussels' articulate a British aversion to the involvement of 'foreigners' in domestic British affairs. However, calling European federalism 'socialist' has confused the issue. What such attacks really express, perhaps, is disagreement with the kind of federalism adopted by Christian Democrats such as Kohl and Wilfried Martens, the Belgian Prime Minister. Shortly after the Bruges meeting, Martens said that elimination of trade barriers would make closer political unity inevitable, leading to 'some form of loosely constructed federal European government' responsible not only for economic affairs but also defence and foreign relations. Martens agreed with Mrs Thatcher's 'apprehension about an unbridled European bureaucracy' and 'centrally imposed overregulation', but came to the opposite conclusion: the answer lay in an all-European executive body 'answerable to a genuinely European and sovereign legislature'. National states would retain some powers to control crime and immigration, and 'given Europe's history, steeped in diversity, a highly decentralized form of government is undoubtedly preferable'. But European government there would be. Five Christian Democrat Prime Ministers, including Kohl, Martens and Ruud Lubbers, the Dutch Prime Minister, met in Brussels in late October 1988 to re-affirm this line.

The Commission, angered by the charge that the EC is controlled by 'appointed bureaucrats', has also joined the debate. To focus on the

Commission, officials point out, is to ignore the Council of Ministers and the Parliament, which take decisions for the Twelve as a whole. In an interview in *Le Figaro*, Delors said in October 1988 that only the British Prime Minister dissented from the goal of economic and monetary union, 'because national currency is seen as a symbol of national sovereignty'. He himself was mistakenly seen as 'a sort of red demon who wants to blow on the embers of outdated socialism'. Andriessen departed from remarks on farm reform in Dublin on 20 October to make the 'personal' observation that Mrs Thatcher's views were based on a 'profound misunderstanding'. The Commission's real aim was to enhance competition and enterprise, limit central regulation 'to the minimum level required for coherence' and give the regions a greater say in their own economic development.

Lord Cockfield told the Swiss Institute for International Studies in Zurich the same month that, although the concept of European Union was not defined in the Treaty of Rome, it clearly meant economic and political union. The EC was avoiding 'provocative terms' like single currency 'in view of the sensitivities of certain member states', but 'no-one need have any doubt about what is intended or where we are going'.

Federalism: the end of the nation state?

Peter Sutherland, the former Commissioner for Competition, has called for 'a reasoned debate, avoiding emotional polemics' on how Europeans could deal with the loss of sovereignty resulting from 'our common commitment to the 1992 programme'. He wrote in *The Times* on 22 October 1988:

> It is important to remember that with the ratification of the European treaties, concessions of sovereignty to autonomous European institutions have already occurred. An embryonic federal structure is in place, even if its powers are confined to certain areas . . . There is no vast bureaucracy in Brussels which seeks to impose itself on member states. It is inconsistent to criticize the institutions of the Community for being appointed rather than elected democratically and at the same time to ignore the claims of the European Parliament for powers which alone can develop control on a common European basis.

Delors backs this up. He told the Belgian daily *Le Soir*:

> It is the Council and not the Commission which takes the real decisions. It is regrettable that attacks on the Brussels bureaucrats have become a scapegoat and a way of avoiding having to give concrete answers to what should be done to implement the Single European Act.

However, the problem of the 'democratic deficit' is not so easily solved. If transfer of sovereignty is inevitable, is the right answer to devolve further powers from Westminster, the Bundestag and the Assemblée Nationale to the European Parliament? The same Britons who supported European unification in the MORI post-Bruges opinion poll obviously thought not: 67% opposed giving greater power to Strasbourg, with only 25% in favour. Sheer volume of work, and the integration process, are pushing the European Parliament towards more frequent sessions (perhaps two weeks a month instead of one) and will almost certainly press for meeting in Brussels rather than in Strasbourg. This is not the same, however, as the evolution of a European government.

The idea of a European government, in any case, arouses horror in some quarters. Responding to Commissioner Sutherland, William Cash, Conservative MP for Stafford and a member of the Commons Select Committee on European Legislation, claimed in *The Times* on 25 October 1988 that European federalism was being introduced by stealth:

The EC in principle has just about the right framework now. It will
develop and must be reformed. The advantages it offers will help
us to compete successfully with other continental giants. But
political union on the same scale is unnecessary, and could provoke
unwelcome hostility.

Others who are unhappy about the transfer of sovereignty involved in 1992 fall back on a cautious 'step-by-step' approach. On the other hand, as Sir Nicholas Henderson—former British Ambassador in Bonn, Paris and Washington, and chairman of the Channel Tunnel Group—pointed out in *The Independent* on 13 October 1988, 'a step-by-step approach is very reasonable, but it is also reasonable to believe that the steps must be leading somewhere'. He added:

For many of the peoples of Europe the nation state has proved in
this century to be not only inadequate to their needs, but
disastrous. Without wishing to sacrifice national tradition or
nationhood, they aspire to a new and wider identity.

What is needed, in other words—especially in an era when there is likely to be further pooling of security and defence interests—is a redefinition of the nation state itself. In their recent study of *Options for British Foreign Policy in the 1990s* (Royal Institute for International Affairs, October 1988) Christopher Tugendhat and William Wallace confront this directly:

There is now a structural contradiction not only between the logic
of international industrial and economic integration and the
national framework of popular loyalty, but also between the

increasing integration of defence and security policies and the underlying rationale of the nation state. The force of this contradiction has not yet filtered through to the British electorate.

Wallace regards national sovereignty as a Victorian creation, and points out that Mrs Thatcher has no qualms about allowing Japanese or other foreign takeovers: 'Like Hugh Gaitskell during the debate over Britain's first application to the EC, the Government seems determined to defend the myths of British history and constitution against the realities of the contemporary global economy.' The shade of Churchill is invoked by both sides: in 1953 he observed that 'We are in Europe but not of it, linked but not comprised, associated but not absorbed'. But in *The Times* on 23 June 1989 Edward Heath claimed that the Conservatives had lost electoral support because of Mrs Thatcher's 'aggressive and nationalistic rhetoric', a contrast with Churchill's 1948 view that some sacrifice of sovereignty was involved in 'the gradual assumption by all nations concerned of that larger sovereignty which alone can protect their diverse and distinctive customs and characteristics'.

Defining Europe: the global context

One side-effect of Mrs Thatcher's Bruges speech is that it may have helped to emphasize to British voters that the underpinning of the nation state (popular loyalty to the state within defined borders, management of common economic resources within the same borders, taxation to raise revenues, the maintenance of nationally defined police and armed forces) needs re-examining as some of these functions begin to take on a pan-European character. Traditionally, a nation defines itself by what its citizens have in common, or—what is not quite the same thing—by ways in which it differs from other nations. Ultimately, nation-states are given internal coherence by their response to perceived external threats. In the past, such threats, whether commercial or military, have come to Britain from across the Channel, in centuries of trading wars and military conflicts with France, Germany and other Continental countries, one (the Second World War) within living memory. Popular stereotypes of Germans, French and Italians are still based on the last war.

However, as 1992 approaches, the perceived military threat is from the Soviet Union to Western Europe as a whole, while the perceived commercial threat—again to Europe as a whole—comes from the United States and Japan. Europe itself, meanwhile, grows more compact: the Channel Tunnel will reduce train journey time between London and Paris from 5½ hours to 3, between London and Brussels from 5 hours to 2½, and between London and Amsterdam from 10 hours to 5.

Certainly, the rest of the world increasingly looks on Europe as a unit, and deals with it as such. The United States, Japan, Comecon and EFTA are becoming increasingly alarmed at the prospect of being shut out of

'Fortress Europe', with the EC building barriers against the outside world while demolishing frontiers inside the Community. World competitors fear that in sectors such as cars and textiles, EC quotas, replacing national ones, will be adjusted to the most protectionist EC states; that non-EC companies with subsidiaries in Europe will have to prove that their products have a 'minimum local content' and therefore count as European; and that the 1992 integration programme in services such as banking and insurance is premature when the GATT is still in the very early stages of discussing an international liberalization system.

The US administration of President George Bush takes the view that world trade stands to gain from the single European market, and Washington under Bush is seeking closer co-operation with Brussels and EC capitals. However, the United States also privately warns European officials that the plan for an 'open' EC could give way to protectionism if 'backsliding, narrow national interests' prevail, and that protectionist pressures in a Democrat-dominated Congress are also powerful.

Moscow is also focusing on 1992: Gorbachov closely questions every West European visitor to the Kremlin about the implications of the single European market for the world. Russia not only fears the rise of a powerful, united trading bloc in Western Europe, it is also concerned about the potential destabilizing effect on Eastern Europe at a time when Soviet control over the Soviet bloc is already loosening. The EC of 1992 can provide an enlarged market for Eastern Europe, and restructured Russia will be more open to the EC: but whether this adds up to Gorbachov's idea of a 'common European home' is another matter. The West remains democratic and the East undemocratic, even with concessions to pluralism in Hungary and elsewhere.

Enlargement: twelve is an optimum number

In October 1988 the Commission launched the slogan 'Europe—a World Partner' to reassure the outside world. Willy de Clercq, the former External Relations Commissioner, observed that the aim of 1992 was to revitalize world trade and enable the EC's global partners to enjoy 'the considerable advantages of 1992, on the basis of reciprocity'. Lord Cockfield explained that the EC would only demand reciprocal access to a foreign market in, say, banking when a non-EC enterprise tried to gain access to Europe after 1992: the rights of foreign firms with already-established subsidiaries would be guaranteed. However, he also warned that 1992 would 'sharpen the cutting edge of EC industrial competitiveness'. If this frightened non-EC countries, 'then they had better pull their socks up'.

Increasingly, the Commission uses the term 'foreign' in official documents to mean 'non-EC'. The reaction of some EFTA countries (many of which border directly on the EC) has been to draw closer to the EC. In July 1989 Austria took the step of applying for full membership. On the other hand, the Commission and the Council have made it clear that twelve is an optimum number, at least for the foreseeable future, and that the EC is still fully occupied with the consequences of absorbing Spain and Portugal in 1986. Turkey applied for membership in April 1987, but, quite apart from specific drawbacks—the Turkish human rights record, a weak economy, a Muslim (albeit secular) culture and the prospect of a flood of Turkish migrant workers into Europe—adding a thirteenth member is not an EC priority.

A Norwegian application might be looked on more favourably. However, at the European Parliament in October 1988 Mrs Gro Harlem Brundtland, the Norwegian Prime Minister, made it clear that Oslo had no desire to re-open the wounds of the 1972 referendum campaign. She even rebuked 'impatient voices in EFTA countries calling for a direct, bilateral approach to the issue of membership', and said that the answer lay in active co-operation with the EC.

The introduction of more democratic systems in formerly Communist East European countries raises the long-term possibility that Poland or Hungary might eventually join. But as Douglas Hurd pointed out in his first speech to the Commons as Foreign Secretary in November 1989, 'nothing is to be gained by forcing the pace.' The EC, Hurd said, was 'not likely to receive new full members in the near future . . . We are not attracted by the notion that we should in some way dilute the strength of the Community by enlarging it.' Instead, 'new forms of association' could be found by building on trade and co-operation agreements with East European nations or encouraging them to join the larger Council of Europe, provided they fulfilled the criteria of human rights and democracy.

The United States, meanwhile, remains convinced that 1992 spells protectionism, and is not keen to see the EC enlarged further. It has a further fear: that Cocom, the Co-ordinating Committee for Multilateral Export Controls, based in Paris, will lose the ability to police exports of sensitive high-technology equipment to the Communist world after 1992, on the grounds that the Commission wants the EC to be a single destination for US technology.

From Rhodes to Strasbourg via Madrid

Making industry and commerce more competitive on a European rather than national basis will also have painful consequences within Europe itself. This—together with belated resentment over the partial loss of political sovereignty—could lead to a popular reaction against integration. According to Sir John Harvey-Jones, former chairman of ICI (quoted in the *Observer* on 23 October 1988):

> We are looking at a degree of attrition that we have not experienced at any time. In my judgement, at least half the European companies will disappear.

The EC has twelve major boilermaking companies, the United States only six: the EC has ten competing turbine manufacturers, the United States only two. Something will have to give, and the consequences could be important. Hence the Commission's concern over a 'social dimension' to soften the blow. Hence also the argument that the single market inevitably entails monetary union, which, in turn, implies close co-ordination of economic and social policy, if not a supranational body to supervise such co-operation. In the defence field, Lord Kennet has argued that sovereignty is already something of a chimera, with the UK independent deterrent made up of US nuclear weapons, US presidential control of weapons deployed in the UK and 'effective US sovereignty' over US bases in Britain.

Is there room for compromise on the great issues raised by 1992, from economics to defence? At the end of October 1988 Delors, speaking in the European Parliament and appealing to his critics to resolve the dispute over 1992 in a spirit of 'friendship and honesty', hinted that there was. The 30-year-old history of the EC showed that 'misunderstandings' had to be settled quickly before they became 'uselessly dramatized', he said, adding: 'You can be proud of your country and at the same time be a European.'

However, Delors was firm on the Single European Act, which meant the abolition of physical, technical and fiscal barriers, and firm, too, in denying that the Commission was 'going beyond its responsibilities' under the Act. He warned of the danger that the EC could once again be paralysed by a political crisis.

On the eve of the Rhodes EC Summit in December 1988 Delors said in Paris that 'we will sort things out with Mrs Thatcher in the end', and indeed the summit was relatively uncontroversial.

Reflecting the debate over how far frontier controls could be abolished if the fight against terrorism and crime is to be effective, the summit's communiqué affirmed the EC's commitment to a Europe without frontiers, while it linked this to 'progress in inter-governmental co-operation to combat terrorism, international crime, drug trafficking and trafficking of all kinds'. This co-operation must be increased, the communiqué said, leaving room for argument between now and 1992 over how the EC can achieve free movement yet control crime. At Rhodes, Mrs Thatcher made clear that she did not regard any alternative to border controls proposed so far as adequate. Equally, the Rhodes summit, which was a 'pause for breath' at the halfway stage to 1992, only briefly addressed key 1992 problems which must be solved in the next two to three years.

On harmonization of taxation, which President Mitterrand maintained was a prerequisite for free capital movement but which Mrs Thatcher insisted was not, the Rhodes summit merely discussed the hope of a 'convergence of views', and asked the Council of Ministers to speed up its work 'so that tax measures, to the extent that they are necessary for the establishment and operation of the internal market, could be adopted in accordance with the timetable set'.

On the 'social dimension', the summit agreed in vague terms on the need for a 'Social Charter' along the lines of that adopted by the Council of Europe, and called for safety in the workplace; a fight against unemployment through economic growth; and a 'constructive dialogue between management and labour at Community level in accordance with Article 118b of the Treaty'. However, the question of worker participation and the European company statute remain unresolved.

The Rhodes communiqué noted 'with particular satisfaction' the smooth, steady and dynamic development of the Community as it moves towards 1992 as well as the fact that 'at the halfway stage towards the deadline of December 1992, half of the legislative programme necessary is already nearly complete'. It called for 'further appropriate harmonization or approximation where necessary', an ambiguous phrase which could allow compromise but could equally well lead to disputes, and warned that 'the pace of work must be speeded up in future'. The summit identified areas which were lagging, such as transport, energy, animal and plant health controls and the free movement of people within the community.

The Madrid summit of June 1989 undoubtedly marked a watershed, with France pressing for a fast pace of progress towards economic and monetary union based on the Delors report, and Mrs Thatcher insisting that the EC need not go beyond such moves as the liberalization of capital movements and closer economic co-ordination. After Madrid, the French immediately began setting the agenda—and the pace—for the Strasbourg summit at the end of the French Presidency. Mitterrand declared in July 1989 that 'what cannot be agreed by 12 may be done among 11, 10 or 9'. Mrs Thatcher retorted that Britain was ahead of France in having abolished exchange controls and industrial subsidies, adding: 'I look forward to the day when France follows our lead.'

Although Anglo-French tensions increased in the run up to Strasbourg, the summit passed without the rancour which has marred many previous meetings. The trade-off between President Mitterrand and Herr Kohl over German re-unification and the inter-governmental conference on economic and monetary union left Mrs Thatcher in a minority of one, forcing her to put a brave face on the outcome. 'She was outnumbered and she knew it. There was nothing she could do,' said one senior member of the West German delegation. Nevertheless, Mrs Thatcher was noticeably less strident in arguing her case—a change of tone rather than substance —which prompted many observers to suggest a belated attempt to 'polish up her pro-European credentials.'

EC leaders will now gather in December 1990, when Italy holds the rotating presidency of the Council of Ministers, with a view to making the necessary changes needed in the institutional structure of the Community to pave the way for full economic and monetary union. Also on the agenda are proposals to increase the powers of the European Parliament, in an effort to meet criticisms of the so-called 'democratic deficit'. However, Mrs Thatcher pointed out that Britain had tabled an alternative to the Delors Plan, based upon competing currencies, which would also be up for discussion. The inter-governmental conference is likely to take three or four years to complete, and while Britain will be under tremendous pressure to conform with the wishes of its Community partners, it nonetheless retains its national veto—all Treaty revisions have to be approved unanimously.

In the meantime, Ireland, which holds the chair in the first half of 1990, is likely to be more concerned with regional aid for the EC 'periphery', perhaps putting controversial federalist issues on one side. However, Italy, which is noted for its federalist, pro-European fervour, is likely to return them to the top of the Community's agenda. The Presidency falls to Luxembourg and the Netherlands in 1991, and then to the United Kingdom and Belgium in 1992.

Economic co-operation and complementary measures

For the immediate future, the question is not so much how to achieve European Union as how to co-ordinate European political and economic systems and policies more closely for the world of 1992. In his monograph on *Europe After the Crash* (CEPS Paper No. 37, Brussels, 1988) Charles Bean, Reader in Economics at the London School of Economics, outlines three scenarios one year after the stock market crash of October 1987: an 'optimistic' one in which West Germany 'eschews fears about growth in government debt' and France and Britain 'stop worrying about a worsening of their current accounts and undertake fiscal measures that tackle supply-side problems as well as sustaining demand'. There are also two 'pessimistic' options, one in which a further fall in the dollar risks renewing the financial turbulence witnessed in 1987, with EC states 'individually boxed in by budgetary concerns', feeling that there is little room for generating domestic demand while protectionist pressures rise in the United States; and another in which the Europeans 'acquiesce in a renewed decline of the dollar' to moderate protectionist pressures, but at the risk of a recession and higher unemployment.

This gloomy possibility lends added importance to proposed 'complementary economic measures' which EC states might agree on to accompany the internal market. One of the main aims of the Common Market, after all, is to achieve a high standard of living for its citizens. Complementary measures include:

1 A vigorous competition policy, which necessarily entails EC-level regulation (with the aim, paradoxically, of achieving deregulation);

2 A common external policy, allowing the EC to avoid the 'Fortress Europe' approach feared by other global trading blocs;

3 Exchange rate stability, preferably with sterling inside the EMS;

4 Co-ordination of government intervention in markets; joint research and technology programmes;

5 Common rules on trade marks, copyright, property and counterfeiting;

6 Harmonization of company law;

7 A flexible regional development policy; and

8 A co-ordinated macroeconomic policy, with joint monetary targets and a joint EC approach to international monetary matters, with the ECU as a reserve currency.

European Union—or a 'concert of independent states'?

As all these arguments unfold over economic policy, taxation, the social dimension and EC security policy there is one overriding question to which only 1992 and the Europe it creates can provide the answer: whether an integrated Europe means co-operation among sovereign nations or the merging of nation states into a federal Europe. The Single European Act preserves unanimity and the national veto in key policy areas, and does not commit EC states to European Union. The Commission argues that 'movement towards a European Union cannot be accomplished without the agreement of all Europeans'.

On the other hand, once begun, the integration process will lead to whatever destination the dominant political figures of Europe wish. In October 1988 the European Parliament made clear what that goal was by passing a resolution (formulated by an Italian Communist MEP, Carlo Graziani) calling for a common EC security policy; a European Central Bank and single currency; further transfer of powers from Westminster and other national parliaments to the European Parliament; and European citizenship.

Such visions seem far-fetched, and may remain just that—visions. Lord Young observed in May 1989 that 1992 should mean the 'Thatcheriz-ation of Europe': Britain could not accept 'the transfer of sovereignty' involved in such schemes as monetary union. 'Distant horizons are perhaps attractive to those getting bored or irritated with the nitty-gritty detail of creating a single European market.' *The Times* commented on 18 May 1989 that extension of the Commission's powers had to be 'vigilantly monitored and where necessary combated', with Europe-wide regulations kept to the minimum, but added that sharing of sovereignty was a consequence of the Single European Act and 1992. Some, such as Dr Peter Ludlow, director of the Centre for European Policy Studies in Brussels, foresee a revival in secular form of the concept of European Christendom, based on modern European ideas of democracy and human rights.

In his meeting with the Pope in December 1989 Gorbachov—a lifelong Marxist—referred to the importance in Europe of 'the moral values which religion has generated and embodied for centuries.' On a visit to the European Parliament shortly beforehand, Dr Robert Runcie, the Archbishop of Canterbury, spoke of the need for European unity to respond to 'the challenge of sudden large-scale change in Central and Eastern Europe'. Those hesitating about European Union—including its social aspects—should remember Shakespeare's *Julius Caesar*, Dr Runcie said: 'There is a tide in the affairs of men, which, taken at the flood, leads on to fortune . . . On such a full sea are we now afloat, and we must take the current when it serves.'

Many will find echoes of the current debate on the future of Europe in Gibbon's *The Decline and Fall of the Roman Empire*, in which he reflects that Europe was once divided into 'twelve powerful though unequal kingdoms . . . what secured modern freedom was the emergence out of the fragments of the old empire of a new European polity comprising a concert of smaller, independent states'. Almost as if anticipating the lessons of European history for the 1992 debate, Gibbon concludes: 'The benefits of such an interlocking fabric of rival states, and the balance of power thereby created, were great by contrast to the stifling, deadening uniformity of empire.'

Many will share Gibbon's distaste for 'deadening uniformity', preferring instead 'a concert of independent states'. On the other hand, the drive for integration is based on the assumption that union is enlivening, not deadening, and that the Europe of the late twentieth century has no option but to pool its resources if it is to survive in the modern world and achieve the aims for which the EC was created in the first place. The outcome of the struggle between these two concepts of 1992 will determine what kind of Europe we live in, what kind of Europe the world has to deal with, and what Britain's place in Europe is to be.

Appendix 1   EUROPE'S TOP TEN COMPANIES

Company	Country	Turnover (£ million)	Profits (£ million)
Royal Dutch Petroleum	Netherlands	33,494	3,325
British Petroleum	UK	33,101	3,290
IRI	Italy	24,022	85
Daimler-Benz	West Germany	23,912	1,523
Shell	UK	22,329	2,404
Siemens	West Germany	19,318	805
Volkswagen	West Germany	19,268	695
Fiat	Italy	17,252	1,345
Deutsche Bundespost	West Germany	17,082	718
Philips	Netherlands	16,199	269

Source: The Times 1000.

Appendix 2   EUROPE'S TOP TWENTY BANKS

Bank	Country	Assets (£ billion)
Banque Nationale de Paris	France	114.4
Barclays	UK	104.6
Crédit Lyonnais	France	103.9
Deutsche Bank	West Germany	99.3
National Westminster	UK	98.6
Crédit Agricole	France	92.0
Société Générale	France	78.3
Dresdner Bank	West Germany	75.1
Paribas	France	70.6
Union Bank of Switzerland	Switzerland	62.7
Commerzbank	West Germany	58.6
Swiss Bank Corporation	Switzerland	58.0
Midland Bank	UK	55.7
Bayerische Vereinsbank	West Germany	52.8
Lloyds Bank	UK	51.8
Amsterdam Rotterdam Bank	Netherlands	48.5
Banca Nazionale del Lavoro	Italy	48.4
Rabobank	Netherlands	46.6
Westdeutsche Landesbank Girozentrale	West Germany	46.2
Bayerische Hypotheken und Wechselbank	West Germany	43.9

Source: The Times 1000.

Appendix 3   VAT RATES IN THE EC

Country	Lower	Standard	Higher	VAT as percentage of GDP
Belgium	6/17	19	25	7.67
Denmark	None	22	None	9.84
West Germany	7	14	None	6.34
Greece	6	18	36	—
France	5.5/7	18.6	28	9.19
Ireland	0/10	23	None	8.22
Italy	2/9	18	38	5.48
Luxembourg	3/6	12	None	6.04
Netherlands	5	19	None	6.83
Portugal	0/8	17	30	—
Spain	6	12	33	—
UK	0	15	None	5.22

Source: *Completing the Internal Market*, European Commission White Paper, 1985.

Appendix 4   EUROPEAN COMMISSION DIRECTORATES GENERAL

DG I	External Relations
DG II	Economic and Financial Affairs
DG III	Internal Market and Industry
DG IV	Competition
DG V	Employment, Social Affairs, Education
DG VI	Agriculture
DG VII	Transport
DG VIII	Development
DG IX	Personnel and Administration
DG X	Information and Culture
DG XI	Environment, Consumer Protection, Nuclear Safety
DG XII	Science and Research
DG XIII	Telecommunications, Information Industries, Innovation
DG XIV	Fisheries
DG XV	Financial Institutions and Company Law
DG XVI	Regional policy
DG XVII	Energy
DG XVIII	Credits and Investments
DG XIX	Budgets
DG XX	Financial Control
DG XXI	Customs Union and Indirect Taxation
DG XXII	Co-ordination of Structural Instruments
DG XXIII	Small and Medium Enterprises (SMEs)

Secretariat General   Statistical Office
Spokesman's Service   Official Publications
Interpreting and Conference Service   Source: European Commission.

Appendix 5 USEFUL 1992 CONTACTS AND ADDRESSES

Commission of the European Communities
rue de la Loi 200
1049 Brussels
Belgium
Tel: 010 322 235 1111

EC UK Information Offices:
8 Storey's Gate
London SW1P 3AT
Tel: 01-222 8122

4 Cathedral Road
Cardiff CH1 9SG
Tel: 0222 371631

7 Alva Street
Edinburgh EH2 4PH
Tel: 031 225 2058

Windsor House
9♡15 Bedford Street
Belfast
Tel: 0232 40708

European Business Information Centres:
Scottish Development Agency
Rosebery House
Haymarket Terrace
Edinburgh EH12 5EZ
Tel: 031 337 9595

Birmingham Chamber of Industry and Commerce
PO Box Harborne Road
Birmingham B15 3DH
Tel: 021 454 6171

Northern Development Company
Bank House
Carilo Square
Newcastle-upon-Tyne
Tel: 091 261 0026

Department of Employment
Small Firms and Tourism Division Limited
Ebury Bridge House
Ebury Bridge Road
London SW1W 8QD
Tel: 01-730 5874

European Documentation Centres in the UK:
The Library
University of Aberdeen
Meston Walk
Aberdeen AB9 2UB
Tel: 0224 4021

Library
Wye College
Wye
Ashford
Kent TN25 5AH
Tel: 0233 812401 × 242

University Library
University of Bath
Claverton Down
Bath BA2 7AY
Tel: 0225 826826 × 559

The Library
Government Publications Dept
Queens University
Belfast BT7 1LS
Tel: 0232 245133

William Kendrick Library
Birmingham Polytechnic
Birmingham B42 2SU
Tel: 021 356 6911

Main Library
University of Birmingham
PO Box 363
Birmingham B15 2TT
Tel: 021 414 3344 × 58

J B Priestley Library
University of Bradford
Richmond Road
Bradford BD7 1DP
Tel: 0274 733466

The Library
University of Sussex
Brighton BN1 9QL
Tel: 0273 678159

Law Library
University of Bristol
Queens Road
Bristol BS8 1RJ
Tel: 0272 24161

The Library
University of Cambridge
West Road
Cambridge CB3 9DR
Tel: 0223 61441

Arts and Social Studies Library
University College
PO Box 430
Cardiff CF1 3XT
Tel: 0222 874262

The Library
University of Essex
PO Box 24
Colchester CO4 3UA
Tel: 0206 862286

The Library
New University of Ulster
Coleraine BT52 1SA
Tel: 0265 4141

Lanchester Polytechnic
Priory Street
Coventry CV1 5FB
Tel: 0203 24166

University of Dundee
Perth Road
Dundee DD1 4HN
Tel: 0382 23181 × 4101

Official Publications Section
University Library
Stockton Road
Durham DH1 3LY
Tel: 091 374 3041

Centre of European Studies
University of Edinburgh
Old College
South Bridge
Edinburgh EH8 9LY
Tel: 031 667 1011

Centre for European Legal Studies
Exeter University
Law Faculty
Rennes Drive
Exeter EX4 4RJ
Tel: 0392 77911

The University Library
University of Glasgow
Hillhead Street
Glasgow G12 8QE
Tel: 041 339 8855 × 67

George Edwards Library
University of Surrey
Guilford GU2 5XH
Tel: 0483 571281

Brynmor Jones Library
University of Hull
Cottingham Road
Hull HU6 7RX
Tel: 0482 46311

The Library
University of Keele
Staffs
Tel: 0782 621111 × 300

Library Building
University of Kent
Canterbury
Kent CT2 7NU
Tel: 0227 66822

University of Lancaster
Library
Lancaster LA1 4YX
Tel: 0254 62501

The Library
Leeds Polytechnic
Calverly Street
Leeds LS1 3HE
Tel: 0532 462925

University of Leeds
20 Lyddon Terrace
Leeds LS7 9JT
Tel: 0532 31751

University Library
University of Leicester
University Road
Leicester LE1 7RH
Tel: 0533 522044

Liverpool and District Science
and Industry Research
Council
Central Libraries
William Brown Street
Liverpool L3 8EW
Tel: 051 207 2147

EC Unit Room 61
Polytechnic of Central
London
309 Regent Street
London W1R 8AL
Tel: 01-580 2020

The Library
Queen Mary College
Mile End Road
London E1 4NS
Tel: 01-980 4811

The Library
Polytechnic of North London
Prince of Wales Road
London NW5
Tel: 01-359 0941

Reference Division
Department of Printed Books
Overseas Section
British Library
Great Russell Street
London WC1B 3DB
Tel: 01-323 7602

The Library
RIIA
10 St James Square
London SW1Y 4LE
Tel: 01-930 2233

European Depository Library
Central Reference Library
City of Westminster Library
St Martin's Street
London WC2 7HP
Tel: 01-798 2084

British Library of Political
and Economic Science
The Library
10 Portugal Street
London WC2A 2HD
Tel: 01-405 7686

The Library
Loughborough University
of Technology
Loughborough LE11 3TU
Tel: 0509 222344

John Rylands Library
University of Manchester
Oxford Road
Manchester M13 9PP
Tel: 061 273 3333

The Library
Newcastle Polytechnic
Ellison Place
Newcastle-upon-Tyne NE1
8ST
Tel: 091 232 6002 × 4136

The Library
University of East Anglia
University Plain
Norwich NR4 7TJ
Tel: 0603 56161 × 2412

The Library
University of Nottingham
Nottingham NG7 2RD
Tel: 0602 506101 × 374

Bodelian Library
University of Oxford
Oxford OX1 3BG
Tel: 0865 277201

Frewen Library
Portsmouth Polytechnic
Cambridge Road
Portsmouth PO1 2ST
Tel: 0705 827681 × 401

The Library
University of Reading
Whiteknights
PO Box 223
Reading RG6 2AH
Tel: 0734 874331 × 131

The Library
University of Salford
Salford
Lancs
Tel: 061 736 5843

The Library
Sheffield City Polytechnic
Pond Street
Sheffield S1 1WB
Tel: 0742 20911 × 2494

Faculty of Law
University of Southampton
Southampton SO9 5NH
Tel: 0703 559122

The Library
University of Warwick
Coventry CV4 7A

British Library
Document Supply Centre
Boston Spa
Wetherby
LS23 7BQ
Tel: 0937 546045

Robert Scott Library
Polytechnic of
Wolverhampton
St Peters Square
Wolverhampton WV1 1RH

Source: European
Commission

**Private EC Consultancies and
Advisers:**
Allott & Lomax
Fairbairn House
Ashton Lane, Sale
Manchester M33 1WP
Tel: 061 962 1214

Advocacy Partnership
Limited
16 Regency Street
London SW1P 4DB
Tel: 01-630 1235

Ceres
Station House
Station Road, Wylam
Northumberland NE41 8HR
Tel: 0661 853982

CSM European Consultants
Limited
Eagle House
109 Jermyn Street
London SW1Y 6HB
Tel: 01-839 4544

CTA Economic Export
Analysts Limited
96 London Road
Reading RG1 5AU
Tel: 0734 66 8381

David Perchard Associates
23 Kingsbury Avenue
St Albans AL3 4TA
Tel: 0727 43227

European Strategy Council
18 Bolton Street
London W1Y 7PA
Tel: 01-493 0049

GJW Government Relations
64 Clapham Road
London SW9 0JJ
Tel: 01-582 3119

Galactic Trading Company
Limited
European Trade Index (1992)
38♡40 Clareville Street
London SW7 5AW
Tel: 01-244 8697

Halcrow Fox & Associates
Vineyard House
44 Brook Green
London W6 7BY
Tel: 01-603 5783

Hambros Bank Limited
41 Bishopsgate
London EC2P 2AA
Tel: 01-588 2851

McAvoy Wreford Bayley
36 Grosvenor Gardens
London SW1W oED
Tel: 01-730 4500

Randall's Parliamentary
Serice
7 Buckingham Gate
London SW1E 6JY
Tel: 01-828 2277

Sallingbury Casey Limited
25 Victoria Street
London SW1H oEX
Tel: 01-799 1020

Spicers Centre for Europe
Information Division
4th Floor
Cavendish House
Albion Street
Leeds LS1 6AG
Tel: 0532 442629

SRI International
Menlo Park House
4 Addiscombe Road
Croydon CR0 5TT
Tel: 01-686 5555

Westminster and Whitehall
Consultants Limited
25 Victoria Street
London SW1H oEX
Tel: 01-222 2025

Appendix 6   THE SECOND DELORS COMMISSION 1989–92

1   Jacques Delors (France) President of the European Commission
2   Christiane Scrivener (France) Fiscal Affairs and the Customs Union
3   Martin Bangemann (West Germany) Internal market
4   Peter Schmidhuber (West Germany) Budget
5   Leon Brittan (UK) Competition Policy and Financial Services
6   Bruce Millan (UK) Regional Development
7   Abel Matutes (Spain) Mediterranian Policy, Relations with Latin America, and North South issues
8   Manuel Marin (Spain) Cooperation and Development (Lome), and Fish.
9   Carlo Ripa di Meana (Italy) Environment, Nuclear Safety, and Civil Protection
10   Filippo Maria Pandolphi (Italy) Science, Research and Development, Telecommunications, and Joint Research Centres
11   Frans Andriessen (Netherlands) External Relations
12   Henning Christopherson (Denmark) Economic and Monetary Affairs, and Coordination of the Structural Funds
13   Raymond MacSharry (Ireland) Agriculture
14   Antonio Cardosa (Portugal) Personnel and Administration, Energy, and Small and Medium Enterprises
15   Vasso Papandreau (Greece) Employment, Industrial and Social Affairs, and Education
16   Karel Van Miert (Belgium) Transport, Credit and Investment, and Consumer Protection
17   Jean Dodelinger (Luxembourg) Audio Visual and Cultural Affairs, Information and Communication, and Citizens' Europe

---

Appendix 7   SELECT BIBLIOGRAPHY

The basic texts for 1992 remain the European Commission's White Paper *Completing the Internal Market*, June 1985; the Commission's Mid-Term Report on the Internal Market, December 1988; and the Treaties establishing the European Communities, incorporating the Single European Act and the Treaty of Rome, all issued by the Office for Official Publications of the European Communities, Luxembourg.

Other useful publications include:

Europe Without Frontiers—Completing the Internal Market, Commission of the European Communities, 1987.

The European Challenge 1992: The Benefits of a Single Market, by Paolo Cecchini and others, Wildwood House, 1988.

Pocket Guide to the European Community, by Dick Leonard, Basil Blackwell and The Economist Publications, 1988.

The EEC: A Guide to the Maze, by Stanley Budd, Melville Crawford Associates, Edinburgh, 1985.

The Economics of the Common Market, by Dennis Swann, Penguin, 1984.

Europe: More than a Continent, by Michael Butler (former UK Ambassador to the EC), Heinemann, 1986.

Making Sense of Europe, by Christopher Tugendhat (former Commissioner), Viking, 1986.

Europe's Domestic Market, by Jacques Pelkmans and Alan Winters, Chatham House Papers No. 43, Royal Institute of International Affairs, 1988.

The European Community. Past, Present and Future, edited by Loukas Tsoukalis, Blackwell, 1983.

The European Community: Progress or Decline? by Karl Kaiser, Royal Institute of International Affairs, 1983.

1992: Implications and Potential, by James Elles, Conservative MEP for Oxford and Buckinghamshire. The Bow Group, 1988.

VAT: The Zero Rate Issue, European Parliament discussion paper, by Ben Patterson, Conservative MEP for Kent West, 1988.

Common Standards for Enterprises: Document, Commission of the European Communities, Florence Nicolas, Office for Official Publications, Luxembourg, 1988.

Vacher's European Companion (quarterly), 29 Tufton Street, London SW1P 3QL.

Eurojargon: A Dictionary of EC Acronyms, Abbreviations and Sobriquets, by Anne Ramsay, Capital Planning Information, The Grey House, Broad Street, Stamford, Lincs PE9 1PR.

Europe 1992 Directory, published by Coventry Polytechnic Commercial Development Unit, Priory Street, Coventry CV1 5FB, in collaboration with the DTI Information Technology Unit.

Appendix 8 HIGHLIGHTS OF THE SINGLE EUROPEAN ACT

Article 8a
The Community shall adopt measures with the aim of progressively establishing the internal market over a period expiring on 31 December 1992, in accordance with the provisions of this Article and of Articles 8D, 8C, 28, 57(2), 59, 70(1), 83, 99, 100a and 100b and without prejudice to other provisions of this Treaty.

The internal market shall comprise an area without internal frontiers in which the free movement of goods, persons, services and capital is ensured in accordance with the provisions of this Treaty.

Article 8b
The Commission shall report to the Council before 31 December 1988 and again before 31 December 1990 on the progress made towards achieving the internal market within the time limit fixed in Article 8a.

The Council, acting by a qualified majority on a proposal from the Commission, shall determine the guidelines and conditions necessary to ensure balanced progress in all the sectors concerned.

Article 8c
When drawing up its proposals with a view to achieving the objectives set out in Article 8a, the Commission shall take into account the extent of the effort that certain economies showing differences in development will have to sustain during the period of establishment of the internal market and it may propose appropriate provisions.

If these provisions take the form of derogations, they must be of a temporary nature and must cause the least possible disturbance to the functioning of the common market.

Article 99
The Council shall, acting unanimously on a proposal from the Commission and after consulting the European Parliament, adopt provisions for the harmonization of legislation concerning turnover taxes, excise duties and other forms of indirect taxation to the extent that such harmonization is necessary to ensure the establishment and the functioning of the internal market within the time limit laid down in Article 8a.

Article 100a
1 By way of derogation from Article 100 and save where otherwise provided in this Treaty, the following provisions shall apply for the achievement of the objectives set out in Article 8a. The Council shall, acting by a qualified majority on a proposal from the Commission in co-operation with

the European Parliament and the Economic and Social Committee, adopt the measures for the approximation of the provisions laid down by law, regulation or administrative action in Member States which have as their object the establishment and functioning of the internal market.

2 Paragraph 1 shall not apply to fiscal provisions, to those relating to the free movement of personsnor to those relating to the rights and interests of employed persons.

3 The Commission, in its proposals laid down in paragraph 1 concerning health, safety, environment protection and consumer protection, will take as a base a high level of protection.

4 If, after the adoption of a harmonization measure by the Council acting by a qualified majority, a Member State deems it necessary to apply national provisions on grounds of major needs referred to in Article 36, or relating to protection of the environment or the working environment, it shall notify the Commission of these provisions.

The Commission shall confirm the provisions involved after having verified that they are not a means of arbitrary discrimination or a disguised reaction on trade between Member States.

By way of derogation from the procedure laid down in Articles 169 and 170, the Commission or any Member State may bring the matter directly before the Court of Justice if it considers that the Member State is making improper use of the powers provided for in this Article.

5 The harmonization measures referred to above shall, in appropriate cases, include a safeguard clause authorizing the Member States to take, for one or more of the non-economic reasons referred to in Article 36, provisional measures subject to a Community control procedure.

Article 100b

1 During 1992, the Commission shall, together with each Member State, draw up an inventory of national laws, regulations and administrative provisions which fall under Article 100a and which have not been harmonized pursuant to that Article.

The Council, acting in accordance with the provisions of Article 100a, may decide that the provisions in force in a Member State must be recognized as being equivalent to those applied by another Member State.

2 The provisions of Article 100a(4) shall apply by analogy.

3 The Commission shall draw up the inventory referred to in the first subparagraph of paragraph 1 and shall submit appropriate proposals in good time to allow the Council to act before the end of 1992.

Article 148

1 Save as otherwise provided in this Treaty, the Council shall act by a qualified majority of its members.

2 Where the Council is required to act by a qualified majority, the votes of its members shall be weighted as follows:

Belgium	5	Ireland	3
Denmark	3	Italy	10
West Germany	10	Luxembourg	2
Greece	5	Netherlands	5
Spain	8	Portugal	5
France	10	United Kingdom	10

For their adoption, acts of Council shall require at least:

—fifty-four votes in favour where this Treaty requires them to be adopted on a proposal from the Commission,

—fifty-four votes in favour, cast by at least eight members, in other cases.

3 Abstentions by members present in person or represented shall not prevent the adoption by the Council of acts which require unanimity.

Declaration on Article 8a of the EEC Treaty

The Conference wishes by means of the provisions in Article 8a to express its firm political will to take before 1 January 1993 the decisions necessary to complete the internal market defined in those provisions, and more particularly the decisions necessary to implement the Commission's programme described in the White Paper on the Internal Market.

Setting the date of 31 December 1992 does not create an automatic legal effect.

Declaration on Articles 13 to 19 of the Single European Act

Nothing in these provisions shall affect the right of Member States to take such measures as they consider necessary for the purpose of controlling immigration from third countries, and to combat terrorism, crime, the traffic in drugs and illicit trading in works of art and antiques.

Appendix 9   GLOSSARY OF EC TERMS

ACP states
The 66 African, Caribbean and Pacific countries party to the Lomé Convention

ACPM
Advisory Committee on Programme Management

Agrimed
Mediterranean Agriculture

Aqua Europa
European Federation for Water Treatment

ASSILEC
Association of Dairy Industries of the EC

BCC
Business Co-operation Centre

BEUC
European Bureau of Consumer Councils

BRITE
Basic Research in Industrial Technologies for Europe

BTR
Basic Technological Research

CAOBISCO
Association of the Sugar Products Industries of the EC

CAP
Common Agricultural Policy

CARICOM
Caribbean Community and the Common Market

CCC
Consumer Consultative Committees

CCT/CET
Common Customs Tariff/Common External Tariff

CEFIC
European Council of Chemical Industry Federations

CEN
European Committee for Standardization

CENELEC
European Committee for Electrotechnical Standardization

CEOP
European Committee of Workers' Co-operative Production Societies

CERN
European Nuclear Research Centre

CFP
Common Fisheries Policy

CICI
Confederation of Information Communication Industries

CID
Centre for Industrial Development

Cohesion
A term meaning reduction in disparities between regions

Comecon
Council for Mutual Economic Assistance

COMETT
Community in Education and Training for Technology

Comitextil
Co-ordination Committee for the Textile Industries of the EC

COPA
Committee for Agricultural Organizations in the EC

CORDI
Advisory Committee on Industrial Research and Development

COREPER
Committee of Permanent Representatives (i.e. EC ambassadors in Brussels)

Co-responsibility levy
A tax paid by farmers as a contribution towards the cost of storing farm surpluses

COST
Committee on European Co-operation in the field of Scientific and Technical Research

CPC
Community Patent Convention

CRM
Committee for Medical and Public Health Research

Democratic deficit
The need for greater democratic accountability of EC institutions as a result of European integration

DG
Directorate General

EAGF
European Agricultural Guidance and Guarantee Fund

ECE
Economic Commission for Europe (UN)

ECSC
European Coal and Steel Community

ECU
European currency unit (mecu = million: becu = billion)

EFTA
European Free Trade Association

EIB
European Investment Bank

EMCF
European Monetary Co-operation Fund

EMS
European Monetary System

EMU
Economic and Monetary Union

EP
European Parliament

EPC
European Political Co-operation

EPU
European Political Union

ERASMUS
EC programme to promote student mobility

ERDF
European Regional Development Fund

ERM
Exchange Rate Mechanism

ESA
European Space Agency

ESC
Economic and Social Committee

ESPRIT
European strategic programme for research and development in information technology

ETSI
European Telecommunications Standards Institute

ETUC
European Trades Union Confederation

EURATOM
European Atomic Energy Community

Eureka
European programme for high-technology research and development

Euro-Coop
European Community of
Consumer Co-operatives
Eurofer
European Federation of the
Iron and Steel Industry
EUROPMI
European Committee for
Small and Medium-sized
Industries
EUROSTAT
The Community's statistics
office
EVCA
European Venture Capital
Association
FAO
Food and Agricultural
Organization (UN)
FAST
Forecasting and Assessment
in Science and Technology
FIPACE
International Federation of
Self-generating Industrial
Users of Electricity
FIPMEC
International Federation of
Small and Medium-sized
Enterprises
GATT
General Agreement on Tariffs
and Trade
GSP
General System of
Preferences
IDN
Integrated Digital Network
IEA
International Energy
Association (OECD)
IGADD
Intergovernmental Authority
on Drought and
Development
IGC
Intergovernmental
Committee
IMF
International Monetary Fund

IMP
Integrated Mediterranean
Programmes
IPM
Integrated Pest Management
ISDN
Integrated Services Digital
Network
IT
Information Technologies
ITTTF
Information Technology and
Telecommunications Task
Force
JET
Joint European Torus
JRC
Joint Research Centre
LDCs
Least Developed Countries
MCA
Monetary Compensation
Amount
MFA
Multi-Fibre Arrangement
MFTA
Medium-term Financial
Assistance
MGQ
Maximum Guaranteed
Quantity
MS
Member States of the EC
NCI
New Community
Instruments (EIB)
NGO
Non-governmental
Organization
OCTs
Overseas Countries and
Territories
OECD
Organization for Economic
Co-operation and
Development
OJ
Official Journal of the EC
POCO
see **EPC**

QR
Quantitative Restrictions
RACE
Research and development in
advanced communications
technologies for Europe
SCAR
Standing Committee on
Agricultural Research
SEA
Single European Act
Set aside
Taking land out of
production
SMEs
Small and medium-sized
businesses
STABEX
Stability in Export Revenue
(Lomé Convention)
Stabilizer
A mechanism for controlling
farm output
STMS
Short-term Monetary Support
Sysmin
System for Safeguarding and
Developing Mineral
Production
Systran
Co-ordination of National
Policies Relating to Machine
or Machine Assisted
Translation
UKREP
United Kingdom Permanent
Representation to the EC (i.e.
the British Embassy to the
EC)
UNICE
Conference of Industries of
the European Communities
VAT
Value Added Tax
WEU
Western European Union

Appendix 10   EC SUMMITS 1983–9

Stuttgart, June 1983 (West German Presidency): Agreed budget needs reform, especially in view of coming enlargement, and Common Agricultural Policy must be brought into line with market realities.

Athens, December 1983 (Greek Presidency): Stuttgart declaration reaffirmed.

Fontainebleau, June 1984 (French Presidency): Principles of budgetary discipline agreed; British budget rebate agreed.

Dublin, December 1984 (Irish Presidency): Laid down internal market without frontiers and the key to growth and jobs.

Milan, June 1985 (Italian Presidency): Disagreement over Single European Act giving European Parliament more power and defining 1992 as date for completion of internal market.

Luxembourg, December 1985 (Luxembourg Presidency): Single European Act finally agreed.

The Hague, June 1986 (Dutch Presidency): Limited sanctions against South Africa. Budget reform deferred.

London, December 1986 (British Presidency): Further progress on internal market and Community co-ordination against threat of terrorism.

Brussels, June 1987 (Belgian Presidency): Disagreement (Thatcher veto) over proposed budget reform based on package put forward by Jacques Delors, the president of the European Commission. Britain said farm controls too weak.

Copenhagen, December 1987 (Danish Presidency): Further refinement of Delors reforms, but still not enough to satisfy Britain. Agreement to hold extraordinary summit in Brussels in February 1988, to solve the crisis before the Hanover summit of June 1988 and the passing of the Presidency to Greece.

Brussels, February 1988 (West German Presidency): Delors reforms agreed.

Hanover, June 1988 (West German Presidency): Delors Committee on Economic and Monetary Union set up. 1992 declared 'irreversible'. Delors confirmed as President of the European Commission for a second term.

Rhodes, December 1988 (Greek Presidency): Presentation of European Commission's mid-term report on progress towards the completion of the internal market by 1992. 'Slippage' identified as cause of growing concern.

Madrid, June 1989 (Spanish Presidency): Delors report on economic and monetary union debated. First stage adopted.

Paris, December 1989: special one-day summit, called after upheavals in Soviet bloc, agreed to link economic aid to Eastern Europe to political reform.

Strasbourg, December 1989 (French Presidency): Endorses principle of German re-unification, sets date for inter-governmental conference to reform the Treaty of Rome, and approves the creation of a European Development Bank and the European Social Charter.

Appendix 11   BASIC STATISTICS OF THE TWELVE

Country	Population (millions)	GDP (£ billion)	Exports (inside) (£ million)	Exports (outside) (£ million)	Imports (inside) (£ million)	Imports (outside) (£ million)
France	54	339	29,770	30,794	36,943	32,768
Britain	56	296	26,885	34,772	29,010	38,349
Italy	57	236	22,317	26,008,	22,803	30,535
West Germany	62	431	53,990	58,339	51,035	50,357
Holland	14	87	31,341	12,073	21,756	18,999
Ireland	3	11	3,950	1,774	4,382	1,699
Belgium	10	53	24,087	10,405	23,694	13,166
Spain	38	109	5,760	7,357	5,669	13,630
Greece	10	23	1,557	1,410	3,075	3,334
Luxembourg	0.5	2	(exports and imports included in Belgian figures)			
Portugal	10	14	1,617	1,400	1,903	3,391
Denmark	5	38	5,207	5,577	5,315	5,600

Source: The European Commission.

Appendix 12   EC's EXPORTS AND IMPORTS WITH MAJOR TRADING PARTNERS FOR 1987 (IN £ BILLION)

Trading partner	EFTA	USA	Japan	Comecon*
GNP	378.853	3,750.936	1,539.678	1,649.69
Exports to	33.0003	50.3303	0.5326	13.3519
Imports from	57.8753	39.3484	24.3299	17.1353
Population (millions)	33	240	121	393

* Excluding Cuba, Vietnam and Mongolia.
Source: European Commission et al.

Appendix 13 THE EC IN CONTEXT

ECONOMIC BLOCS, WITH DATES OF MEMBERSHIP
★ European Community (EC)
▲ Benelux Customs Union, 1947
▼ Council for Mutual Economic Assistance
 (CMEA/COMECON)
● European Free Trade Association (EFTA)

MILITARY PARTITION, WITH DATES OF MEMBERSH
■ North Atlantic Treaty Organization (NATO)
○ Brussels Pact, 1948
□ Warsaw Pact Organization

The Twelve								
		FDR (W. GERMANY)	★ 1957 ■ 1955	ITALY	★ 1957 ■ 1949	PORTUGAL	★ 1986 ■ 1949
BELGIUM	★ 1957 ▲ ■ 1949 ○	FRANCE	★ 1957 ■ 1949 ○	LUXEMBOURG	★ 1957 ▲ ■ 1949 ○	SPAIN	★ 1986 ■ 1982
DENMARK	★ 1973 ● 1960–72 ■ 1949	GREECE	★ 1981 ■ 1952	THE NETHERLANDS	★ 1957 ▲ ■ 1949 ○	UNITED KINGDOM	★ 1973 ● 1960 ■ 1949 ○
		IRISH REPUBLIC	★ 1973 ● 1970–72				

AUSTRIA	● 1961	TURKEY	★ applied for EC membership 1987 ■ 1952	ALBANIA	▼ 1949–61 □ 1955–68	ROMANIA	▼ □
FINLAND	● (ass. member 1961–85)			BULGARIA	▼ 1949 □ 1955	USSR	▼ □
ICELAND	● 1970 ■ 1949			CZECHOSLOVAKIA	▼ 1949 □ 1955	YUGOSLAVIA	▼
NORWAY	● 1960 ■ 1949			GDR (E. GERMANY)	▼ 1950 □ 1955		
SWEDEN	● 1960			HUNGARY	▼ 1949 □ 1955		
SWITZERLAND	● 1960			POLAND	▼ 1949 □ 1955		

Appendix 14   DECLARATION OF THE EUROPEAN COUNCIL
ON EUROPE AND THE WORLD (RHODES,
DECEMBER 1988)

1 Reaffirming its commitment to achieve concrete progress towards European Unity on the basis of the Single European Act,
—determined to strengthen and expand the role of the European Community and its Member States on the international political and economic stage, in co-operation with all other States and appropriate organizations,
—and aware that the completion of the internal market in 1992, which is already inspiring a new dynamism in the Community's economic life, will equally affect the Community's political and economic role in the world,
—the European Council reaffirms that the Single Market will be of benefit to Community and non-Community countries alike by ensuring continuing economic growth. The internal market will not close in on itself. 1992 Europe will be a partner and not a 'Fortress Europe'. The internal market will be a decisive factor contributing to greater liberalization in international trade on the basis of the GATT principles of reciprocal and mutually advantageous arrangements. The Community will continue to participate actively in the GATT Uruguay Round, committed as it is to strengthen the multilateral trading system. It will also continue to pursue, with the United States, Japan and the other OECD partners, policies designed to promote sustainable non-inflationary growth in the world economy.
2 The Community and its Member States will continue to work closely and co-operatively with the United States to maintain and deepen the solid and comprehensive transatlantic relationship. Closer political and economic relations with Japan and the other industrialized countries will also be developed. In particular, the Community wishes to strengthen and to expand relations with EFTA countries and all other European nations which share the same ideals and objectives. Open and constructive dialogue and co-operation will be actively pursued with other countries or regional groups of the Middle East, and the Mediterranean, Africa, the Caribbean, the Pacific, Asia and Latin America, with special emphasis on interregional co-operation.
3 The European Council emphasizes the need to improve social and economic conditions in less-developed countries and to promote structural adjustment, both through trade and aid. It also recognizes the importance of a continuing policy to tackle the problems of the highly indebted countries on a case-by-case basis. It looks forward to the successful conclusion of the negotiations for the renewal of the Convention between the European Community and its 66 African, Caribbean and Pacific partners during the coming year.
4 The European Community and its member states are determined to play an active role in the preservation of international peace and security and in the solution of regional conflicts, in conformity with the United Nations Charter. Europe cannot but actively demonstrate its solidarity to the great and spreading movement for democracy and full support for the principles of the Universal Declaration on Human Rights. The Twelve will endeavour to strengthen the effectiveness of the United Nations and to actively contribute to its peace-keeping role.
5 Against the background of improved East–West relations, the European Council welcomes the readiness of the European members of the CMEA to develop relations with the European Community and reaffirms its willingness to further economic relations and co-operation with them, taking into account each country's specific situation, in order to use the opportunities available in a mutually beneficial way.
The European Council reaffirms its determination to act with renewed hope to overcome the division of our continent and to promote the Western values and principles which Member States have in common. To this effect, we will strive to achieve:
—Full respect for the provisions of the Helsinki Final Act and further progress in the CSCE process, including an early and successful conclusion of the Vienna follow-up meeting;
—The establishment of a secure and stable balance of conventional forces in Europe at a lower level, the strengthening of mutual confidence and military transparence and the conclusion of a global and verifiable ban on chemical weapons;
—Promotion of human rights and fundamental freedoms, free circulation of people and ideas and the establishment of more open societies; promotion of human and cultural exchanges between East and West;
—The development of political dialogue with our Eastern neighbours.
6 The European Community and the Twelve are determined to make full use of the provisions of the Single European Act in order to strengthen solidarity among them, co-ordination on the political and economic aspects of security, and consistency between the external policies of the European

Community and the policies agreed in the framework of the European Political Co-operation. They will strive to reach swift adoption of common positions and implementation of joint action.

7 The European Council invites all countries to embark with the European Community as world partner on an historic effort to leave to the next generation a Continent and a world more secure, more just and more free.

Appendix 15 DECLARATION ON ECONOMIC AND MONETARY UNION ADOPTED BY THE EUROPEAN COUNCIL (MADRID, JUNE 1989)

1 The European Council restated its determination to progressively achieve economic and monetary union as provided for in the Single European Act and confirmed at the European Council in Hanover. Economic and monetary union must be seen in the perspective of the completion of the internal market and in the context of economic and social cohesion.

2 The European Council considered that the report by the committee chaired by Jacques Delors, which defines a process designed to lead by stages to economic and monetary union, fulfilled the mandate given to it at Hanover. The European Council felt that its realization would have to take account of the parallelism between economic and monetary aspects and allow for the diversity of specific situations.

3 The European Council decided that the first stage of the realization of economic and monetary union would begin on 1 July 1990.

4 The European Council asked the competent bodies to carry out the preparatory work for the organization of an intergovernmental conference to lay down the subsequent stages: that conference would meet once the first stage had begun and would be preceded by full and adequate preparation.

INDEX